International Sale of Gc

International Sale of Goods

James Crabtree, Stephenson Harwood
Simon Davidson, Holman, Fenwick & Willan
Colin Ferris, Stephenson Harwood
T. R. Marshall, Holman, Fenwick & Willan
Stephen Paull, Holman, Fenwick & Willan
Bridget Wheeler, Holman, Fenwick & Willan

Croner Publications Ltd
Croner House
London Road
Kingston upon Thames
Surrey KT2 6SR
Telephone: 081–547 3333

First published 1991

Published by
Croner Publications Ltd,
Croner House,
London Road,
Kingston upon Thames,
Surrey KT2 6SR
Tel: 081–547 3333

While every care has been taken in the writing and editing of this book, readers should be aware that only Acts of Parliament and Statutory Instruments have the force of law, and that only the courts can authoritatively interpret the law.

Typeset and printed by Redwood Press Ltd
Melksham, Wiltshire

Contents

Foreword

The lawyers who have contributed to this publication work in firms in the City of London which have been providing legal services and advice to the international transportation community for over 100 years. During that period there have been substantial developments in the law concerning contracts for the sale and purchase of goods and their transportation around the world. In disputes arising from such transactions it is vital to understand who has title to goods which have been damaged and, for insurance purposes, who bears the risk of loss during transit.

Many existing text books on the subject are large volumes written with the specialist practitioner in mind. They are not designed for commercial people who wish to acquire some understanding of the legal principles involved without becoming too concerned with legal complications and detail. This book is therefore designed for commercial people but has been written by lawyers experienced in dealing with problems arising within the international transportation community on a daily basis.

Members and former members of my firm have contributed their expertise to produce a book written in clear and sensible English and in a manner which can readily be understood by business men and women with no previous legal knowledge.

I do not pretend that the book will give answers to every legal problem which may arise. If problems do arise to which the book does not give an answer, there will doubtless be such lawyers in the City of London for another 100 years who are well placed to offer their particular experience to resolve these problems for you.

Archie Bishop
Senior Partner
Holman, Fenwick and Willan

Acknowledgement

We would like to thank the following members of staff at Holman, Fenwick & Willan for giving up their time to assist on the preparation of this book and for the endless patience they have shown.

Ioannis Alexopoular
Antony Concagh
Belinda Hackett
Jayne Lewis
Philip Midgen
Pauline Flanagan
Annette Pointon
Jenny Starkey
Joanna Wingar

We would like to extend our special thanks to Samantha Bennett who has edited the text on endless occasions and has generally co-ordinated the production of this book with Croner Publications Ltd.

Introduction

Even if all the implications are as yet unclear, no one in business in Europe, or trading with Europe, can be unaware that by 1992 the single European market is intended to become a reality. The Single European Act 1987 sets this deadline and defines the objective of the Single Market as:

> . . . an area without internal frontiers in which the free movement of goods, persons, services and capital is ensured in accordance with the provisions of [the Treaty of Rome].

It is proposed that deregulation will remove (or, at least, substantially reduce) existing national artificial barriers to free trade (and ban new ones) among Community members. It is more likely, in the future, that Europeans will cross borders as they now cross from one town to another within their own country, and that factories and distribution systems will largely be able to treat national borders with similar indifference.

Although much Community legislation is being created to reach the goal of a single market, a great deal of existing law will continue to apply. Thus, the traditional English law provisions governing the making of contracts, agency, carriage of goods by road, insurance and the rules governing contract generally should, whilst still evolving, largely survive the transition into the "brave new world" of the Single Market and, where relevant, operate with fewer hindrances than before.

What is clear is that any businessman or woman engaged in international trade, in or with Europe, should have a passing knowledge of the legal structures and devices that underpin the legality of this trading and define the limits of the applicable rights and obligations.

This book is not designed to provide definitive answers to all questions or solutions to all problems that may be encountered, but it is hoped that readers will gain an appreciation of the problems to be wary of and find some practical ideas as to how these can be avoided or overcome.

Of course, it is not only Europe which is, to use the Department of Trade and Industry's slogan, becoming "open for business". Increasingly this applies to the rest of the world and with the changes in eastern Europe, this process promises to expand even more rapidly. English law has long provided much of the grease to the wheels of international trade, embracing as it does all the areas referred to above.

Anyone engaged in the fields of activity to which this book relates will know that, frequently, the only English connection that a contract may have is to prescribe English law and jurisdiction for the resolution of disputes. Both the cause and result of this common practice is that London has developed a unique expertise, with an arbitration system and specialised courts familiar with the arcane problems associated with international trade, together with professionals experienced with those difficulties being able both to represent the parties and to hear and deal with the disputes.

In their work as solicitors in the City of London, dealing with international trade and finance matters, all the authors of this book have daily experience of the problems discussed. However, this book is intended only as an introduction to an enormous subject. It is safe to assume that the law will continue to change and difficulties and complications will wax and wane for as long as there are disagreements between commercial people and lawyers to act on their behalf! Nevertheless, this book should help to guide the wary, lead them away from making some mistakes and assist them in understanding the implications of any problems that do prove unavoidable.

1

Making the contract

Introduction

The international supply of goods generally requires a combination of arrangements, not simply for the sale and purchase of the goods, but also for their carriage. This is usually by road or sea, but may be by rail and air, or even inland waterway, or a combination of these methods. The carriage of goods may also involve the need to retain the services of others to load and discharge the consignment. Arrangements may also be required to insure the goods during transit. Finally, the whole transaction may need to be financed.

Common to all these arrangements in the commercial world is a contract; an agreement which the law is able to enforce. Should any question or dispute arise concerning the rights of the parties under the contract, the first essential step for them or their advisers, and any court, is to confirm that a contract has been made and the terms that have been agreed.

The purpose of this chapter is to outline the factors relevant to the making of the contract and its terms. Where English law is concerned, the issues which arise in relation to the making of any of the contracts involved in the international sale of goods, their carriage, handling, insurance or financing do not differ from those applicable to commercial contracts generally. This is, however, an area where in practice many problems continue to arise, not only on the issue as to when or whether a contract has been made or concluded, but also on the issue of what terms have or have not been included. A recurrent area of difficulty continues to be the incorporation of standard or printed terms which often appear as an afterthought.

Many of the elements involved in the international supply of goods are the subject of detailed statutory codes, some based on international conventions and some not. The question of whether a contract has been made has, hitherto, fallen outside the scope of these and the position remains governed under English law by the case law developed by the courts over generations.

Although the English statutory code covering the sale of goods—the Sale of Goods Act 1979 and the Supply of Goods and Services Act 1982—leaves untouched the underlying position concerning the making of the contract, the drafters of the two recent conventions to harmonise international trade by the adoption of uniform rules have recognised the importance of this issue. The Hague Convention of 1964 included not only a Uniform Law on the International Sale of Goods but also a Uniform Law on the Formation of Contracts for the International Sale of Goods. These Conventions represented the culmination of work started under the auspices of the League of Nations in 1930. Brought into force in the United Kingdom by the Uniform Laws on International Sales Act 1967, the Conventions have effectively remained a dead letter. Under the Act they only apply where the parties have so provided, which in practice is extremely rare.

More recently, the question of a uniform law has been taken in hand by the United Nations Commission on International Trade Law (UNCITRAL) and the result of its deliberations has been the Vienna Convention on Contracts for the International Sale of Goods 1980. To date the United Kingdom has not acceded to this but the indications of the current DTI consultative paper generally support the possibility of accession to the Convention which is already in force in a number of European countries, including France, Italy, the Netherlands, Denmark, Sweden and Norway as well as the USA. The Vienna Convention, like its predecessor, makes specific provision concerning the "Formation of the Contract". There is considerable overlap between the Convention approach and that of English law in this area but there are some significant differences. The Convention, as its title suggests, is solely concerned with the sale transaction; the formation of the other ancillary contracts for carriage, insurance or finance are unaffected.

Reaching agreement

For the present, however, the English law position remains, based on the established case law, that an agreement derived from an offer by one party and accepted by another, supported by consideration and entered into with an intention to create legal relations, where both parties are of full capacity, will result in a valid and binding contract. Any such agreement will be enforced in accordance with not only its express terms but also those to be implied by law or from the dealings of the two parties and the background circumstances against which agreement has been reached.

To ascertain the existence of the required agreement, English law has traditionally focused attention on finding an offer on the one hand and a matching acceptance on the other. It is not enough that an offer is acknowledged, it is necessary for there to be an agreement to the terms offered.

In deciding whether a contract does or does not exist, English law is only concerned with what has been said or written or what can be inferred from a particular course of conduct; the unexpressed reservations of one or other party will be of no effect—"like a thing writ in water". It is not, however, always easy to distinguish or isolate in the context of protracted negotiations, the exact stage at which agreement has been reached by the parties. They may begin to perform before agreement is actually reached and negotiations may continue even after a contract has been agreed.

The offer

No particular formality is usually required by English law for the making of an offer capable of leading to a binding contract. It can be made orally, in writing or even by conduct.

The essential elements are:

(a) that the party making the offer does so with the intention that it can be accepted by the other party without further negotiation and
(b) that the offer is in terms which are sufficiently certain to be capable of enforcement.

Where the Vienna Convention is applicable its definition of an offer includes a requirement that it be addressed to one or more specific persons; however, in practice this is unlikely to represent a significant change.

Invitation to treat

Although the offer is the first step to the final agreement, it is not usually the first step so far as the parties are concerned. That may be an "invitation to treat". This term covers any approach or proposal, whether indirectly through advertising or directly to a specific party, which is intended not to be accepted as such but to lead to an offer, as in a tender.

Advertising, circulars, catalogues, price lists

General proposals for concluding a contract, whether addressed to persons generally in the form of advertising or in the form of circulars, catalogues or price lists, are regarded not as offers to supply what in effect would be an unlimited quantity, but instead to invite offers to buy from intending purchasers. It has been suggested that an advertisement from a manufacturer might stand in a different position (*Partridge v Cruttenden* [1968]). This seems unlikely; no such distinction has been suggested in relation to price lists (*Grainger v Gough* (1896)).

Where the Vienna Convention applies, a proposal which is not addressed to specific persons (and this will probably cover both advertising and the circulation of catalogues or price lists) will be similarly regarded as inviting an offer, although the contrary can be indicated by the party making the proposal.

Tender

In the absence of any provision binding the party inviting tenders to accept the lowest offer, a request for tenders, no matter how detailed the terms will, nevertheless, be an invitation to the parties requested to put forward an offer. This will be so whether this is a specific invitation addressed to a limited list of chosen contractors or widely advertised in the national or international press. The responses of the parties requested to tender will constitute offers on the terms of the tender for acceptance by the party putting out the request to tender.

Furthermore, an invitation to tender can give rise to an implied contractual obligation on the invitor to consider tenders which conform with the conditions of tender (*Blackpool Fylde Aero Club Limited v Blackpool Borough Council* [1990]).

It is possible, although rare, for this approach to be displaced by the specific terms of the tender. The inclusion of an express provision to accept the lowest or highest price will result in the invitation to tender being looked at as an offer capable of acceptance by the making of the lowest or highest tender.

In general, the conclusion of any of the contracts involved in the international sale of goods will be preceded by negotiations and not every exchange between the parties can necessarily be characterised as either an invitation to treat or an offer.

Subjects

An approach by one party that may otherwise constitute an offer capable of acceptance will not be so where from its terms the party making the offer intends that agreement will not be immediately binding. Perhaps the most common example of this is where the terms given are expressly stated to be "subject" to some further requirement.

"Subject to contract"

In property transactions the almost universal usage is of the words "subject to contract" to prevent agreement being reached until the contract is finally signed on both sides. The use of such a subject in international trade is rare. In this context the intention of the parties that the agreement reached will be subsequently drawn up in writing will not normally prevent a conclusion that agreement had in fact been reached based on an earlier exchange of telexes or similar communication. This is particularly so in relation to negotiations for the chartering of ships where the agreement is often seen as being reached on the exchange, usually by brokers, of the "recap" telexes. The drawing up and signature of the charter usually follows much later, sometimes after the voyage has been completed! This approach can be displaced if the parties make this clear during the negotiations and agreement will only become binding on signature (*British Steel Corporation v Cleveland Bridge Limited* [1984], page 10 below). This is also so even if the words "subject to contract" or similar are not expressly used (*Sopanata v Hvaljslsk Polaris A/S* [1952]). In practice, such a finding is more likely where long term business is involved.

More common in international trade are more limited subjects to cover a specific requirement of one of the parties such as "subject to confirmation", "subject to board approval" or "subject to receiver's approval". Recognition is given particularly to "subject to details" as being a broking shorthand intended to make clear that there is no binding agreement until the "subject" is displaced either by actual agreement on the details, the waiver of any outstanding points or the execution of a formal contract.

In the *"Junior K"* [1988] owners and charterers agreed on the terms for a charterparty "subject to details of Gencon charterparty". In the event the owners decided not to continue with the negotiations. It was decided that the fixture was conditional on the details of the Gencon form and there was no contract until agreement had been reached on those details.

It is important to distinguish the position where a "subject" prevents agreement being reached from cases where an agreement is actually reached but performance of one or both parties is subject to some condition being complied with.

In *Brauer v James Clark (Brush Materials) Ltd* [1952], negotiations led to an agreement to supply Brazilian brush fibres to the United Kingdom "subject to Brazilian Export Licence". The sellers could not obtain the licence except at a loss-making price. In defence to the buyer's claim for non-delivery, the sellers argued that liability only arose if the subject was lifted. It was decided that a contract had been concluded binding the sellers to deliver provided they could obtain the necessary licence through reasonable endeavours.

Certainty

Given the basic approach of the law that the parties are left to agree their own terms, the courts are not able to fill any gaps or add any terms that might otherwise be regarded as useful, usual or reasonable. If no certain meaning can be given to a supposed offer then this cannot give rise to a contract.

In *G. Scammel and Nephew Ltd v H. C. & J. G. Ouston* [1941] a provision was added to a written contract of sale for a motor lorry: "for finance on hire purchase terms over a period of two years". The buyer failed to complete and denied that any contract existed. It was decided that the term as to finance was too vague and uncertain to constitute an enforceable contract.

Withdrawal of an offer

An offer may be withdrawn at any time before acceptance. This is the position even where the party making the offer has said that the offer will be kept open for a period. The withdrawal only takes effect when actually brought to the notice of the party to whom the original offer was addressed. This is an issue on which the Vienna Convention, if brought into force in the United Kingdom, would have a significant impact as it says that an offer stated to be irrevocable could only be withdrawn if the withdrawal reaches the person receiving the offer on or before the time the offer is received. Otherwise under the Convention an offer that is stated to be or can reasonably be considered to be irrevocable, if only for a certain period, cannot be revoked.

Under English law, at present, it is only where the party making an offer has been paid or received some other benefit or consideration independently solely to maintain the offer that such a promise would be binding. This would be more usually regarded as a formal option.

Where an offer has been made it will normally be considered to lapse, in the absence of any specific provision, if it is not accepted within a reasonable time; the length of such time will depend on the circumstances.

An offer is considered automatically to lapse if expressly rejected, whether directly by a refusal or indirectly by any counter-proposal.

Acceptance

To constitute an agreement an offer must be accepted. As with an offer, unless the offer itself has required otherwise, acceptance may be:

(a) verbally, as by telephone
(b) in writing, as by letter, telex, cable or fax
(c) or by conduct, as where goods are simply dispatched in response to an order.

In general, silence or inactivity do not constitute acceptance. In a number of cases concerning moribund arbitrations, agreements have been derived from long periods of inactivity. It is doubtful that such principles extend beyond such cases and in any event the "agreements" reached have been limited to the abandonment of an existing agreement. For the present, the orthodox position is that some more positive step is required and the Vienna Convention requirements are not dissimilar to this.

Time of acceptance

The acceptance must normally be communicated or advised to the party making the offer. The time and place when this takes place depends in part on the mode of acceptance.

Acceptance by telephone, telex and (probably) fax is complete when received by the other party, even if not read or, it has been suggested, heard where the party who has failed to hear has not asked for its repetition.

Acceptance by letter or telegram is complete, and the contract binding, when the letter or telegram is handed in or when posted and properly addressed. This takes effect even if the acceptance is lost *en route*. This is probably best regarded as an arbitrary rule putting the risk of postal delays on the party making the offer in cases where communication by letter has been chosen. This rule may also be applicable where the parties have used despatch riders or couriers, although this cannot be stated with certainty. Use by the accepting party of the post or courier when these are likely to be affected by strike action will displace this rule and acceptance will only take place when the communication reaches the other party.

The Vienna Convention, if brought into force in the United Kingdom, would have the effect of reversing the rule for international sale transactions. The position would then be that in all cases (including post) acceptance takes effect on receipt and not on sending. The different rule under the Convention for postal communications gives an opportunity to withdraw the acceptance which is not otherwise available under English law and this is permitted provided this withdrawal arrives no later than the "acceptance" it is seeking to forestall.

These are general guides and any specific requirement in the offer terms will oust them. Any requirement that acceptance be by "notice in writing" requires the acceptance actually to reach the party making the offer and any time limit for acceptance contained in an offer will have to be obeyed. In contracts incorporating the Uniform Laws on International Sales the specific provisions of the Hague Convention will apply.

Acceptance by conduct

Acceptance by conduct is also recognised. An offer to buy can be accepted simply by despatching the goods, for example. An acceptance of this nature tends, in practice, to give rise to greater difficulties than the more straightforward verbal or written acceptance. A court, however, once convinced of the fact of a basic agreement will strive to resolve uncertainties.

For instance, in the case *Steven v Bromley & Son* (1919), charterers agreed to load a full cargo of steel, but in the event loaded partly general merchandise. Owners sued for extra freight for general cargo. It was decided that shipment of general cargo did not fall within the agreement to ship steel and a new contract of carriage at the current rate of freight was to be implied from the offer derived from the charterers' delivery to the ship of general merchandise to be paid for at the current rate of freight and the owner's acceptance by loading.

In striving to resolve the uncertainties inherent in a situation where acceptance has been by conduct a court is likely to look, as a guide, to the parties' intentions. Where relevant, these will be derived from the previous dealings between those parties and also any draft agreements prepared by them but not otherwise finalised, where the actual performance of the contract has followed.

In the case *Brogden v Metropolitan Railway Company* [1877] parties negotiated an annual contract for the supply of coal. A draft agreement was prepared to be signed and approved by the seller. On reaching the buyer the draft was put in a desk drawer and left there. There were no further negotiations. Soon afterwards the seller began to supply coal and subsequently disputes arose as to quality and quantity. The seller argued that there was no concluded agreement. It was decided that the conduct of the parties in the shipment of and payment for the coal established the existence of the contract on the terms of the draft approved by the seller.

An important, and common, aspect of this approach is in its application to the incorporation of standard trading terms, which is dealt with separately on page 12.

A note of caution should be sounded in this context, as it is not in every case where the parties have conducted themselves as though agreement had been reached that this will be found to be the case. An important feature of the *Brogden* case above is that the placing of the draft in the drawer effectively marked the end of negotiations. Where performance is taking place in parallel with written or verbal negotiations which break down, there will be no agreement even though considerable work may have been done or substantial sums laid out in the faith that agreement would eventually be reached. A good example of this is the case *British Steel Corporation v Cleveland Bridge and Engineering Co. Ltd* [1984]. In negotiations for the supply of steel work, the buyer issued a letter of intent, indicating its intention to issue a formal sub-contract on its own terms at prices offered by the seller. The buyer asked the seller to start manufacture immediately, which it did. Disputes arose as to the delivery schedule and no formal sub-contract document was finalised. It was decided that there was no concluded contract because the continuing negotiations showed uncertainty as to the terms and there was no formal contract document as envisaged by the letter of intent. This prevented acceptance by the seller's conduct in delivering the steel work.

A seller who has actually supplied goods is not left completely without remedy and may be awarded what a court considers to be a reasonable price. A similar result could follow where a service had been supplied, such as the carriage of goods, without any firm agreement on the freight or other remuneration having been reached. The court may fix a reasonable sum on what is known as a "quantum meruit" basis.

No such remedy, in the absence of agreement, is available where the issue is one of non-performance or where a partially completed transaction has to be unravelled. Considerable loss and expense can be involved in such situations. In one such case the Government of Hong Kong had to vacate 83 flats it had occupied in advance of agreement being reached, when the overall deal collapsed. An argument that the continuing negotiations and continuing performance was a binding representation that agreement would be reached was rejected. It was also doubted that such a result could ever be reached when the negotiations were expressly subject to contract or similar condition.

Retrospective acceptance

In those situations where performance and negotiations take place concurrently, the parties' intention will usually be that the negotiations will be successful and lead to agreement being reached, and that the agreement so reached will be back dated to cover any goods supplied or work already done. In *Trollope & Colls v Atomic Power Construction Ltd* [1963] a sub-contractor tendered to the contractor for a nuclear power authority for the construction of power stations. Substantial changes were made to the work to be done at the request of the authority. Three months later work started. Ten months later in April 1960 the contract terms were finally agreed. It was decided that the tender was an offer which was finally accepted when the parties agreed the terms in April 1960. This acceptance was expected to, and did have, retrospective effect to cover all work that had already been done.

Acceptance must be unqualified

Acceptance must correspond with the terms of the offer being accepted. A willingness to take a quantity different from that offered is no more an acceptance than a willingness to pay a different price. In each case the purported acceptance will take effect as a counter-offer. This, as it has been said, "kills" the original offer which can no longer be accepted, unless reoffered. This would equally be the position if an additional term or terms were put forward.

This is to be distinguished from an enquiry as to whether the party making the offer would be prepared to vary it, which will preserve the original offer for acceptance unless expressly withdrawn. The distinction between a counter-offer and an enquiry can be a fine one, and the use of a question mark should not be regarded as necessarily guaranteeing the continuation of the offer.

Exact correspondence word for word is not essential and the express proposal of a term which would be implied, in any event, will not prevent agreement. Similarly, a new term which is for the benefit of the party making the offer may not prevent acceptance. Where the Vienna Convention applies, express provision is made to the effect that terms which do not "materially" alter the original offer constitute an acceptance unless immediately objected to. As matters of price, payment, quality, quantity, time and place of delivery, terms concerning the parties' liabilities to each other and terms concerning the settlement of disputes are to be regarded as "material", in practice the position is probably little different from the current situation.

Acceptance must be certain

As with the offer, any uncertainty in the acceptance may be fatal to agreement being concluded. A simple yes to an offer giving alternatives is just as unhelpful in this context as any other. This is illustrated in *Peter Lind & Co. Ltd v Mersey Docks & Harbour Board* [1972] where a contractor tendered for the construction of a freight terminal giving both a fixed and a fluctuating price. The dock company wrote accepting "your tender". It was decided that the dock company letter was imprecise as it did not specify which tender was being accepted, so no contract was concluded.

Agreement reached

Two important consequences flow from the focus on the offer from one party and the acceptance by the other as constituting a binding contract which the law will enforce. These are:

(a) that it is only the terms agreed or to be regarded as forming part of the exchange which are binding and
(b) that it is only the parties to the agreement who are bound by it.

Incorporation of standard terms

A perennial problem arises in relation to the incorporation of standard terms to which no reference has been made at the time of the conclusion of the agreement. This is a problem perhaps more prevalent with the sale contract than the shipping insurance or finance elements of a transaction.

It is a matter of some importance whenever performance by the parties does not proceed as smoothly as planned. In sales where the security for a period of credit is the seller's retention of title clause or similar, this can be absolutely crucial. In the event of the insolvency of a buyer before payment, no receiver or liquidator will miss the opportunity to avoid such terms given by any failure to have the applicability of the standard terms agreed at the time the contract was concluded. Even where it can be said that one of the alternative principles looked at below applies, the failure to make this clear at the outset almost inevitably leads, in a dispute with a liquidator, to the seller's claim to any proceeds being discounted unless the matter is to be tested in court.

There are, however, certain circumstances in which the standard terms of one of the parties will form part of the terms agreed or, at least, be regarded as agreed, despite the absence of any reference to them in what would otherwise be seen as the offer and the acceptance.

Initial arrangements made informally

Where the original arrangements of the parties are informal, particularly where they are oral, the subsequent despatch of a document which includes one party's standard terms can be viewed as confirming and supplementing what had been agreed, particularly where these would be expected. In *Interphoto Picture Library Limited v Stiletto Visual Programmes* [1988] an advertising agency requested a photo library which they had never used before to forward some pictures. The request was made over the telephone. The pictures were sent round with an invoice incorporating the library's terms including charges for holding the pictures. The agency kept the pictures for weeks and received a huge bill. It was decided that, given the informal nature of the initial contact, the terms were incorporated but that the unusual and extortionate charges could not be relied on unless they had been specifically brought to the attention of the user, which they had not.

Course of dealing

Standard terms may be applicable even though not referred to directly where they have been used habitually or referred to in a course of dealing between the parties. It is not yet clear how many transactions constitute a course of dealing but a consistent course rather than scattered transactions is sought.

The basis of this approach is that by using standard terms, as for example on the back of an invoice, one party shows an intention to rely on them, and the other party, if raising no complaint over a period, is taken on subsequent deals to accept their applicability even though they are not expressly referred to at the time such subsequent agreements were reached. In *British Road Services Ltd v Arthur Crutchley* [1968] the carrier deposited whisky with a warehouse over a long period and on each occasion the carrier's delivery note was stamped "received under [warehousemen's conditions]". It was decided that if it had only happened once it was doubtful that the warehousemen had done enough but the regularity and frequency over the years was sufficient, combined with the references in the invoices to the warehousemen's terms, for them to apply.

Usual trade terms

In certain areas an intention to contract on standard terms, especially where these are well known or customary in the trade, will be inferred even without any previous course of dealing. The applicability of the conditions of carriage of bills of lading is probably an example of this principle.

Battle of the forms

Another facet of the problem is where each party in the negotiations is putting proposals on its own terms. On a strict analysis no agreement may be reached but where the parties have acted on the basis that an agreement has been concluded and substantially performed the contract, a court is likely to want to find a contract and will look at all the exchanges to assess which terms should prevail. The crucial issues will be the extent to which notice was given of the terms and the extent to which one or other party can be said to have acquiesced in them.

One of the best examples of this problem is *Butler Machine Tools Ltd v Ex Cell O Corporation (England) Ltd* [1979]. In negotiations a seller of a machine tool quoted a price of £75,000 to a buyer. The quotation incorporated the seller's terms. The buyer placed an order referring to its own terms. The seller returned a tear-off slip on the buyer's order form acknowledging the order and the buyer's terms. A covering letter returning this referred to the seller's own quotation. The seller's terms allowed an increase in price which it was claiming. It was decided that the buyer's order was a counter-offer which destroyed the offer in the seller's quotation and which the seller accepted by returning the tear-off slip so the buyer's terms applied.

The device of seeking to include a term in standard conditions that party's terms are to prevail will not be effective, unless backed by the necessary action to impose the terms including that provision in the first instance.

Parties

As generally any agreement results in an offer from or on behalf of one party and its acceptance by another, the consequence is that those parties, from whose communications the agreement has resulted, are the ones bound by the agreement and the only persons entitled to sue or be sued in respect of that agreement.

In *Dunlop Pneumatic Tyre Co. v Selfridge & Co. Ltd* [1915] a tyre manufacturer supplied tyres to wholesalers on terms that they were to ensure that any retailers adhered to the manufacturer's list of prices. The retailer failed to do so and the tyre manufacturer sought to enforce the prices. It was decided that no third party rights could arise by way of contract and only a person who is a party to a contract can sue on it.

Since there was no contract between the manufacturer and retailer, the claim was unenforceable.

This is a principle known in legal terms as the doctrine of privity of contract. In the vast majority of cases it presents little difficulty and reflects the reality of the position as understood by the parties in negotiation, although there are exceptions.

Involvement of agents

The involvement of agents is commonplace in any international transaction and agents properly so called will, in accordance with normal agency principles, not themselves be a party to any contract concluded through their efforts. Occasions arise, however, when it is far from clear whether a person's role is that of agent or principal to the contract. A variation on this arises where a party, in fact acting as agent, has not disclosed this and the party in the dark will be able to look to both the agent or the true principal for satisfaction. This is considered further in Chapter 3.

Collateral contracts

In certain situations, where three parties have been involved in a transaction which results in agreement between two of the parties, on the faith of a representation by the third party, a further agreement may be implied between the third party (that is the party making the representation) and the party relying on the representation. This further agreement is said to be collateral to the main agreement. In the present context this is a situation most likely to arise in relation to a sale contract and which can arise where, for example, a buyer has chosen a specific product on the strength of representations made by a manufacturer or dealer other than the actual seller.

In *Wells (Merstham) Ltd v Buckland Sand & Silica Ltd* [1965] a sand merchant represented to a plant grower that one of its grades of sand would be suitable for growing chrysanthemums. The grower bought the recommended sand from its usual supplier. The sand in fact contained harmful chemicals which killed the plants. The grower claimed against the sand merchant. It was decided that the grower's actions in buying the grade of sand on the faith of the representation of the sand merchant constituted a collateral contract between grower and merchant and it was immaterial that the purchase had actually been from another party.

Irrevocable credits

A particular exception which is of relevance in the international sale of goods is the position between the seller and a bank issuing a letter of credit on behalf of the buyer. The application of the orthodox approach which requires an offer and a matching acceptance would lead to the view that no agreement existed; in some instances there is little or no contact at all between the seller and the paying bank until presentation of the documents under the letter of credit. In what is perhaps best regarded as an anomaly, English law has adopted the pragmatic approach, recognising the need for enforceable rights between the seller and the buyer's banker, even if there is no obvious legal principle which quite provides such a result.

Bills of lading

Another exception relevant to international trade concerns the application of the terms of the contracts of carriage between shipowner and cargo owner as contained in or evidenced by a bill of lading between cargo owner and any of the shipowner's sub-contractors, especially stevedores. Terms seeking to provide for the position of stevedores and others are now commonplace in liner bills of lading. Such terms are often known as "Himalaya" clauses, after their introduction to close the gap exposed by a Mrs Adler's successful claim against the master and crew members of the P&O liner of that name, following her fall from an inadequately secured gangplank onto the quay at Trieste. The purpose of the claim was to avoid the application of the exclusions from liability of P&O's standard ticket terms which would otherwise have applied.

Once again, the pragmatic approach can probably be said to have triumphed over legal theory, and the standard forms of clause are now given effect in England (*Eurymedon* [1974]), if not in all common law jurisdictions, as constituting an agreement binding cargo owner and stevedore or other sub-contractors despite the absence of any real contact between the two and probably very little, if any, awareness as to each other's actual identity.

Requirements

The fact of agreement between the parties does not necessarily result, as a matter of English law, in there automatically being a binding contract.

For that agreement to constitute a binding contract the following requirements must also be met, namely that:

(a) there is consideration for the agreement
(b) the parties intended to create legal relations
(c) there is compliance with any formalities
(d) both parties have capacity to enter such a contract.

Consideration

English law also requires that where agreement has been reached, it should have been reached for "consideration". This is the requirement that a promise by one party is matched by some benefit to that party from the other, or by some detriment to the party in whose favour the promise has been made. In a straightforward case the consideration for the promise to supply goods is the payment by the other party of the price. The need for consideration does not feature in a number of Continental jurisdictions and the Vienna Convention reflects this—consideration not being a requirement either for the original agreement or any variation.

The rationale

The rationale for this requirement is to distinguish between promises the law should enforce, such as contractual promises, and those which are not intended to be binding, such as the promise of a gift.

Adequacy

The requirement is that there is some benefit, not that the benefit should be regarded as reasonable or adequate. Indeed, it can be patently inadequate, as in the case of the proverbial peppercorn, or, a more modern example, used chocolate bar wrappers.

Impact—the initial agreement

In the context of international agreements for the sale, carriage and financing of goods in a commercial context a requirement that there be consideration for the agreement is not of great practical importance. The consideration for the promises made by seller, carrier or bank in the form of price, freight or fees and interest are fairly obvious.

The most relevant exceptions to this are in the context of the difficult cases posed by the relationship between paying bank and seller/beneficiary under a letter of credit, and the relationship of stevedores and other sub-contractors of a shipowner to the bill of lading holder which have been considered later in this book.

Impact—subsequent variation

The requirement for consideration as it applies to an agreement initially concluded between two parties applies equally to any agreement on a variation or amendment of that contract and, potentially, this latter requirement can pose considerable practical difficulty. A promise to undertake what is already promised is not generally regarded as consideration and, hence, there is often no consideration from a party in whose favour a variation of, say, the time for delivery or the time for payment, has been made.

Many of the potential problems which this request may otherwise cause are avoided, by reason of the application of the principles of waiver and estoppel which are considered below. However, these do not always provide an answer. This can be an issue especially where the insolvency or threatened insolvency of a party is involved. Very recently in a building case the court has found that an agreement by a contractor to make top up payments to a sub-contractor, whose financial situation would otherwise prevent the work being completed, was enforceable as the contractor obtained the benefit of avoiding penalty payments to the building owner, even though the sub-contractor did no more than it was already required to do. There seems no reason why this approach should not apply to international trade transactions.

This question is also relevant to the problems posed by agreements secured by duress, which are considered on page 39.

Waiver or forbearance

Although a waiver is in principle little more than a variation without consideration, a waiver by a party is enforceable against that party by the party in whose favour the waiver was made and the party who has agreed a variation cannot refuse to accept the varied performance by the other. No claim will arise on either side in the event that the agreement is performed as varied.

The absence of consideration does, however, allow the party making the allowance or waiver to retract it, so far as this is still possible, provided reasonable notice is given.

In *Nichimen Corporation v Gatoil Overseas Inc.* [1987] Brent crude was sold on terms that a buyer provided a letter of credit in acceptable terms by a certain date. Following a major fall in the market, the seller allowed an additional fixed period within which to provide a letter of credit which the buyer failed to do. It was decided that although the seller had waived the original time limit, by substituting a new date, it had not waived its right to terminate the contract if the buyer failed to provide a letter of credit by the new date.

Estoppel

A variation to an agreement without consideration will also be enforced where:

(a) there is a representation or assurance by words or conduct made by one party to the other,
(b) intended to affect legal relations and to be acted on accordingly, and
(c) which is acted upon by the party to whom it is made.

If these requirements are met, the court will not allow the party which made the representation or assurance to go back on its word and it must accept the position as qualified by its own actions, even if there is no consideration.

As with waiver, the effect is merely to suspend the enforceability of the term in question and the party waiving its rights is entitled to revert on reasonable notice. Again there will be occasions when events intervene to deprive the party of the opportunity to go back to the original agreement.

Part payment of a debt

Part payment of a debt occupies a special category by reason of the much criticised rule in the case of *Foakes v Beer* (1884), that a creditor is not bound by an undertaking to accept part payment in full settlement of a debt. This does not apply strictly to claims other than debt (damages, for example) or where there is a *bona fide* dispute as to the amount due. Any benefit to the creditor such as a marginally earlier payment date will displace the rule, as will payment by a third party or where agreement has been reached as part of a composition agreement involving other creditors. Where none of these exceptions apply, the equitable doctrine of estoppel outlined above can be relied on. There is, however, some question whether, as this is merely suspensory, a creditor, on giving notice, can demand the full sum due. So far no one seems to have been willing to sacrifice their reputation to test this. In one case, concerning payments for the use of a patent, where "compensation" instalments had been waived, it would seem to have been assumed that these could not subsequently be recovered, although the "compensation", was, on notice, restored to the proper level for the future.

Promises under seal

The rule that consideration is not applicable in respect of a promise or contract in a deed under seal is likely to have been amended by the Law of Property (Miscellaneous Provisions) Act 1989 so that the exception is that now no consideration is required in respect of a promise or contract contained in a deed, so long as that deed complies with the formalities of the Law of Property (Miscellaneous Provisions) Act 1989.

For individuals the deed must be in writing on any substance which can constitute a document and it must be signed and delivered. Signature must be witnessed and attested, and the instrument must make it clear from its face that it is intended to be a deed.

S.130 (2) of the Companies Act 1989 states how a company may execute a deed. It must either be sealed or signed by a director and secretary of the company or by two of its directors, and it must also be clear from the face of the instrument that it is intended to be a deed.

Intention to create legal relations

An agreement, even if supported by consideration, will not represent a binding contract unless there was also an intention to create a legally binding arrangement. This is an aspect which has its main role in a domestic or employment context. In the field of international trade the impact is likely to be limited. The author has seen it argued that empty jute bags supplied with three shipments of barley were supplied under an agreement which, with regard to the bags, was not legally binding since they were provided "to help out". The buyer had paid US$ one million just for the bags and was justifiably unimpressed. In a sense also, agreements subject to some further requirement also represent circumstances where, at least at the time initial agreement is reached, the parties do not intend to be legally bound. Where the Vienna Convention applies there is no separate requirement of an intention to create legal relations as such.

Agreements expressly binding in honour

An arrangement which expressly provides that it is not to be the subject of legal jurisdiction and is only to constitute an expression of intention binding in honour will not be regarded as intending to create legal relations.

In *Rose & Frank v Compton Bros* [1923] a distribution agreement between manufacturers of paper tissue and distributors provided that "this arrangement is not entered into as a formal legal agreement and shall not be subject to legal jurisdiction and is only a definite expression and record of the purpose and intention which [the parties] honourably pledge themselves . . ." It was decided that the document did not constitute a binding contract and no liability arose from the manufacturer's termination of the agreement without notice.

Letters of comfort

A similar issue arises with regard to letters of comfort or letters of awareness which may well be intended, at least by the party giving them, not to be legally binding. This is a question to be determined from the actual wording of the letter.

In *Kleinwort Benson v Malaysia Mining Corporation* [1989] a dealing subsidiary of a mining company sought an additional loan facility from a bank. The bank sought a parent company guarantee. This was refused and a letter of comfort provided instead in terms that "It is our policy to ensure that the business of [the borrower] is at all times in a position to meet its liabilities to you under the above arrangements". It was decided that the letter did not express any contractual promise and the parent assumed a moral, not a legal, liability.

Formalities

Whilst in practical terms the recording of any contract or agreement in writing is to be encouraged from the point of view of certainty,

English law no longer requires this as essential for any contract to be enforceable, except in certain situations such as contracts for the sale of land.

So far as the main elements involved in the international sale of goods are concerned, there are no formalities required by the law before any agreement reached can be enforceable. As we have seen on page 3, agreements reached orally and those inferred from the conduct of the parties are equally enforced by the courts.

Jurisdiction agreements

Although the overall agreement may be regarded by the courts as enforceable, a term of that agreement making provision for the referral of any disputes which arise to the jurisdiction of the courts of a particular country or to arbitration is likely to be required to be in writing to be effective.

The contract should also contain a choice of law clause. If, as is common, no provision is made, traditionally in case of disputes the court has but to look for the system of law with which, taking all the background circumstances into acount, the contract has its closest connection. From 1 April 1991 this question will need to be answered by reference to the Rome Convention on Law Applicable to Contracts which was brought into force by the Contracts (Applicable Law) Act 1990.

Under the Convention, if the parties do not include a choice of law clause then the governing law will be that of the country of the party making the "characteristic performance". This overlaps but is not entirely square with the traditional English approach. The parties are also bound by any "mandatory rules" of the country with which "all the other elements relevant to the situation at the time of the choice are connected". Therefore the parties cannot circumvent such rules by deliberate choice of law.

What is less clear is how far the laws of another country will encroach. In its narrowest sense this adds little to the approach of the court in cases of illegality under foreign law. For example, in *Ralli Bros v Compania Naviera Sota y Aznar* [1920] the choice of English law did not entitle the parties to disregard Spanish fiscal laws in respect of the payment and receipt of freight in Spain. What is likely is that the Convention's terms will be given some wider scope, but at this early stage it is difficult to predict how much impact a reference back to a foreign system of law will have in practice, except that taking advice on two systems of law in cases of dispute will involve additional expense.

The convention does not apply to certain types of contract such as bills of exchange, cheques, promissory notes, bills of lading, arbitration agreements and agreements on the choice of court.

Term giving jurisdiction over disputes to the courts of a country

The requirements that may apply in this instance result from the provisions of the Brussels Convention on Jurisdiction and the Enforcement of Judgments in Civil and Commercial Matters brought into force by the Civil Jurisdiction and Judgments Act 1982 and in effect since 1986. Under the terms of the Convention (Article 17) any term providing for the courts of any one of the eleven Member States of the European Community which are signatories (Spain and Portugal have yet to adhere to this) to have jurisdiction to be effective must be:

(a) in writing or
(b) evidenced in writing or
(c) in international trade or commerce in a form which accords with the practices in that trade or commerce of which the parties are or ought to have been aware.

Similar rules apply under Article 17 of the 1988 Lugano Convention on Jurisdiction and Enforcement of Judgments in Civil and Commercial Matters made between the Member States of the European Community and European Free Trade Association.

Perhaps strangely, a special rule applies to a party based in Luxembourg (Article I of Protocol annexed to the Brussels Convention). To be binding on such a party, that party has to have expressly and specifically agreed to such a provision. It is unclear whether this agreement should be in writing but it would be sensible to ensure this.

Terms giving jurisdiction over disputes to arbitration

An agreement to refer any disputes to arbitration can be verbal but unless that agreement is reduced to writing in some way, the powers of the courts to supplement the powers of the arbitrators and to give effect to any arbitration agreement by the enforcement of an award cannot be invoked.

It is sufficient for this purpose that the arbitration agreement, if not part of the principal agreement itself, can be found in writing by reference to another document. Even in the case of a verbal agreement it will be sufficient if the parties have agreed expressly or impliedly that the terms as set out in a document are to form the basis of at least part of the contract.

In *Zambia Steel & Building Supplies Ltd v James Clark & Eaton Ltd* [1986] 100,000 MT of sheet glass was contracted to be sold C&F Dar es Salaam. Some arrived damaged. The contract was comprised in quotations incorporating the seller's terms and including an Arbitration Clause. The final conclusion of the agreement had been verbal. It was found that the contract was partly in writing and partly unwritten. It was legitimate to look to any evidence to prove assent to the written terms and on the facts the agreement to arbitrate was one of the terms in writing.

A special rule may apply, however, that specific words making reference to the arbitration clause expressly are required where it is wished to incorporate in a contract the terms of the arbitration clause of another contract between different parties. This has long been the rule applying to the incorporation of charterparty arbitration clauses into bill of lading contracts where a general incorporation of all terms and conditions does not incorporate the arbitration clause unless stated in the terms. Despite much criticism, this long established rule has been recently re-confirmed (*"Varenna"* [1983]). A more recent decision (*Pinetop v Unione Italiana* [1987]), has extended the rule to contracts of reinsurance, which suggests that the rule may be of wider application. This has not, hitherto, been the practice as regards sales terms, including trade association standard terms, and it is doubtful whether the extension of the rule applying to bills of lading, which can and will usually be transferred to third parties by assignment or negotiation, is justified in other areas.

Capacity

Individuals

Where an individual is concerned, the main requirement affecting the ability to contract is that the party is not a minor. Individuals under the age of 18 are regarded in law as minors or infants and special rules apply to contracts to which they are a party. For present purposes the most important rule is that a minor is not bound by a trading contract, which will include a contract of carriage as well as a contract of sale, and cannot be made liable for failure to deliver or, without a court order, failure to pay. Special rules also apply with regard to lunatics and parties contracting whilst drunk, who may avoid a contract if the other party has sought to take advantage of their situation.

Corporate bodies

The question of capacity is potentially more important for corporations, particularly limited companies. These exist under a statutory or chartered framework and their ability to contract is governed by the limitations of that framework.

In the case of a limited company incorporated under the Companies Act 1985 or its predecessors, whether private or plc, the relevant framework is the objects clause in the Memorandum of Association.

In the case of corporations set up under their own Act of Parliament, usually now quasi-government organisations, the terms of the Act itself will provide the limits.

Under what is known as the "ultra vires" (beyond its powers) doctrine any act, including what would otherwise be a contract, which is not authorised by the statute or the objects clause is void and unenforceable by either party.

In *re Jon Beauforte (London) Limited* [1950] a company set up to operate a business as costumiers and gown makers instead undertook the manufacture of veneer panels. In the liquidation, claims were made by suppliers to the veneer panel business. It was found that the company did not have the power to undertake the business and could not be bound by the supply contracts which were void.

In practical terms it is rare in the international sale of goods context that this should be an issue. This is largely the result, despite judicial disapproval in 1918, of the practice to have, for even the smallest business, the most widely drawn objects clauses. The writer has seen a company intended to run a family farm having powers (amongst others) to run dancing troupes and jugglers and other circus acts! This is, however, not always so and the doctrine may have a role with ancillary arrangements such as the giving of guarantees. Such a case arose recently when a government development corporation sought to avoid a guarantee it had given, on the grounds that its statute of incorporation (ordinance) did not permit the giving of the relevant guarantee; in the event, on the construction of the ordinance, the defence failed (*Den Norske Creditbank v Sarawak Economic Development Corporation* [1989]).

Additionally, much of the force of the doctrine has, for those dealing with companies, been removed by the harmonisation of the position of English law with that of Europe by s. 34 of the Companies Act 1985 (superseding s. 9(1) of the European Communities Act 1972). This provision deems any transaction decided on by the directors as within the company's powers, in favour of any third party who is unaware of any relevant limitation on the company's powers. This only assists third parties dealing with companies incorporated under the Companies Act and is of no help to the company itself.

Partnerships

Although various procedural rules give a partnership some of the attributes of a separate entity, it really has no such status and its capacity is that of its individual members, personal or corporate.

Avoiding the agreement

There are, however, certain situations where despite the agreement which has (or has apparently) been reached, the circumstances in which that agreement has been reached or in which it is to be performed are such that English law will allow one or both parties to avoid the agreement.

These situations are:

(a) where the agreement has been reached
   (i) through the mistake of one or both parties
   (ii) through the misrepresentation of one party
   (iii) through the duress of one party
(b) where the terms of the agreement or its performance would involve illegality.

Mistake

Mistake has an impact on an otherwise valid agreement in one of two ways:

(a) where a fundamental mistake of one or other party is such that in truth no agreement between the parties has taken place, mistake is said to "negative the contract"
(b) where both parties have made a mistake about a fundamental issue, this is said to "nullify the contract".

In either case the party mistaken may avoid the agreement which had otherwise apparently been reached.

No real consent

To negative the apparent consent of the parties, it is essential that the mistake was crucial to the conclusion of the contract and, but for the mistake, the contract would not have been concluded. It is not every mistake which will enable the contract to be avoided, as otherwise any party who had miscalculated on the profitability of a particular deal would be able to avoid the agreement on that basis.

The mistake, to be operative, will need to be known to the other party or induced by that other's negligence, or to have resulted in a genuine ambiguity as to what the parties agreed.

The situations where the parties' apparent agreement is *initiated* by the fundamental mistake of one of the parties have generally concerned:

(a) a mistake as to identity of the other party
(b) where one party intends to deal with one thing and the other with a different one
(c) where one intends to deal on one set of terms and the other on a different set.

Mistake as to person

Cases of this nature generally concern rogues and impostors who have misled an innocent party into parting with money or other property. The mistake has, however, to be a fundamental one as to the actual identity of the other party; a mistake as to an attribute such as credit-worthiness, for example, would not be sufficient.

Mistake as to subject-matter

Where one party intends to deal with one thing and the other something else, the "contract" would be void.

In *Raffles v Wichelhaus* (1864) there was a sale of 125 bales of cotton ex *Peerless* from Bombay. Unknown to either party there were two vessels of the same name. The seller tendered goods from the second vessel which the buyer was entitled to refuse having intended to buy from the first.

Mistake as to terms

A mistake as to the terms of the contract will avoid it. This could perhaps also be explained on the basis that there is in reality no certain agreement between the parties.

In *Hartog v Colin Shields* [1939] a seller agreed to sell hare skins. In error it offered the goods at a price per pound, instead of a price per piece. The value of a piece was one-third of the price per pound. In negotiations reference had always been made to the price per piece. It was decided that the buyer could not reasonably suppose that the seller's offer represented its real intention and must have known of the mistake and this prevented a binding contract coming into existence.

Mutual mistake

Unlike the mistake which is said to negative the agreement, a mistake, to have the effect of nullifying the agreement, has to be one that is made by both parties and, as such, either party will be entitled to avoid the contract. The mistake of the party must not have arisen out of a belief entertained without any reasonable ground and deliberately induced in the mind of the other, otherwise the right to avoid the contract will be lost by the party who has created the false impression.

In *McRae v Commonwealth Disposals Commission* [1950] the Commission sought tenders for disposal of a wreck which the successful tenderer found did not exist. The Commission attempted to avoid the contract on the grounds of mistake. It was decided that the Commission was liable as it had failed to take steps to confirm the existence of the wreck.

If the right to avoid the contract for mutual mistake is to remain, the contract must not make provision for the possibility that the assumed position is mistaken. The latter point can raise difficult questions as to the extent of the risk undertaken by one of the parties. A mistake as to the actual existence of the goods or any other subject-matter is likely to entitle the mistaken party to avoid the contract. More difficult questions will arise where the mistake concerns a specific feature of goods, and the issue will be whether the parties have contracted on the basis that some specific thing or feature existed, or whether one of the parties has undertaken the risk of its existence.

In *Amalgamated Investment and Property Co. Ltd v John Walker & Sons Ltd* [1977] the buyer of a warehouse refused to complete the purchase on the grounds of common mistake when, unknown to both parties, the warehouse was listed as a building of historic interest. It was found that listing was a risk which any developer took; in any event the mistake, to justify avoiding the agreement, had to concern an existing fact and not a future expectation and the warehouse was not listed at the time of the agreement.

S.6 of the Sale of Goods Act 1979 makes express provision that a sale contract for specific goods will be void where unknown to the seller the goods no longer exist.

Quantity

A similar rule to that which applies where goods do not exist at all also applies where there is a mistake as to the quantity which will also nullify the contract where the contract makes no provision for shortages.

In *Barrow Lane and Ballard Ltd v Phillips & Co. Ltd* [1920] a seller sold a parcel of 700 bags. Unknown to either party the warehouse in which they were stored had wrongfully released part of the consignment. Only 591 bags remained. It was decided that the parcel of 700 was to be regarded as an indivisible whole and the contract was void, as the full parcel no longer existed, unknown to the seller.

It has also been suggested that an assignment of a five year lease would not be the same as an assignment of a three year one; presumably the same principle would be applicable to time charters of a vessel.

Quality

In the absence of misdescription, mistake as to quality is not normally sufficient to nullify a contract.

In *Harrison & Jones v Bunten and Lancaster* [1953] the sale of "Sree Brand Calcutta Kapok" was not void even though unknown to both parties the goods in question were contaminated.

This is not to say that a mistake as to quality will never result in avoiding the contract, but what is required is a mistake as to an essential attribute of the subject-matter. A buyer may not be completely without remedy in the circumstances of the *Harrison* case as, in such a case this may give rise to a claim for breach of the warranties as to merchantable quality or fitness for purpose.

Mistake in the contractual documents

There are two particular situations which can arise where the contractual documentation is affected by the mistake of the parties:

(a) the document as prepared in error fails to record the exact terms as actually agreed or
(b) one of the parties signing the document misunderstood its nature or content.

With regard to (a), provided clear, irrefutable evidence can be shown of the supposed error, the court has the power to rectify the written document to reflect the underlying agreement of the parties which the document was intended to do, but in the event through error did not do so.

In *Rowley & May v Aperghis* [1923] the court allowed rectification of a contract to supply sultanas to include a force majeure clause. The contract was in a form which customarily included a specific type of force majeure clause which through inadvertence had not been added in the contract in question.

With regard to (b) the principal rule is that a party signing a document is bound by it whether it has been read or understood or not, and in the commercial context there are few instances where this will be avoided. The most likely area where this may have some impact would be in the context of personal or family guarantees which the cases show to be an area where not all those signing such guarantees fully understand the position.

The main exception is in favour of persons who, without explanation, have no real understanding of the purport of the document in question, whether this is through lack of education, illness or incapacity. The rule may also apply to those unable to read the language of the document.

As with other elements of mistake the difference between the document as signed and the document intended to be signed must be radical, substantial or fundamental, to be judged by the seriousness of the practical result, provided reasonable care has been taken by the signatory. Signature of a document without having any idea as to its effect will lose this protection (*Avon Finance Co. Ltd v Bridger* [1985]).

Another facet of the rule is that a party who has signed in one capacity whilst intending another will be able to avoid the signature and this will also be the approach where a party signs a document which has been "slipped in" for signature amongst a number of others without attention being drawn to its presence.

Misrepresentation

Non-disclosure

The starting point of English law is that parties in negotiation are not required to disclose all that they know that may be relevant to the business in hand. A different rule applies in respect of insurance contracts where public policy requires that the insured should act with utmost good faith. In such a case full disclosure of all matters which may have an effect on the risk being undertaken is required. Failure to make such a disclosure will entitle the insurer to avoid the insurance contract.

Where, however, during negotiations a statement or representation is made which is in fact untrue this will, in certain circumstances, lead to the party who has been misled being entitled to avoid the contract and also, in some instances, to damages as well as, or instead of, the right to set aside the contract.

The dividing line between non-disclosure and an implied misrepresentation can be a fine one; in one old case it was held that the owner of a cow who said nothing about its soundness impliedly represented that the cow was sound by simply taking it to the market. The particular circumstances of this case are now covered by the statutory implied terms contained in the Sales of Goods Act 1979 and Supply of Goods and Services Act 1982 concerning merchantable quality and fitness for purpose.

Misrepresentation

A party will be entitled to avoid and have set aside, where this is still practical, any contract where during the negotiations there had been a misrepresentation by the other party inducing that first party to enter into the contract where the misrepresentation was:

(a) one of fact or of an opinion based on fact or facts known solely to the person giving that opinion
(b) a material one
(c) relied on by the party to whom it was made.

This assumes that the misrepresentation does not itself become a term of the contract. Once a representation becomes a term it is a breach of that term which will give rise to a right in damages, or in more serious cases the right to terminate the contract, as with any other terms. These issues are dealt with in Chapter 9.

Representation of fact

Opinion

A general statement of opinion given by someone not professing any particular expertise in the subject-matter which proves to be wrong will not give rise to any legal consequence; the same applies to any advertising hype or sales talk. This is particularly so where the opinion is based on facts known to both parties.

The statement, if it is to give the innocent party any remedy, is required to be one of an existing fact and not a simple statement of opinion or belief. A statement of opinion or belief may nevertheless give rise to a right to avoid the contract:

(a) where the opinion given or the belief expressed does not genuinely reflect that party's view
(b) where the opinion is or would be expected to be particularly within the knowledge of the person making the statement.

    In *Smith v Land and Home Property Corporation* (1884) on a sale of a hotel the seller described the tenant as "very desirable". Rent had not been paid and before completion the tenant became insolvent. It was found that wherever facts were within the knowledge of only one of the parties, the statement of opinion, such as that as to the desirability of the tenant, included an implied statement that facts were known to that party which justified the opinion. As rent had been in arrears, the reference to the tenant as "desirable" constituted a misrepresentation.
(c) This also extends to the situation where the statement is made honestly but the party making it has carelessly failed to confirm the facts on which it appears to be based.

Strictly, a representation as to the future cannot be complained of unless it becomes a term of the contract, but where the statement misrepresents a current intention it can give rise to a right to avoid the contract.

In *Edgington v Fitzmaurice* (1885) a company raised funds said to be intended for the completion of alterations to the company's premises and the purchase of vehicles to develop its trade. The real object was to enable the directors to discharge pressing liabilities. It was found that the statement of the directors' current intention was a statement of fact which had been misrepresented, allowing the lenders to avoid the loan.

Materiality

A misrepresentation has no effect unless it would be regarded as material to a reasonable person in deciding whether to accept the terms on offer or, indeed, whether to enter the contract at all.

The main exception to this is where the misrepresentation was made intentionally, as in the case of fraud, in which event materiality is not an issue.

Reliance

Unless relied on as inducing entry into the contract in question, the misrepresentation is of no effect. Reliance is not avoided because the party misled also relied on other inducements to enter into the contract. If, however, a party relies on something which is true to the exclusion of a matter which is untrue, any right to relief will be lost.

Reliance is also unaffected by the failure to make use of an opportunity to find out the truth. This does not apply where that other party does take that opportunity or seeks to test the accuracy of the statement but does not discover the truth.

Effect of misrepresentation

Avoidance of the contract

Until recently the primary remedy in cases of misrepresentation was the ability of the party which had relied on the misrepresentation to have the contract set aside at its option, provided that what had been received under the contract could be returned in exchange for what was given. This right is available whether the relevant misrepresentation was innocent or careless and negligent or intentional and fraudulent. This remedy was only available, however, where it was still possible to restore the parties to their initial position. If the subject-matter of the contract has been so changed that it could not be restored, the right to avoid the contract is lost (where, for example, the goods have been consumed). Precise restitution is not required, provided substantial restitution can be made together with an account for any profits made on the one hand and an allowance for any deterioration on the other (*Erlanger v New Sombrero Phosphate Co.* (1878)).

The right to set aside the contract has to be taken up very promptly on discovery of the truth. The right will be lost if the party continues with the contract either expressly or, more likely, by conduct (*Long v Lloyd* [1958]). Even where the truth is not discovered, the right to set aside a contract for an innocent misrepresentation will be lost after a period of time within which the truth could reasonably be expected to have been discovered.

Indemnity

The process of setting aside a contract may also include an award of an indemnity for expenses which entry into the contract had resulted in. This additional recovery is much more limited than a right to damages and only covers expenses, duties paid on goods would be an example. The indemnity provided does not cover recovery of loss of profits or similar; losses of this nature can only be recovered where a right to damages proper arises, which is considered in the next section.

Damages

Two overlapping principles provide for the right to damages for misrepresentations. On the one hand, there is the common law right to damages available in cases of a fraudulent or negligent misrepresentation and on the other there is statutory provision by virtue of the Misrepresentation Act 1967. The latter provides an alternative right which extends even to damages for innocent misrepresentation where the court considers this a more appropriate remedy than setting aside the contract.

Exclusion of liability

Common law allows a party to exclude by an appropriate notice or disclaimer any responsibility for misrepresentation, except probably for fraud. The Misrepresentation Act 1967, now superseded by s. 11(1) of the Unfair Contract Terms Act 1977 prevents exclusion of liability for misrepresentations before the contract is made, unless the court considers such a provision as being reasonable; it is for the party seeking to exclude liability to prove that the exclusion is reasonable.

Illegality

The general principle is that for reasons of public policy the courts will not enforce an otherwise binding agreement reached by the parties where to do so would involve the enforcement of an agreement to commit a crime or other breach of the law, or where to do so would require the court to assist a party who has been guilty of conduct which is either illegal or contrary to public policy.

Whilst easy to apply to a clear case such as an action or account between a partnership of highwaymen, this is not so easy in the wide variety of situations in which one or both parties may find themselves transgressing the regulations of modern legislation which may impinge directly or indirectly on any international trade transaction.

The following is not intended as an exhaustive review of cases where the parties' obligations are cut across by illegality, but is intended as a guide to the more significant categories in the field of international trade.

Object of the contract is illegal

A contract the making of which itself is illegal will not be enforced. An example of this is the position with the writing of insurance business under the Insurance Companies Act 1974, which must be duly authorised by the Department of Trade and Industry. Similarly, enforcement will be refused where the main aim of the contract is either illegal, in the sense that the object of the contract is the contravention of some statutory provision, or contrary to the policy of common law, which will include an agreement to commit a civil wrong, such as the defrauding of a third party. In the context of international trade perhaps the most likely examples of illegal contracts would be those involving the sale or the carriage of goods contrary to government embargoes or other restrictions.

The primary concern of the English court will be with rule of English law, whether statute or otherwise, irrespective of whether the contract is actually to be performed in England, but the question of illegality is not confined solely to the contravention of the rules of English law. Where the contract is to be performed abroad or is governed by foreign law, the English courts will have regard to the provisions of such laws; this includes foreign revenue and fiscal laws which are not otherwise enforced by the English courts.

Recognition of the impact of foreign law is limited to those which apply in places where the contract provides expressly or implicitly that one or other party is to perform one or some of its obligations. Recognition does not extend to foreign laws which prevent a party from performing in a way that was merely intended rather than required. Failure to obtain domestic foreign exchange control permission by a foreign party will not be an answer to a claim for non-payment in London, for example.

In *Ralli Brothers v Compania Naviera Sota y Aznar* [1920] a charterer agreed with an owner to charter a vessel for the carriage of goods to Spain. As a result of exchange rate fluctuations the freight agreed in the contract exceeded the maximum limit allowed under Spanish law. It was decided that English courts would not enforce payment of the excess over that allowed by Spanish law, as the freight was to be both paid and received in Spain.

Where, however, the statutory restriction represents not a total embargo but some form of rationing or licensing, the defence of illegality will not be available, similarly where the issue is one of exchange control permission (*Toprak Mahsulleri Ofisi v Fingrain* [1979]). A party contracting against this background, whether foreseen or not, will be held to the undertaking of absolute liability, in the absence of any relevant exception, and it is for the parties concerned to satisfy themselves of their ability to meet their contractual obligation from the restricted or rationed quantity. In practice, the standard form commodity contracts of the commodity associations, such as GAFTA, make specific provision to cover such eventualities.

Another category of contracts contrary to English public policy which may be material in the context of international trade are arrangements or agreements whereby a commission or other bribe is paid to obtain influence with the representatives of a government or quasi-government body in circumstances where the party undertaking the lobbying does not disclose a financial interest.

In *Montefiore v Menday Motor Components Co. Ltd* [1918] an aircraft manufacturer agreed with an intermediary to pay sums for the use by that intermediary of influence with the Air Ministry for the procurement of contracts in favour of the manufacturer. It was decided in the action by the intermediary for his commission that the agreement was unenforceable as being contrary to public policy.

This principle will also be applicable to the lobbying of representatives of a foreign government where the policy of the foreign government parallels that of English law (*Lemenda Trading Co. v African Middle East Petroleum Co.* [1988]).

Legal object—illegal performance

A similar or related situation arises where the contract is *prima facie* for a legal object but the mode of performance adopted by one or both parties is illegal. Where the contract has yet to be performed the contract may be enforceable, provided that it could yet be performed in a legal manner, even though that may not have been the initial intention of the parties.

In *Fielding and Platt Limited v Najjar* [1969] a manufacturer agreed to sell machinery to a buyer in the Lebanon. It was intended by the parties that the machinery would be imported under the cover of false invoices. The manufacturer resorted to action to enforce the agreement. It was decided that although the issue of false invoices would represent an illegal performance of an otherwise legal contract, the issue of such false invoices was not a term of the contract, which could still be performed legally and was therefore enforceable.

The courts may not, however, be too astute to discover theoretical ways in which the contract may be performed legally. This was shown in the case *Foster v Driscoll* [1929] where a distiller of Scotch whisky agreed with a buyer for the sale of such whisky for shipment to North America. The intention was that the whisky would be shipped to the United States during prohibition. It was found that the possibility that the whisky may be shipped to Canada or New Foundland did not prevent the contract being illegal.

Legal contract—illegal benefit

The courts will also not lend their aid to a party seeking to enforce an otherwise legal contract where to do so would enable that party to benefit from criminal conduct, although this may not necessarily be directly related to that contract. In the commercial context, this particularly applies in relation to claims under an otherwise valid and legal insurance contract.

In *Euro-Diam Ltd v Bathurst* [1987] a seller had agreed with a buyer that goods which should have been shipped to Iran would be invoiced at less than the true price, in order to deceive the Iranian customs authorities. This involved the sellers in a breach of the Customs and Excise Act. Whilst in transit the goods were stolen and in a claim by the seller against the carrier, the carrier sought to rely on the false invoice. It was found that the breach of the Customs and Excise Act did not prevent the seller claiming against the carriers for the value of the goods lost.

Collateral illegality

The issues already considered arise in situations where a party seeks to or is forced to found his or her claim on an illegal contract, or the terms of a legal contract which can only be performed in an illegal manner. This is to be distinguished from situations where that party's claim is not founded on any illegal contract or an illegal act but where conduct, which is otherwise reprehensible, becomes apparent in the course of the proceedings. In this instance, public policy does not necessarily require that the contract is unenforceable.

In *St John Shipping Corporation v Joseph Rank* [1956] a shipowner loaded a vessel such that on sailing the vessel's load line was overloaded. This was a breach of the requirements of the Merchant Shipping Act. In a defence to an action for freight the cargo owner claimed illegality. It was decided that whilst the owners may be subject to a fine there was nothing in the policy of the Merchant Shipping Act which required a contract of affreightment to be unenforceable and the owner's claim for freight was allowed.

The relative culpability of the parties

In cases where the making of the contract itself or its performance is expressly prescribed by a particular statute, the fact that one or indeed both the parties did not intend this will be immaterial.

The exception to this is where the statute is considered to have been passed to benefit a particular class of persons, in which case the contract may be enforceable by an innocent party of the class which the statute is seeking to protect

Where, however, the possible illegality of the contract involves questions of public policy generally, the courts adopt a more pragmatic approach and will look at the relative culpability of the parties. A party seeking to avoid a contract on the basis of illegality would not be allowed to do so where that party is the chief culprit or beneficiary from any such illegality. Where, however, both parties are equally aware of the illegality, neither party will be able to enforce the contract. The same approach will apply in cases where false invoices have been raised in relation to an otherwise legal sale in deciding whether the illegality provides a defence to an action. A crucial issue will be the extent to which the seller is involved in or knew of the use of the invoices to mislead the authorities or any other third parties.

Action seeking to recover money or property

The impact of an illegal contract may be avoided where a party is able to claim for delivery of goods, or for damages for their wrongful conversion, where this can be based on a proprietary or possessory title, even if this is ultimately derived from an illegal contract (*Bowmaker v Bryants Instruments* [1945]).

Severance

In cases where a party is seeking to avoid a contract solely on the grounds of illegality the courts have the power to strike out any illegal terms where this can be done, whilst still leaving the substance of the contract intact. Where the contract in its entirety provides for an illegal object, this remedy will not be available.

In *United City Merchants (Investments) Limited v Royal Bank of Canada* [1982] an English company sold manufacturing equipment to a Peruvian company and agreed to a scheme to double the price so that the Peruvian company could exchange Peruvian currency for the excess amount in breach of Peruvian exchange control regulations. It was decided that it was the task of the court to penetrate any disguise presented by the contract's language and to refuse to enforce the illegal element but to the extent that the contract did not offend exchange control regulations it was enforceable.

Duress

A number of circumstances have been recognised where contracts which would otherwise be valid but which had been concluded in circumstances which the law regarded as unfair could be avoided. The role of these doctrines was, and still is primarily, for the protection of individuals, and they have limited application in the context of commercial transactions. The principal exception to this is the refusal of the courts to enforce agreements entered into by one party under duress. This has seen an increasing role in commercial affairs as a result of the recent recognition that the doctrine, originally developed in relation to threats of physical violence and subsequently damage to property, could also extend to commercial and financial pressures.

The basic principle is that a contract may be avoided by a party who can show that agreement to the contract was only apparent and that as a result of duress or coercion, there was no true consent. The key issue is whether the circumstances show true coercion, in which case there is no consent, or merely a "grumbling acquiescence" where there is.

In *Atlas Express Ltd v Kafco (Importers and Distributors) Ltd* [1989] a haulier sent a lorry with instructions that it was only to load if the seller of basketware agreed new rates. The haulier's management personnel then left the office. The seller, fearing the loss of a major contract and with no opportunity to make representations, signed a revised agreement as demanded. It was found that the revised agreement had been signed under compulsion and was not a genuine renegotiation. The haulier's refusal to complete the contract as originally agreed was without justification and the tactics adopted entitled the seller to avoid the revised terms.

Commercial pressure, of itself, is not sufficient. In assessing the position, important issues will be whether at the relevant time the party alleging coercion protested, whether there was an alternative course of action available, the possibility of an adequate legal remedy, availability of independent advice, and, crucially, whether after entering the contract steps were taken to avoid it at the earliest opportunity.

This last point is one of importance, and it is clear that failure to repudiate any agreement concluded under duress as soon as the party oppressed regains its freedom of manoeuvre will be regarded as an affirmation of the new agreement and the right to avoid the contract will be lost.

In *North Ocean Shipping Co. v Hyundai Construction Co.* [1978] an owner contracted with a shipyard for the building of a tanker. Due to exchange fluctuation, the shipyard, without any justification, demanded an additional ten per cent. The owner was advised that the claim had no legal basis and rejected it but subsequently having reached an advantageous agreement for the future use of the vessel, finally succumbed to the pressure of the yard, which included threats to terminate the contract. It was decided that the agreement for the revised price was made under compulsion, but the owner's failure immediately on delivery of the vessel, when it was free from the duress, to protest constituted an affirmation of the agreement to pay the extra ten per cent.

2

The contract of sale

So far as English law is concerned the regime applicable to the contract of the sale of goods is the same whether the sale is a domestic one or international. That regime is derived from the judge-made common law of past centuries as codified first in the Sale of Goods Act 1893 and consolidated in substantially the same terms by the Sale of Goods Act 1979.

The ambit of the Sale of Goods Act 1979 can be said to be confined to "pure" contracts for the sale of goods. More recently the Supply of Goods and Services Act 1982 has been passed applying the implied terms as to title and fitness for purpose to contracts falling within the major gaps left by the earlier legislation, especially in relation to service and hybrid contracts.

Aside from this central core of statutory provision, there are other statutes which have a more limited impact in this area, namely:

(a) The Unfair Contract Terms Act 1977 which makes provision for the regulation of exemption clauses, save where reasonable. For present purposes its impact is limited by the exceptions for contracts for the international sale of goods and the carriage of goods by sea.

(b) The Factors Act 1889 which concerns the position of agents holding goods for sale or purchase and who are able, vis-à-vis third parties, to give a good title which they themselves may not possess.

(c) The Latent Damage Act 1987 which is primarily concerned with product liability but will have an impact in so far as the seller may be responsible for any injury caused by the goods.

(d) The Uniform Laws on International Sales Act 1967 giving limited force to the Hague Convention of 1964 on a Uniform Law on the International Sale of Goods. The Convention annexed to the Act itself provides a comprehensive, if different, code but its application is limited to contracts where the parties expressly provide for its application under s. 1 of the Act. In practice this is rare.

Application of general principles

Despite the statutory codification of the law of sale of goods most of the general principles considered earlier apply equally to contracts for the sale of goods. The Sale of Goods Act 1979 itself lays down no requirements concerning the reaching of agreement. It does, however, make specific provision in s. 4(1) of the Act so that the contract may be made in writing or by word of mouth, or partly in writing and partly by word of mouth, or may be implied from the conduct of the parties. S. 3(1) again confirms that questions of capacity are also regulated by the general law and certain special provisions deal with the question of necessaries for individuals which are of little relevance in a commercial context. Whilst the general rules as to consideration apply, the application of the Act is restricted by s. 2(1) to contracts "for a money consideration called the price".

Whilst the price will usually be expressly agreed at the time of the contract, this is not essential; it may be fixed at a later stage if the parties so agree or by a course of dealing between the parties, if any. In an extreme case, where no price is agreed, the buyer must pay a reasonable price.

In many cases this limitation of the Act to contracts involving the payment of a price will be barely perceived as a limitation but it will have an impact in cases of sale by barter, counter-trade or exchange.

This particular distinction has given rise to questions of whether a particular agreement is to be regarded as one for barter or two related agreements, each for a price, which are then mutually set off. The answer to this will depend on the terms of the specific agreement.

This is one of the gaps plugged by the Supply of Goods and Services Act 1982 which expressly covers contracts for the transfer of goods, whatever the nature of the consideration (s. 1(3)).

Sale of goods

Under the Sale of Goods Act 1979 a contract of sale was recognised as being either:

(a) a sale where the contract transferred the property in the goods to buyer from seller (s. 1(4)), or
(b) an agreement to sell where the transfer of the property was to take place at a future time or subject to some condition which would be fulfilled later (s. 1(5)).

The principal importance of the distinction is that under the former, the buyer acquired, in addition to its contractual rights, rights based on ownership or possession, whereas under the latter the buyer's rights were purely contractual until property in the goods passed.

It is the latter category, namely the agreement to sell, that is of primary importance in the international context and the passing of property represents one of the principal issues to be provided for in the contract.

Goods

Until the passing of the Supply of Goods and Services Act 1982 it was important to distinguish contracts for the sale of goods from contracts more properly regarded as those for the supply of services, and many fine distinctions were drawn. So far as the question of warranties as to title and fitness for purpose are concerned, this is no longer an issue as combined contracts for the supply of goods and services now fall under the more recent Act.

The distinction will still be important to have in mind so far as the provisions of the Sale of Goods Act 1979 concerning the effects of the contract are concerned as this Act forms a more complete code than that in the later Act.

The basic rule adopted is that in each case the question is whether the substance of the contract is for the sale of a chattel or goods, or instead one for the performance of work.

For the purposes of the two Acts "goods" is not exhaustively defined but is probably to be given a very wide meaning and the Latent Damage Act expressly extends the word to cover electricity. What is not included, however, are land buildings and fixtures on the land, except that growing crops are included as "goods" as is any other thing attached to the land which it is agreed will be severed before sale.

Conditions and warranties

Unless the terms of the contract negative them by express agreement, there will be implied in any contract for the sale of goods, whether strictly so called or otherwise, warranties as to title, fitness for purpose or merchantable quality.

Title

S. 12 of the Sale of Goods Act 1979 and s. 2 of the Supply of Goods and Services Act 1982 imply a condition that the seller has the right to sell the goods or will have at the time property is to pass.

There is also an implied warranty that the goods are free of any encumbrances not disclosed at the time the contract is made, and that the buyer will enjoy quiet possession.

These warranties will not apply where the contract shows that only a limited title is intended to be passed as where the seller only passes on such title as it has itself.

Quality or fitness

On sales in the course of business there is an implied term that the goods are of merchantable quality, save where defects are expressly brought to the buyer's attention or they were readily apparent on inspection. If the buyer makes known a specific purpose for the goods to the seller prior to the purchase, there will also be implied a term that the goods are fit for that particular purpose whether or not that is a common use (ss. 14 and 4 respectively).

Where the sale is by description, there is implied a term that the goods will correspond to that description and if the sale is by sample and description, it is not sufficient that the bulk corresponds to the sample but does not correspond with the description (ss. 13 and 3 respectively).

Effects of the contract

The section concerned with the effects of the contract is primarily about the passing of property, risk and title.

Apart from the basic rule provided for by s. 16 that property in unascertained goods cannot pass and that no property passes until ascertainment, the provisions are *prima facie* rules which can be displaced by the specific terms of the contract actually agreed by the parties.

In the context of the international sale of goods a considerable number of recognised types of contract have been developed, the operation of which have an important impact on the questions of passing of property, risk and title, although in themselves the contract types are delimited primarily by operational factors which have little direct bearing on these questions.

Classic International Sale Contract

Incoterms

There are many "standard" international sale contracts regularly adopted by parties trading across borders. These impose varying responsibilities on the parties and range from the minimum requirements to sellers of EXW, through the gambit of obligations under FCA, FAS, FOB, CFR, CIF, CPT, CIP, DAF, DES, DDU to, probably the most onerous, DDP. In Appendix A we include a glossary of the most commonly used contracts in this regard.

The rights and duties of buyers and sellers in relation to each of these contracts vary. Incoterms, produced by the International Chamber of Commerce, attempt to set out in some detail the trading practice concerning the varying duties of buyers and sellers in relation to such contracts.

It is particularly important to appreciate when, under a classic CIF or FOB contract, title and risk passes as this may radically affect the rights of the parties to exercise liens or retain the goods if things go wrong (see Chapter 9). It should, moreover, be understood that simply because a contract is described as being CIF, it may not necessarily have the classic qualities of such a contract; indeed it may, by virtue of certain terms expressly agreed between the parties, take effect as something of a hybrid. By way of an example, a classic FOB contract would mean that the parties had agreed that title and risk in the goods passed on shipment of those goods. In those circumstances, in the event of the bankruptcy of the buyers, regardless of whether or not the goods have been paid for, the trustee in bankruptcy would have obtained title and risk in the goods from the time of shipment regardless of whether payment had been made. Regularly, however, because of the distances separating buyers and sellers, special arrangements are made for the finance of international sales which require payment for the goods to be made by way of letter of credit, the bank paying on receipt of, for example, a shipped bill of lading. An FOB contract which makes provision for payment to be made in this way may well take effect as a hybrid, the sellers reserving title to themselves (in spite of the contract being expressed to be an FOB contract) until such time as they actually receive money. In such circumstances the buyers' trustee in bankruptcy would not obtain title until payment was made (we elaborate on this below and the contents of Chapter 7 explain in rather more detail the concepts of property and risk and how they pass).

CIF: cost, insurance, freight

A sale CIF is usually followed by the named port of destination, eg a sale of 1000 tons alumina CIF Oslo is a sale of alumina for delivery to Oslo.

A CIF contract is one of the most common types of export sale contract. It places reduced responsibility on the buyers and a much greater burden on the sellers.

It is for the sellers to arrange for the shipment and insurance of the goods to the port of destination agreed by the parties. From a business point of view it is often suggested that a CIF sale is not a true sale of goods at all but rather is a sale of documents. This is because, under a classic CIF contract, documents evidencing the cost, insurance and freight (commonly an invoice, assigned insurance policy and bill of lading) are tendered to the buyers as representing the goods sold. One of the characteristics of a CIF contract is this representation of the goods in question by documents, and title to those goods passes upon presentation of those papers on their being taken up and paid for by the buyers. Conversely, risk in the goods passes upon shipment.

It is for the parties to agree between themselves what documents they require to represent the goods. Commonly, these will include a sales invoice, a certificate of quality and quantity, a shipped clean on board bill of lading, an insurance certificate, and other specially agreed documents. Commonly, a contract will simply require tender of "shipping documents", which comprise:

(a) a clean bill of lading evidencing a contract of carriage by sea to the agreed place of destination
(b) a marine insurance policy covering the usual marine risks and any additional agreed risks
(c) a sales invoice in an appropriate form.

These documents should provide "continuous documentary cover" from port to port of all the relevant goods.

Duties of the buyer under a CIF contract

These can be expressed succinctly: to pay the price upon tender of proper documents.

In a classic contract, delivery and payment are concurrent conditions. The buyer's duty to pay arises upon tender of documents. Unless there is express agreement between the parties, buyers are not permitted to prevaricate pending payment against documents nor to ask to be able to examine the goods. So long as documentation conforms to contract, the duty to pay is absolute. There are a number of things buyers can do to protect themselves from being required to pay against documents which may turn out to be misleading. For example, the common insistence on the inclusion of certificates for quality and quantity in the shipping documents is such a precaution. Even if buyers suspect that the goods may not be in conformity with contract, they are obliged to pay (so long as the documentation reveals no discrepancy). The only exceptions to this rule are:

(a) sellers' fraud or
(b) a dramatic difference in the commodity shipped from that contracted for (eg peas instead of beans).

Buyers are not obliged to make payment against documents which do not conform with the requirements of the contract—for example, a bill of lading which is not "clean" or which reveals that the goods have been shipped outside the agreed shipment period.

The loss of the goods does not excuse the buyers from their obligation to make payment. So long as the documentation is in order the fact that it is known that the goods have been lost does not excuse the buyer. The buyer will, however, obtain the insurance policy with the documentation and so will have some comfort there. If the goods have been lost, however, by reason of an uninsured peril the buyer is not relieved and has a duty to make payment against the documents although he or she may maintain an action for breach of contract in appropriate circumstances against the seller thereafter.

Different considerations arise in the event of the purchase of non-ascertained goods, that is the purchase of generic not specific goods. As a matter of English law property in such unascertained goods does not pass until there is *appropriation*. On this basis the sale of a part of a bulk cargo will result in the title passing to the purchasers only on appropriation (identification of the relevant part) which is usually at discharge.

On this basis if there is a CIF sale of part of a bulk cargo documents may be presented whilst the goods are in transit and payment duly made, but title will not pass prior to discharge. This is considered in more detail in Chapter 7, but is a little appreciated area of difficulty with particular problems for banks. The difficulty that may be experienced by banks is best illustrated by an example.

Example

Shady Company, a seller of crude oil, enters into a series of contracts for the sale of parcels from a bulk cargo with a number of purchasers. The sales are expressed to be CIF, cash against documents. A series of bills of lading are drawn up for each of the parcels sold. Whilst the cargo is on the high seas the purchasers make payment against shipping documents and obtain bills of lading. Several of the purchasers are themselves in a shaky financial condition and their banks hold the bills of lading as security pending the delivery of the cargo (by prior agreement with the purchasers). Shady Company becomes insolvent and a receiver is appointed whilst the goods are still afloat. Because the sale was for a part of a bulk cargo, property in the goods is not transferred until the goods are ascertained (ie identifiable) (s. 16 of the Sale of Goods Act 1979). Accordingly, although the purchasers have all paid for their parcels of the cargo, they have not obtained title in the usual way because their parcel is still an unidentified part of the whole, and the cargo is still retained by the receiver. The bank's security is illusory. Even s. 1 of the Sale of Goods Act 1979 (which we deal with in detail in Chapter 6) which would normally give a bill of lading holder protection does not assist because title to the cargo has not been obtained by reason of an endorsement of the bill of lading; indeed title has not been obtained at all.

The situation would have been quite different if Shady Company had been selling a number of caterpillar tractors identifiable by their registration numbers. The goods would have been ascertained immediately and upon payment against shipping documents title would have passed to the purchasers, and the bank's position would not have been imperilled.

These two examples illustrate a loophole in the present law on the sale of bulk cargoes, which is currently the subject of consideration in a working paper by the Law Commission, and may be resolved in the new Carriage of Goods by Sea Act.

Payment
Buyers have a duty to make payment in accordance with a specific agreement, in default of which, payment must be made at the sellers' place of business. The debtor must seek out the creditor. Contractual stipulations as to the method of payment must be strictly performed.

Place of delivery
There may be other duties imposed on buyers. They may be required to choose one of several destinations, in which case they are under a duty to notify the sellers in reasonable time before the beginning of the shipment period to enable the goods to be shipped within the time limit.

Duties of the seller under CIF contract

These duties can be summarised as to ship or obtain goods in accordance with contract; to procure and prepare sufficient documentation; to tender.

(a) *Shipment/procuration of goods*
Sellers have two options; they can either organise the shipment of the goods from port of origin to port of destination themselves or they may buy afloat. If the contract is for the sale of generic goods, the sellers must appropriate goods of the contract description to the contract. They must give notice of appropriation.

(b) *Sufficiency of documentation*
Because a CIF contract can loosely be described as a sale of documents, the purchasers have a right to reject both documents and goods if they are on their face defective, and this will operate to retransfer the risk in those goods back to the sellers and for title to remain with the sellers.

The policy of insurance must cover risks which it is customary for the particular trade to cover in relation to the cargo and the voyage in question for the duration of the voyage. There are several specific authorities as to the sufficiency of insurance certificates supplied, but these generally provide that an acceptable policy is the usual one in relation to the particular trade. The value of insurance is also important and it is usual for the policy of insurance to provide for a ten per cent increase above the insurance value of the goods (Incoterms endorse this practice). Difficulty can arise when the buyers or sellers dealing in a chain of contracts wish to conceal from other parties the level of loss or profit made on the transactions. In the usual course of events shipping documents can take effect as freely negotiable instruments and may simply be handed from one purchaser to another, thus effecting a transfer of title. To mask profits and losses on the market a practice seems to have arisen of taking out of circulation one particular document (specifically the insurance policy) which gives an indication of the loss or profit taken, and replacing it with the purchasers' own insurance document at the appropriate value for the next transaction. This practice may have the effect of relieving the original insurer of liability altogether or in part and is considered further in Chapter 5.

Another common step taken is for the sellers to arrange open cover for an upper limit of goods shipped within a certain time. That insurance is activated by notice from the sellers to the insurers by a declaration giving details of the consignment in question. The difficulty with such a procedure is that an insurance policy (which is usually required under a classic CIF contract) will not be available for tender, and there may be only a broker's cover note or certificate. These are not equivalent in law to an insurance policy and unless the contract makes specific provision for such reduced evidence of the contract of insurance, the purchasers may be entitled to reject any document of insurance other than the policy itself.

Example

A CIF seller tenders to his or her purchaser a clean shipped on board bill of lading, a properly completed invoice and the policy of insurance insuring the goods against total loss. The general principle is that the buyer may reject documents which are not "usual in the circumstances". It has been held that simple total loss insurance is not "usual" and that a policy of insurance restricted in this way may, therefore, be rejected with impunity.

The invoice must be in strict agreement with the terms of the contract. It is important if a bank has been entrusted with review of the documents before making payment under a letter of credit that the invoice adequately identifies the goods to which it relates, although minute detail is not required.

The bill of lading

Unless specifically agreed to the contrary the bill of lading must be a clean bill (not containing any qualification about the condition of the goods). It should be a shipped bill and not a received for shipment bill. The difference is that a shipped bill on its face records that the goods are actually shipped on board the named vessel. The date on the bill of lading will be the date of shipment. A received for shipment bill simply provides evidence of the fact that goods have been received at the port for shipment but are not necessarily actually on board the chosen vessel. A received bill, partly for this reason, may not take effect as a document of title at common law in the same way that a shipped bill of lading may. A further drawback with the received bill is that it may not provide the buyers with "continuous documentary cover": for example the goods could be damaged prior to shipment on board the vessel (and hence the shipowners would not be liable in the usual course of events to the purchasers), and the insurance policy could well not attach to any period prior to shipment. The received for shipment bill is therefore an inferior document to the shipped bill.

The bill of lading is not a delivery order nor a mate's receipt. A delivery order is quite different from the received for shipment bill.

A delivery order can be one of two documents. There are ship's delivery orders directed to the carriers requiring delivery of goods by the carriers to the purchasers on presentation of documents. Alternatively, there are delivery orders directed to an agent of the sellers which are rather akin to house bills of lading. Such delivery orders consign the goods to a forwarding agent or other entity acting on behalf of the sellers at the delivery port and direct the agent to deliver a section of the consignment to the holder of the order. The more valuable document is the ship's delivery order but neither of the documents is of the same quality as the bill of lading. The reason why delivery orders are frequently necessary is because sellers will often only have one bill of lading for a large consignment and cannot give that single bill of lading to each purchaser. In such circumstances they must take care in their contract to stipulate that they have a right to give a ship's delivery order instead of a bill of lading. The ship's delivery order would not be as good a protection for the buyer because it would give no cause of action against the vessel unless it is "attorned" to the buyer (which would be unusual). To reduce the risk to the purchaser it would be prudent for the contract to make provision for the ship's delivery order "to be countersigned by a banker, shipbroker, captain or mate, if so required".

Mate's receipt

A mate's receipt is a document drawn up by the ship's officer in charge of loading on the basis of a note made by the tally clerk and it will embody any comment or qualification about the condition of the goods received. The qualifications on the mate's receipt should be embodied in the bill of lading. The mate's receipt is, therefore, an acknowledgement by the carrier of the goods received and their condition upon receipt and it is also evidence of the ownership of the goods. The shipowners are entitled to assume that the person named in the mate's receipt or the holder of it is the owner of the goods. In spite of this general presumption, however, the mate's receipt is not a document of title and transfer will not pass possession of the goods and for that reason the document is of a lower order than a bill of lading.

Date

The bill of lading must genuinely bear the date of shipment and must not be backdated. Tender of a bill of lading with a false date of shipment is bad tender under a CIF contract, in the same way as a forged bill would be a bad tender. Buyers are entitled to reject bills of lading which are not "genuine". If payment is made against such a bill, the buyers may have the right to recoup the payment made. The buyers may not, however, always succeed in recovering the entire price as they may have obtained value notwithstanding the fact that the bill of lading was not genuine.

Quantity and quality

The bill of lading must be for the quantity and quality of goods sold. Alterations and erasures in the bill should be avoided if at all possible and indeed buyers may be entitled to reject a heavily amended bill. The bill must make provision for shipment to the port of destination by a reasonably direct route; above all the route must be the usual and customary route, and not necessarily the most direct one. Particularly wide deviation clauses in the bill of lading may be objectionable and a clause "so wide the ship might have called anywhere she liked" may be sufficient reason for buyers to reject the document.

Rejection of the documents

Assuming that the buyers have identified a defect in the documents tendered, they are entitled to reject them. There is a fine distinction between the right to reject documents for being defective and the right to reject them for indicating that the goods may be defective. For example, the contract may require a certificate of quality to be included amongst the shipping documents. All documents may be perfectly acceptable and in accordance with the contract on their face, but the certificate of quality may reveal that the goods are not of the contractual quality. The statement in the certificate of quality does not in itself entitle the buyers to reject the documents. The buyers' right to reject will extend to the goods if they are actually in a defective condition or if it has been agreed (as it often is) that the certificate is to take effect as conclusive evidence.

The buyers are entitled to reject documents which do not comply with the contract even though the goods themselves may be in perfect condition. For example, a bill of lading which contains a date later than the agreed shipment period in itself entitles the purchasers to reject even though the goods may be in first class condition. Commonly, the documents will have been tendered to the purchasers' bank for review by it prior to releasing payment under letter of credit. The bank will scrutinise the documents carefully and if it notes a defect in the documents it is likely to refer to the purchasers for instructions. Depending upon the nature of the defect the purchasers may opt to waive the defect or require the bank to insist upon its rights under the letter of credit and their own rights under the contract of sale and reject. If documents are to be rejected this should be done swiftly (but clearly not in advance of tender). If the buyers waive the right to reject the documents (by indicating that they are going to accept in some way), they may also waive the right to reject the goods for defects which were apparent on the face of the documents (for example if they have become stale and the bill of lading shows an earlier than contract shipment date). There is an independent right to reject the goods, however (which we deal with below), for other defects.

Rejection of the goods

In a classic CIF contract, payment will already have been made by the purchaser against documents before the opportunity to inspect the goods is available. If it subsequently turns out that the goods were not of the contractual description or quality, the buyers may still reject them. If there is a lesser fault with the goods, they may claim damages. Whilst buyers would not usually wish to reject goods, which would cause them no loss even though they are not of contractual quality, they are still entitled to reject them. There is an increasing trend for there to be certificates issued with the shipping document which the parties agree are to be conclusive as to the quality of the goods. In such cases the buyers relinquish an independent entitlement to reject the goods for being of an inferior quality, and must fall back on a right of recourse against the party issuing the certificate if a discrepancy is determined. The remedies of disappointed buyers and sellers are considered in Chapters 9 and 10.

Loss of the goods and risk of deterioration

The following rules apply.

Deterioration

(a) If goods are purchased afloat by the sellers and prior to sale to the buyers they deteriorate, the risk is on the buyers backdated to the time of shipment. It will pass with retrospective effect and the buyers will accordingly bear any risk of deterioration which had already occurred when the contract for sale was made.

(b) If the goods are shipped by the sellers from the port of origin and are sold prior to shipment and during the course of shipment deteriorate, once again risk passes to the buyers on shipment.

(c) If the sellers procure shipment at the port of origin of the goods and then sell goods of a specific description, the risk is on the buyers without retrospective effect if the goods deteriorate after appropriation and with retrospective effect if they deteriorate after contract but before appropriation. This third example is applicable to the sale of a bulk cargo of which a parcel is subsequently appropriated to one particular buyer and between appropriation and contract (appropriation following contract), for example at discharge, the deterioration takes place.

The rules concerning total loss of the goods are similar. Generally speaking, the risk of goods being lost is always on the buyers except in a situation similar to (c) above where bulk goods are shipped, there is a subsequent contract for the sale of goods, and then specific goods are appropriated from the bulk. If the goods are lost after appropriation then clearly the risk is on the buyers; if the goods are lost before the appropriation then title will have remained with the sellers who will bear the risk of loss.

CFR (formerly C&F): cost and freight

A CFR is similar in effect to a CIF contract except that the sellers simply undertake to procure the carriage and delivery of the goods to the agreed destination and receive the price of the goods and freight. It is for the purchasers to arrange their own insurance.

Property and risk will generally pass in the same way under a CFR contract as they do under a CIF contract. It is likely that CFR sellers are under a duty arising by s. 32(3) of the Sale of Goods Act 1979 to give sufficient notice to the purchasers such as to enable them to insure the cargo. Sellers who disregard this duty may themselves be on risk (as quasi insurers) and effective notice should be given promptly.

FOB: free on board

This is another very common export contract and one that is one of the least onerous to the sellers. All the sellers are obliged to do is to place the goods free on board (at their own expense) for transmission to the buyers. It is for the purchasers to procure vessel, insurance, etc. In a classic FOB contract, title and risk will both pass simultaneously when the goods pass the ship's rails.

Sellers are not obliged to make advance arrangements for shipping the goods nor to bear any expense beyond those of ensuring the goods safely on board the vessel.

Duty of the seller

The duty of sellers is to put goods on board. The ship will be nominated or designated by the buyers and the sellers fulfil their obligation to give delivery of the goods by placing them on board. The sellers are responsible until shipment for loss or damage to the goods and for any damage sustained by the goods which is consequent upon their care of them prior to shipment. Accordingly, if the sellers have not taken adequate precautions to maintain the goods in good condition and as a result they deteriorated in transit, they may be liable to the purchasers for breach of contract. For example, if the buyers are selling frozen food and the temperature of the refrigeration plant at the side of the quay is negligently allowed to rise prior to shipment causing later deterioration of the goods, the purchasers may look to the sellers for reimbursement.

The sellers will be responsible for bearing the cost of getting the goods over the ship's rail. They may have to pay for the cost of the loading operation. In certain circumstances the sellers may be obliged to procure a bill of lading, although equally FOB sellers are generally under no liability to pay freight to the shipowners and therefore generally purchasers are responsible for obtaining the bill of lading. The parties may agree who undertakes the task. If it is agreed that the sellers should obtain the bill of lading, similar rules pertain in relation to the format of the bill of lading as for CIF contracts.

Sellers are not obliged to make arrangements for shipment of the goods until the buyers have notified them of the nomination of the vessel. Thereafter, they must act promptly to ensure that the goods are made available within the shipment period agreed. A failure to load within the contractual shipment period is a ground for rejection. The sellers must ship goods conforming to the contract quality. They must be fit for their purpose.

Buyer's duties

Buyers must give prompt shipping instructions. The instructions must be sufficiently clear for the sellers to be in no doubt of what is required of them. The instructions must be effective. It is useless for the buyers to nominate a vessel which will not arrive in time.

Buyers must pay the price agreed. S. 28 of the Sale of Goods Act 1979 provides that the "buyer must be ready and willing to pay the price in exchange for possession of the goods". Accordingly, in the absence of credit arrangements between the parties the price will become payable on tender of the bill of lading or upon delivery of the goods to the ship. The buyers must pay in accordance with the method agreed in the contract or, in the absence of express agreement, must search out the creditors and pay them at their usual place of business.

DES: Delivered ex ship (formerly ex ship)

This form of contract is one of the more onerous contracts for sellers to perform. They are bound to procure delivery of the goods from a ship at a named port of destination, but generally uncleared through customs. All that the buyers are required to do (in addition to pay the price, etc) is to take delivery from the vessel at that place and fulfil all necessary customs formalities. A delivered ex ship contract differs from a CIF contract in that property remains with the sellers until the goods are delivered to the buyers at which time risk will pass. This is in contradistinction to the CIF contract where title will pass on negotiation of shipping documents, and the risk passes on shipment.

Summary

International trading partners regularly deal on the basis of standard contracts. The parties are, of course, free to negotiate variants of these standard contracts. Care must be taken that the payment provisions reached do not have the effect of radically altering the classic standard contract, unless this is so intended.

General points to note

(a) In a CIF contract risk in the goods passes on shipment, title on taking up and paying for shipping documents.
(b) Shipping documents include an invoice, insurance policy and clean shipped on board bill of lading.
(c) Different provisions apply for the passing of title in a bulk cargo afloat where only a part is to be sold.
(d) Purchasers may reject the documents if they appear on their face to be defective and, unless agreed otherwise, may reject goods if they are not substantially in accordance with the contract. Upon such rejection, title and risk will automatically revert to the sellers.

(e) Under an FOB contract title and risk pass on shipment unless the parties have agreed an alternative arrangement, for example payment by letter of credit or cash against document, in which case there may be a presumption that title may well only pass on taking up and paying for such documents.

The glossary in Appendix A gives brief details of the most commonly found international trade contracts.

3

Agency

Introduction

In almost every field of commerce agents of every possible type and standing are used and this is equally so in the field of international trade. Agents, although often referred to as such (eg sales agents, shipping agents, managing agents and so forth) may equally be referred to as representatives or brokers or another specific title such as freight forwarders, but the role and the liabilities remain the same.

The essence of all the varied types of agent, whether independent or employee, is the same basic relationship where one party, the principal, authorises another, the agent, to act on its behalf and the latter agrees to do so. This is the relationship recognised by the law as agency.

This arrangement between principal and agent forms a contract of agency. It is, like any other contract, subject to the general principles concerning the reaching and concluding of agreements considered in Chapter 1.

As is perhaps to be expected in a country were the tenant of a public house is referred to as the landlord, the actual use of the term agent or agency does not always denote that this is the case. An example would be the use of "agency" by the distributor for a major manufacturer which would normally expect to contract in its own right rather than as the agent of the manufacturer.

Whilst as these examples show, the role of agent conjures up an image of an outsider, whether an individual or a company, an agent can equally well be an employee. Surprising though it may seem, this is the more common situation as this may well be the status of any individual acting on behalf of a company. The managing director is as much the company's agent as is its broker.

Of fundamental importance in practical terms is the recognition by the law of the ability of a principal to delegate to an agent the responsibility of entering into an agreement, binding on the principal, with another party, referred to here as a third party.

The law of agency, as well as being concerned with the contract of agency between agent and principal, is also (perhaps more importantly for present purposes) concerned with the position of the parties to the contract concluded through the efforts of the agent.

It is these two strands which form the law of agency, namely:

(a) the impact of the action of the agent on the positions of the principal and third party and
(b) the relationship between the principal and the agent.

Often intertwined, the two are nevertheless separate elements and a breakdown in the relationship between principal and third party will not necessarily affect the relationship of principal and agent and *vice versa*.

The agent's role

The concern of the law of agency is with what has been described as "the true legal Agent" (*Vogel v Kohnstamm* [1973]) who is authorised to act on his or her principal's behalf and binds the principal by so doing.

The term agent is also used rightly or wrongly to include persons who play a lesser role, such as one who represents the principal's interests in seeking customers and promoting the business, and who may act as a channel of communication and negotiate the contract which is ultimately made by the principal and third party. It has been said that this role is better described as that of a representative.

The general principle

The general principle of the law of agency can be stated as follows. There comes into existence a valid and binding contract between a principal and a third party to which the agent is not a party where:

(a) the principal authorises or instructs the agent to enter into a contract with the third party and
(b) the agent has made known to the third party at the time of entering into the contract that his or her role is limited to that of agent and

(c) the agent enters into the contract as authorised with the third party and, in the case of a contract in writing, expressly signs as such.

This represents the most straightforward situation exemplified by the contract through a broker for the sale of goods or the booking of cargo with a shipping line through a freight forwarder.

The general principle and its application is unaffected by the number of agents involved, provided that there is a chain through which the principal's authorisation or instructions are channelled. It is by no means uncommon for two, three or four agents to be involved on behalf of a particular principal and in theory the number is limitless.

In stating the general principle, the simplest case has been taken where only one party has used an agent but the same principle would apply to the situation of the third party.

In practice it is commonplace for agents to be involved on both sides and in extended chains it is not always easy to find the dividing line.

Authority

At the heart of the agent's role is the question of authority to enter into the contract so as to bind the principal. As the agent's role is to act in the interests of the principal and as required by that party in entering into any contract binding on the principal, the agent should have the actual authority of the principal.

A principal may, however, be bound by the actions of the agent in cases where the agent appeared to have the necessary authority but, unknown to the third party, was not in fact so authorised by the principal. In such a situation the agent is said to have apparent or ostensible authority.

Actual authority

Actual authority can take a number of forms:

(a) express authority
(b) implied authority
(c) customary authority.

Common to all these is the approval, whether stated or not, of the principal.

Express authority

This is the most clear cut situation, where the agent acts on an express instruction, written or verbal, or agrees specific terms such as the purchase of a set quantity of a commodity at a certain price, or the chartering of a vessel at a certain rate.

The only formality required is where the agent's duties include the execution of a document under seal, in which case the authority given to the agent must also be under seal—usually a power of attorney.

Implied authority

An agent may have implied authority to undertake certain matters incidental to the tasks for which he or she has express authority.

The existence of such implied authority primarily depends on the particular circumstances of each case.

In the context of a contract of sale there is a question whether an agent authorised to sell is entitled to make representations as to quality or to receive the price.

Similar issues may arise in an operational context. For instance, in the case *Toepfer v Warnico A.G.* [1978] buyers appointed surveyors to supervise loading of fine ground meal. The surveyors failed to stop loading of the cargo which was *coarse* ground. It was decided that the surveyors had no implied authority to vary or waive a condition that the meal be fine ground. A superintendent or surveyor appointed to supervise stowage only had implied authority to give directions binding on the principal relating to matters of stowage.

Customary authority

An agent's customary authority derives from the custom and practice of a particular market or trade in which the principal has asked the agent to act. Authority of this nature differs from express and implied authority which derives from the acts of the principal because authority given by custom will apply even if the principal is unaware of it. In practical terms this principle is of less importance nowadays with the reduction in trading on exchanges.

Apparent or ostensible authority

One of the most important elements of the law of agency is the concept of an agent's apparent, or ostensible, authority (the two terms are interchangeable) to conclude an agreement with a third party which will be binding on the principal even in the absence of actual authority in any form.

Whereas the various forms of actual authority all derive from the relationship between principal and agent, to which the third party is a stranger, apparent authority is a relationship between the principal and third party created by a representation.

To be effective the representation has to be:

(a) made by the principal to the third party
(b) intended to be acted on by the third party
(c) the agent must have authority to enter into a contract on behalf of the principal, of a kind within the scope of the apparent authority and
(d) relied on by the third party.

These requirements inevitably run together and the question of the intention of the principal that a third party will act on the representation is generally implied or assumed from the relevant words or conduct.

In practice, the key representation is commonly made through conduct, although not necessarily so, by permitting the agent to act in some way in the conduct of the principal's business, for example, or by placing the agent in such a position that it is reasonable for the third party to assume that the agent is authorised to make a contract of the kind in question.

For instance, in the case *Freeman & Lockyer v Buckhurst Park Properties (Mangal) Ltd* [1964] the board of a property company had power to appoint a managing director but did not do so. The *de facto* managing director appointed architects for one of the company's developments. It was held that the company was bound by the appointment as the board had allowed the *de facto* managing director to act in relation to the property which the architects relied on as authorising him to contract for their services.

A similar result may follow from the appointment to a specific position. This aspect of agency law is of particular importance in relation to contracts with companies. As a company, not being a physical entity, can only act in relation to the outside world via its agents, the signature of the duly authorised agent of the company, usually one of its officers, acting in the course of its business is the signature of the company. It follows from this that there will be occasions where the company's officers or other agents will bind the company because of their apparent authority to do so. For instance, in the case *Panorama Developments v Fidelis Fabrics* [1971] the company secretary of a textile company hired cars giving the company references. The cars were hired ostensibly for the company's business but in fact for himself. The hire charges were not paid. It was held that the company secretary had apparent authority to enter into contracts connected with the administrative side of the company's affairs and this included car hire.

The opposite result, with a company not being bound, is likely to result where a more junior manager or executive is involved. This was shown in the case *British Bank v Sun Life* [1983] where a bank lent money to property developers on being provided undertakings by a life assurance company, signed by a unit manager of the company whose authority to do so had been confirmed by a branch manager. In fact only certain head office personnel were empowered to sign such undertakings for the company. It was held that the branch manager had no actual authority, express or implied, and there being no evidence that the company had ever held out branch managers to customers as being so authorised, the branch manager had no apparent authority to bind the company.

In a case where the officer of the company is acknowledged as not having the necessary authority it will not be sufficient that the person in question has previously been responsible for communicating the decision of the board or other officers with authority. For instance, in the case of *Mendogas v Armagas* [1987] the buyer of a gas carrier agreed the purchase on terms that the seller continued to charter the vessel for three years. The broker knew the seller would not agree to more than one year and fraudulently induced the chartering manager of the seller to sign a three year charter. It was held that the seller had at no time held out the chartering manager as entitled to fix a three year charter and no question of apparent authority arose. The fact that the chartering manager had communicated decisions of the board on earlier occasions did not entitle the buyer to assume that such authority had been given to the transaction in question.

Common to all the examples considered is the lack of knowledge on the part of the third party of the absence of actual authority and reliance instead on a representation of what appears to be the position even though this is not actually so. It follows that knowledge by the third party of the actual position will prevent any "apparent" position arising. In the *"Liddesdale"* [1899] ship repairers contracted with the master on behalf of the owner to effect certain specified repairs. Instead, equivalent work was done with the approval of the master. It was held that the master's authority having been specifically limited to agreement to the original contract to the knowledge of the repairer, they could not claim under the varied contract.

Authority of necessity

In very restricted circumstances there are situations where a person who has custody of another's goods or property derives authority to act on behalf of the owner of such goods or property from the need to take immediate action for their preservation. This is termed authority of necessity.

The circumstances where such authority arises are very limited:

(a) it must be impossible to communicate with the owner of the goods or property in time to get instructions
(b) the agent must act reasonably, in good faith and in the interests of the owner
(c) the action taken must be justifiable commercially.

There is no necessity to dispose of goods merely because they are causing inconvenience and it is only where goods are of a perishable nature or similar that any such requirement may arise. The view generally taken is that in modern conditions and particularly with today's communications technology, there are unlikely to be many instances where the owner cannot be contacted in time. This may reflect an over-rosy view of telephone links to some third world countries and, indeed, elsewhere in times of trouble.

For present purposes the chief category of agents of necessity are those involved in the rescue of a ship and cargo in peril at sea, namely the master of the ship and salvors. In the *"Winson"* [1982] a master of a vessel which was in peril and who was unable to contact the owners of a cargo entered into a salvage agreement on Lloyd's open form for the provision of services necessary for the preservation of the cargo which had to be offloaded into barges and then stored. It was held that the master had authority to enter into the agreement on the cargo owners' behalf as an agent of necessity.

Traditionally, this category has been classified as one where the agent contracts without any actual authority; however, the practical difficulties involved in obtaining express authority from all relevant interests even where possible, particularly where a number of cargo owners are involved, has resulted in a recognition of what in some cases will be an implied actual authority of the master to take such steps as considered reasonable to preserve the cargo which effectively overlaps with the agency of necessity. For instance, in the *"Choko Star"* [1989] the master of a vessel stranded *en route* from Rosario which, although not in immediate danger, required assistance to refloat, signed a salvage agreement with salvors without reference to the cargo owners, even though it would have been possible to contact them. It was held that a party shipping cargo impliedly authorised the master to take such steps as were reasonably necessary whenever the ship or cargo were imperilled. The master had therefore implied actual authority to retain the salvors on an internationally recognised contract form.

Ratification

A contract may still be binding as between principal and third party even in circumstances where the agent had no actual or apparent authority or authority of necessity where, notwithstanding the agent's lack of authority, the principal adopts or, as it is said, ratifies the contract.

Whilst ratification will probably be express, a principal can ratify by conduct, such as by selling goods purchased by an agent without authorisation.

The principal is required to ratify before the time for performance of the contract or, if no time is set, within a reasonable time; this will be very short where the third party requires to know one way or the other. Ratification also backdates to the time the contract was concluded.

For ratification to be effective it is necessary for:

(a) the principal to have been in existence and have had capacity to contract at the time the contract was concluded

(b) the agent to have purported to act on behalf of and under the authority of the person ratifying.

Principal must be in existence and have capacity

In practical terms this requirement primarily concerns companies. A contract which the company does not have power to enter into cannot be ratified and a subsequent change in the company's power will not be effective to cure such a lack of capacity.

Whilst the provisions of s. 9(1) of the European Communities Act 1972 may affect the position of third parties vis-à-vis the company, the Act makes no change to the ability of the company to enforce a contract beyond its powers.

Agent must have purported to act for the principal

The requirement that the agent must have purported to act for the principal does not necessarily require that the principal is specifically identified but it is necessary that the agent has made known the existence of another who, if not identified, is identifiable as being the intended principal. For instance, in *Keighly v Maxted & Co* [1901] an agent was authorised to purchase corn up to a certain price. The only corn available was at a price above this. The agent purchased the corn on his own behalf. The principal accepted the contract but later refused delivery. It was held that the contract having been made by the agent in his own name, the principal could not ratify and hence was not liable.

The effect of this rule is that an undisclosed principal (this concept is discussed below) cannot ratify a contract, which, unknown to the third party, was purportedly made on their behalf.

Identification of the principal

Disclosed principal

The basic rule in agency law envisages, as will usually be the case, that agents, when contracting with third parties will make clear to them that their role is limited to that of agent.

Where agents have made clear that they are contracting on another's behalf the principal is said to be disclosed.

Where the principal is actually identified, he or she is said to be named and where the principal is not identified specifically but, for example, merely referred to as "my principal" or "client" or similar, he or she is said to be unnamed. Whether named or unnamed the principal is disclosed.

Foreign principal

At one time there was a rule that where an English agent contracted for a foreign principal the general rule did not apply and the agent would be a party to the contract. Following the decision in *Teheran Europe Co. Ltd v S. T. Belton (Tractors) Ltd* [1968] this rule has now effectively been dropped.

Undisclosed principal

In some cases agents intentionally or otherwise fail to make clear the limited role of their involvement even when they intend to act on behalf of the principal. In this instance the principal is said to be undisclosed.

Provided that the agent has actual authority, express or implied, then no question of apparent authority can arise in this instance; the principal may be entitled to sue and be sued on the contract.

There is, however, an important difference from the position with regard to that of a disclosed principal so far as the agent is concerned, in that where the principal is undisclosed the agent, as well as the principal, is liable to be sued and able to sue on the contract (see the next section).

This is not, however, always the case and is subject to restrictions as follows:

(a) An undisclosed principal cannot intervene where this is contrary to the terms of the contract entered into by the agent.

This rule is primarily based on a decision that the principal to an agent who was described as owner in a charter agreement could not adopt the contract, as to do so would be inconsistent with the contract terms describing the agent as owner. It is unlikely that this rule will be extended and its practial importance is doubtful.

(b) An undisclosed principal cannot intervene where the third party wished to deal with the agent or would not have wished to deal with the undisclosed principal.

This issue depends on whether the third party is willing or, at least, leads the agent to believe that they are willing to treat as a party to the contract anyone on whose behalf the agent may have been authorised to contract.

This is likely to be assumed in a commercial context unless the third party makes clear their unwillingness to do so or there are circumstances which should lead the agent to realise that the other party was not so willing.

In a commercial context the factors which are likely to be material to the issue of whether the third party wished to contract with the agent alone, rather than being indifferent to the identity of the contracting party, are whether the third party has particularly relied on the skill or creditworthiness of the agent (see the "*Remco*' on page 72). It is possible that so called personal considerations may arise as, for example, where a party would wish to avoid trading with a competitor.

Agent liable on the contract—the exceptions

In general agents are not a party to the contract between principal and third party which is brought into being through their efforts. They are therefore neither liable under, or able to enforce, the agreement.

The general rule is not always applicable and there are some limited exceptions to the rule where:

(a) agents have contracted in their own name, albeit on behalf of an undisclosed principal
(b) agents, although negotiating as agents, sign in their own name
(c) agents apparently contract on behalf of an unnamed or named principal but are, in fact, the principal and
(d) agents have contracted on behalf of a non-existent principal.

Agent for undisclosed principal

As touched on above, the agent contracting on behalf of an undisclosed principal undertakes a personal liability on the contract. The basis for this is that, to all intents and purposes, the contract appears to be one with the agent and, whilst it is effectively a concession and the undisclosed principal is entitled to intervene in certain circumstances, the original understanding of the position and the agent's role as apparently a contracting party is not wholly displaced.

In cases such as this where the third party has a choice as to which of the principal or agent to hold liable, the third party is only entitled to recover once and will be required to elect which of the two to pursue. A judgment obtained against one will bar proceedings against the other.

Agent signs in own name

Agents will also incur personal liability where, despite making it clear in the context of negotiations that their role is the limited one of agent, when signing the agreement reached they sign in their own name without qualification.

To avoid the impact of this rule it is necessary for agents to ensure either that the position is made clear from the body of the agreement itself or to qualify the signature with words such as "as agent only" or "for and on behalf of".

The basis for this rule is chiefly that evidence of pre-contract communications cannot be admitted to contradict a written agreement.

Agent is in fact the principal

Where a person expressly makes a contract on behalf of a named principal but is in fact the real principal, the so called "agent" may enforce the contract in certain circumstances:

(a) in any case where the contract is subsequently affirmed by the third party with knowledge that the agent is the real principal. This affirmation may be derived from the partial performance of the contract. For instance in *Rayner v Grote* (1846) a party described himself as the agent of another in a written contract for the sale of goods. The buyer paid for and accepted part of the goods and then had notice of the true position. It was held that the "agent" could enforce the balance of the contract as the real principal.

(b) In the absence of any affirmation, the agent may also enforce the contract provided the third party has not made it apparent that the identity of the other contracting party was material, as in the case of contracts where the skill or solvency of the person named could be regarded as relevant. For instance, in the *"Remco"* [1984] a party professing to act as chartering broker but in fact performing as charterer, concluded a fixture on the basis that this was with a subsidiary of a substantial group. It was held that the evidence indicated that the owners regarded the identity of the charterer, whose solvency was important to them, as material, hence the "agent" could not enforce the contract.

Agent for a non-existent principal

Given the conflicting decisions it seems that it is a question of fact in each case whether it is to be inferred that the agent intended to assume personal liability.

The main class of case where this arises is in the context of unformed companies and by s. 9(2) of the European Communities Act 1972 the contract will be presumed to be with the person purporting to act as agent unless agreed to the contrary.

Agent or contractor

In the consideration of the consequences that follow from the intervention of an agent it has largely been assumed that the party acting as agent can be identified as such. In practice it is not always easy to distinguish between parties who are, in fact, contracting as agents rather than as contractors—that is parties to the contract itself.

This is particularly so where a party is seeking to derive the commercial benefits of appearing to contract as principal whilst in fact attempting to limit any potential liabilities by contracting as agent.

A particular example of this is found in the context of carriage of goods. A number of shipping lines (this is primarily those lines not themselves owners of the carrying vessels) apparently operating as principals are, despite the presence of the line name emblazoned in the largest print on the shipping documentation (including the bills of lading), nevertheless acting as agents only. When regard is had to the terms of the actual signature on the bill of lading this will almost inevitably be for or on behalf of the owner of the carrying vessel, not the line, as the small print on the reverse side will usually confirm.

In every case it will be a question of fact whether a party has contracted as agent or principal and in assessing the question of whether a party is contracting as principal or agent regard may be had, not only to the written documentation, but also to the circumstances and background to the negotiations leading to the conclusion of the contract. For instance, in the case of the "*Santa Carina*" [1974] agents for the charterer of a vessel telephoned the agents for a bunker supplier and asked "Can you supply bunkers for this vessel at Penang?" The answer was "Yes, we will arrange it". No mention was made by the charterer's agent that its role was so limited. It was held that it was permissible to have regard to the understanding and background knowledge of the parties and on that basis the supplier's agent knew of the limited role. (Subsequent confirmations were by telex and hence not signed. Had there been an unqualified signature the rule outlined on page 72 would have produced a different result.)

An important fact in such an enquiry will be the form of the party's remuneration. Payment by commission will generally be a pointer to a role as agent and payment of a lump sum or a differential in the price between the possible principal and possible agent, and that between possible agent and third party will be a strong indication that the role is not one of agent but contractor, although this is not necessarily conclusive. For example, the owner of a factory which was being dismantled for shipment to Brazil retained freight forwarders to arrange this. The freight forwarders had contracted with the owner to crate and deliver the machinery to a United Kingdom port for a lump sum. Shipment was arranged through the port of Middlesbrough and the freight forwarders had contracted with the authority to be responsible for port charges. During the shipment one of the machines was dropped. The owner sued the port authority. It was held that the various factors taken together pointed to the freight forwarders' role as being that of contractor and not that of agent and there was therefore no contract between the owner and the authority.

The liability of the agent to the third party

Aside from those situations considered above where the agent is liable to the third party as party to the contract which has been concluded through or with their involvement, the agent will also face a liability to the third party where they have purported to contract on behalf of the principal without actual or apparent authority.

Where the agent has purported to conclude a contract which, by reason of the lack of authority, actual or apparent, is ineffective to bind the intended principal, it does not follow, save perhaps in the anomalous case where the agent has contracted for a non-existent principal, as considered above, that the agent will be a party to the purported contract.

The agent may, however, be liable, not under the terms of the still-born contract but under the general law for breach of warranty of authority. This is what is known as a quasi-contractual remedy. Effectively the remedy provided is of a contractual nature but it arises by operation of law, irrespective of any agreement of the parties.

Where agents have purported to contract on behalf of a principal without the requisite authority, they will be liable for a breach of the warranty and the measure of the third party's damages will be the loss of profit anticipated under the contract which the third party had thought that it had concluded with the principal.

Rights and duties under the agency agreement

The rights of the principal in a commercial context

The terms of any agency agreement will dictate the obligations as between principal and agent, and the primary obligation of agents is to carry out the particular task they have agreed to perform.

In the absence of any express provision to the contrary, there will also be generally implied by law as arising out of the relationship of principal and agent, the following duties on the part of the latter:

(a) obedience
(b) to act with due care and skill
(c) to avoid any conflict of interest
(d) not to take any secret profit.

Obedience

The agent's primary duty is to perform in accordance with the express authority which will usually form a part of the agency agreement, given by the principal. In any matter not covered by the express instructions of the principal, the agent must act in accordance with normal trade customs and usage. In the absence of any such practice, as a guide, the paramount consideration of the agent is the benefit of the principal. In the case of *B. Davis Ltd v Tooth & Co. Ltd* [1937] importers of whisky in Australasia entered into a contract with the agents for the sole agency in New South Wales for particular brands of whisky. Under the terms of the agreement the agents were to devote the principal part of their energies to pushing the sale of the relevant brands. The agents were, however, also allowed to supply other brands where specifically requested by any buyers and to dispose of existing stocks. In the event, the agents' efforts were found to be partial and spasmodic and they continued to allow the advertisement of other competing brands. It was held that the agents were under an obligation to promote the sale of the whisky vigorously. This obligation was not satisfied by inaction or merely by avoiding giving preference to other brands, and by failing to make a steady effort to sell the whisky and in allowing the advertisement of competing brands, the agents had failed to comply with the sellers' requirements.

The contract, although described as a sole agency, is an example of the representative agent or a distributor. The "agents" contracted as the principal in the purchase of the whisky which was sold to customers. This distinction is immaterial for the purposes of considering the respective duties of principal and agent.

To act with due care and skill

It is certainly the case that agents who are receiving some form of payment, by implication hold themselves out as being as skilful and careful as people in that particular trade or profession normally are.

There is some question as to whether the same is required of agents who provide their services free. Where, however, agents expressly or by implication assert that they have certain skills and the principal reasonably relies upon this, they will still be liable for any failure to exercise due care and skill.

Agents retained to sell property or goods would be under an implied duty to exercise all due care and skill to obtain the best price that is reasonably obtainable. For example, agents were employed to sell a block of flats and received an offer from one party which the principal accepted "subject to contract". Subsequently, the agents were notified of a higher offer from another party, which was not notified to the principal. It was held that the agents owed their principal a duty to obtain the best price reasonably obtainable, which included a duty to communicate any better offers. This duty continued until a binding contract of sale had been effected.

Similarly, an independent insurance intermediary must exercise skill and care to obtain the insurance which is best suited to the insured's position. Failure by a broker to effect proper or valid insurance will generally represent a breach of the agent's duty to carry out the principal's express instructions, or failure to exercise proper care and skill in procuring the required insurance. In *Strong & Pearl v S. Allison & Co. Ltd* [1926] a broker was retained to obtain insurance by the owner of a yacht, while the owner was living on board and keeping petrol there for the purpose of using the auxilliary engine. Subsequently the owner gave notice of a change of lay-up berth. The broker obtained a policy in the usual lay-up terms which did not provide cover where persons were on board and petrol remained there during lay-up. On being notified of the change in berth, the broker issued a cover note without first obtaining the insurer's consent. Before that consent was obtained, there was an explosion on board the yacht and the insurer refused to pay. It was held that the broker was in breach of its duty of care and skill in failing to obtain insurance covering the yacht whilst persons and petrol were on board and in failing to advise the owner not to move the yacht, until the insurer's agreement to the change in berth had been obtained.

The obligation to use proper skill and care is a very extensive one and will also apply where the agent is retained to procure the supply of goods or materials. For instance, in *B. Davis Ltd v Tooth & Co. Ltd* [1937] by an ancillary agreement with sole agency for the sale and distribution of whisky, the selling agent undertook to procure for the seller stoppers used instead of corks for bottling whisky. The stoppers obtained contained lead, contrary to the regulations under the Australian Pure Food Act. The presence of lead would have been apparent from a simple test. It was held that in the context of a relationship concerned with the reputation and success of certain brands of whisky, the agent was obliged to use reasonable care in the matter of bottling and the materials employed in that operation. The failure to undertake any check or test of what was in New South Wales an untried device, constituted a breach of duty to use reasonable care.

To avoid any conflict of interest

Agents must not put themselves into a position where their own personal interest and their duty to the principal conflict (eg agents must not sell their goods to the principal when employed to buy goods).

If an agent has any personal interest that might conflict with the principal's interests, it must be disclosed and the principal must consent to the agent continuing to act. If the agent breaks this duty, the principal may set aside any transaction effected by the agent and claim any profits made thereby. This will apply even though the actions taken by the agent may not themselves have been lawful. It makes no difference that the agent has acted without any intention to defraud the principal, as where the agent buys or sells from or to the principal at the ordinary market price.

The principle of the law is that agents are not to place themselves in a situation which under ordinary circumstances would at least provide temptation to do that which is not the best for the principal. For instance, in *Industrial Development Consultants Ltd v Cooley* [1972] the managing director of a design consultancy received an approach, which was communicated to him privately, from a gas board concerning the possible provision of consultancy services in connection with the construction of four depots. The managing director secured his release, allegedly on grounds of ill-health, from the design consultants and set up his own company in competition and secured the contract for the four depots from the gas board. It was held that the contracts obtained by the director's own company had been sought by the design consultancy. The fact that the information concerning the depots had been communicated privately was irrelevant. The managing director had one capacity only in which he was carrying on business at the time: that of managing director of the design consultants and information which was of concern to the design consultancy was information which it was his duty to pass on to his employer. As a director of the company he could not obtain for himself a benefit or profit and the managing director was therefore liable to account to the design consultancy for the work undertaken by his own company.

It should be emphasised that the rule that no agent in the course of the agency, in the matter of the agency, can be allowed to make any profit without the knowledge and consent of the principal, is applied very strictly and no court will take notice of any evidence, suggestion or argument as to whether the principal did or did not suffer any injury, by reason of the dealing of the agent.

It was said in the last century that the safety of mankind required that no agents should be able to put their principal to the danger of such an enquiry. It has been more recently observed that in the nuclear age this may perhaps be something of an exaggeration, but nonetheless eloquent of the strictness with which the rule is applied (see the decision in the *Industrial Development Consultants* case above).

Not to make any secret profit or take a bribe

In many ways the duty of agents is a corollary of their obligation not to put themselves in a position whereby their own interests and those of their principal may conflict. Where this does happen, agents may well be liable to account to the principal for any benefit derived. This is so, even though there be much to say for the fact that the plaintiffs may not have been able to secure a profit for themselves. The application of the rule itself is such that even where the profit obtained is not lawfully acquired, the agent nevertheless will have a duty to account to the principal.

The decision of the court in *Industrial Development Consultants Ltd v Cooley* [1972] that the former managing director of the design consultancy had to account to his former employer for the profits made for the contracts that he secured for himself is an example of this. It was strongly argued in the case that the contracts were obtained as a result of a private approach to the former managing director individually and the design consultancy could not show that they themselves would have obtained a contract.

The liability to account applies even where the secret profit is made after the agent's authority has been determined. For instance, in *Regier v Campbell Stewart* [1939] a potential buyer for a house suitable for conversion into flats instructed an agent to locate a suitable property. The agent offered to the buyer a house that he owned for a price of £500 in excess of that for which it had been purchased... In fact, the prior purchase had been from the agent's brother as nominee and represented a fictitious price, double that for which the property had been bought from an independent third party. It was held that the termination of the agent's authority following the agreement to sell his own house to the buyer did not terminate the duty to act honestly and faithfully, and that the agent's deliberate concealment of the circumstances of the initial purchase constituted a breach of that duty.

The rights of the agent to commission

Agents are only entitled to the payment of commission, or indeed any form of remuneration from the principal, where this right has been expressly or impliedly agreed. Whilst there can be circumstances where the agent's services are given free of charge, in a commercial context at least, agreement to pay some form of remuneration is likely to be readily implied from the nature of an agent's services. If no amount is specified, the agent may be entitled to a reasonable remuneration.

It will be a question of the terms of the agency agreement as to when, if at all, it was the intention of the parties that commission should become payable. There is rarely any major difficulty where the transaction for which the agent has been instructed has been concluded and performed by the principal and third party. In these circumstances the agent will, in the absence of any unusual provisions, be entitled to such remuneration or commission as is agreed.

Difficulties arise, however, where for one reason or another the transaction concluded through the intervention of the agent is not performed or is only partially performed. It is apparent from the decisions of the courts in this area that this will depend largely on the circumstances in individual cases. For instance, in the *"Manifest Lipkowy"* [1988] the sale and purchase of a vessel was concluded through the efforts of a shipbroker. Under the terms of the agreement the broker was to be paid commission of four per cent for division with other brokers involved. In the event, the vessel was not ready for delivery by the agreed date and the buyer cancelled. The broker claimed commission for services rendered in obtaining a concluded agreement from the seller. It was held that in the absence of any express provision as to when commission would be payable, regard should be had to market practice which was that commission was payable only when the purchase price was paid by the buyer. It was impossible to imply a term that the principal would not, by any breach of the sale contract, prevent the agent from earning the commission.

The opposite result has been reached in two cases where there was no market practice to serve as a guide. In *Alpha Trading Limited v Dunnshaw-Patten Limited* [1981] an international trader agreed to introduce to another trader a purchaser for 10,000 tons of cement. The seller agreed to pay the agent a commission per ton. The buyer for the cement was duly introduced but, subsequently, the seller being unable or unwilling to provide the cement, the contract of sale was never implemented. The buyer was released from his obligation to pay the purchase price. The agent claimed to be entitled to be paid his commission. It was held that where principal and agent agreed that, in return for the agent introducing the buyer to the principal the agent would receive commission on any contract concluded, and if a contract was in fact concluded, there would be a term implied that the principal would not commit a breach of the contract with the buyer which would deprive the agent of his commission; the claim was allowed.

The same principle was applied in relation to an agreement for commission on the conclusion of the purchase of 16 new buildings from a shipyard.

It would seem that such a term may not be implied where the commission is derived from the earnings of a property of the principal, as to do so would impose an unreasonable fetter on owners' ability to deal with their own property at will.

The owner of a vessel employed a broker as agent to fix a charter for 18 months for a commission of two and a half per cent of the hire fee. After four months of the charter, the owner sold the vessel to the charterer and the charter was cancelled. It was held that there was no implied term of the contract that the shipowner should not agree to put an end to the charter by the sale of the ship to the charterer. The court would not imply an obligation on any principals to go on conducting their business in order to enable an agent to earn commission.

Similarly, the fact that agents are promised commission, but only if they bring about a sale, will not prevent the principal from disposing of the property through other channels or another agent, with the result that the commission is lost.

The rights of an agent to an indemnity

Provided the agents have acted within their authority, express or implied, the principal is, as a matter of law, in the absence of any agreement to the contrary, obliged to indemnify the agents against any losses, liabilities and expenses incurred in the performance of their duties.

Agents have no right to claim an indemnity in respect of unauthorised actions, unless these are subsequently ratified, and in accordance with general principle no agents have any right to an indemnity for loss caused by their own breach of duty.

The rights of an agent to a lien

Agents are entitled to exercise a lien in the absence of payment of any remuneration or indemnity over goods lawfully in their possession which belong to the principal. It is a question of the construction of the agency agreement as to whether the lien covers all assets of the principal for a general balance of account or particular goods only for sums due to the agent in respect of those specific goods.

The wider general lien is customarily recognised in the case of bankers, solicitors and, of more practical importance in the present context, factors or mercantile agents.

Termination of the agency

Where the agency relationship is one based in contract, as it usually will be in the commercial context, termination of the agreement will be subject to any express terms of the agreement, such as a provision of termination on expiry of a given period of notice.

As the relationship of principal and agent is one involving trust and confidence the agreement may, in the absence of any provision to the contrary, be terminable summarily at any moment. Where, however, the agent is required under the terms of the agreement to expend time and expense on the principal's behalf it is more likely that termination on a reasonable period of notice will be implied.

The insolvency of the principal will also automatically terminate the relationship, as will the liquidation of a corporate agent. With the bankruptcy of an individual the authority will only terminate if the bankruptcy makes the agent unfit for the duties required (see *Interphoto v Stiletto* [1988] on page 13).

Letters of comfort

A similar issue arises with regard to letters of comfort, awareness of which may well be intended by the party giving them not to be legally binding. This is a question to be determined from the actual wording of the letter (see *Kleinwort Benson v Malaysia Mining Corporation* [1989], page 21).

4

Finance

Introduction

The law and the considerations involved in international sale of goods transactions and their financing are complicated. A detailed examination of this area is therefore outside the scope of this book. Accordingly, in the first part of this chapter, consideration is given to an outline of the available methods of financing international transactions. The second part concentrates in more detail on the additional security available to the financial institution in lending transactions, in the form of assignments.

Methods of financing international transactions

General considerations the party will bear in mind when reaching terms of agreement in respect of payment for goods sold will be the time at which such payment will be made, how it will be made, where and in what currency.

The parties my choose any of the following means of payment.

Advance

This is a simple form of finance arrangement whereby cash is payable (generally by telegraphic or mail transfer from the buyer) at the time the order is placed, thus giving the seller maximum protection in that cash is provided in advance.

Open account

This method is usually adopted where the parties have an existing business relationship and therefore the seller has confidence in the buyer and, in particular, the buyer's integrity and financial standing. Under this system the seller sends the documents to the buyer who then, upon checking the documents and confirming that they are in accordance with the contract, pays the seller.

Documentary bill

A documentary bill is a bill of exchange to which the relevant bill of lading covering the goods sold is attached. The purpose is to prevent the buyer from receiving the bill of lading and with it, title to the goods, and disposing of them prior to payment. The seller sends the shipping documents usually via his or her bank to the buyer's bank together with a bill of exchange. The buyer accepts the bill of exchange and his or her bank returns it to the seller's bank. Thus the buyer receives the shipping documents, and the seller receives the bill of exchange which may involve a period of credit given to the buyer.

A bill of exchange involves three parties, the seller, the buyer, and the bank. On the bill the buyer is stated as being the person to make payment. The seller is known as the "drawer" and the buyer is the "drawee". The seller/drawer addresses the bill of exchange (the draft) to the buyer/drawee as promising to pay the payee bank the specified sum on a specified date.

Once the accepted bill is in the seller's hands, it is a negotiable instrument, negotiable at once, and the seller can negotiate it to a third party, usually at a discount, in order to obtain immediate payment from that third party. In due course, upon maturity, the third party recovers the full amount from the drawee.

The Bills of Exchange Act 1882 codifies the practice concerning bills of exchange. They must be in writing and signed by the party who accepts responsibility. By its very nature the bill of exchange will be negotiable either simply by delivery (in which case the promise should be to pay the payee bank) or by order, or by endorsement. The person who holds the document can call for performance of the promise to pay.

The holder will regularly be an endorsee or the payee bank. Significantly, a "holder in due course" or endorsee of the bill can acquire better rights than the person who transferred it and may take the bill free of prior defects (s. 29 Bill of Exchange Act 1882).

Primary liability to pay is on the drawee/buyer although the seller/drawer and payee bank and subsequent endorsees do become liable if there is a default by the drawee and if, for example, the drawee dishonours the bill.

The Act makes provision for foreign bills, ie those bills drawn by a non-British resident or drawn on a person resident abroad, where that bill is payable abroad. By s. 51 of the Bills of Exchange Act 1882, such a bill must be formally protested upon dishonour (that is upon non-acceptance or non-payment). Since this is a different approach from that of foreign laws, the drawee needs to know whether the obligation is to be judged by English law or the applicable foreign law and s. 72 of the Act lays down rules relating to the conflict of laws.

Collection arrangements

The 1978 uniform rules for collections sponsored by the International Chamber of Commerce (ICC) set out the practice in relation to collection arrangements. The rules only apply if incorporated by the parties into the contract, but they are useful guidelines for general reference. In brief, in a collection arrangement the seller will appoint a bank to act as agent and take instructions; the bank will "collect", ie receive documents of title from the seller which will stand for the goods. The price will be paid to seller's bank, or bill of exchange accepted, against the transfer of the documents. Figure 4.1 illustrates the way in which a typical collection arrangement works. Both the bank remitting payment and the collecting bank will generally be the seller's agents.

It is worth noting that the collecting bank may release the documents under "trust" to the buyer prior to the performance of the conditions of the collection order. The buyer becomes trustee of the documents and the collecting bank becomes beneficiary under the trust, thus assuring it of payment for the seller.

Documentary credits

The system of documentary credits is probably the most widely used system for the payment of goods under international sales. The 1983 uniform customs and practice for documentary credits (UCP) is sponsored by the ICC and deals in great detail with every aspect of such credits. Under this system the buyer will make an arrangement with the bank "issuing bank" (IB) to provide finance to the seller. This bank will usually use another bank the "advising bank", in the seller's country, to pay upon presentation of shipping documents. On delivery of such

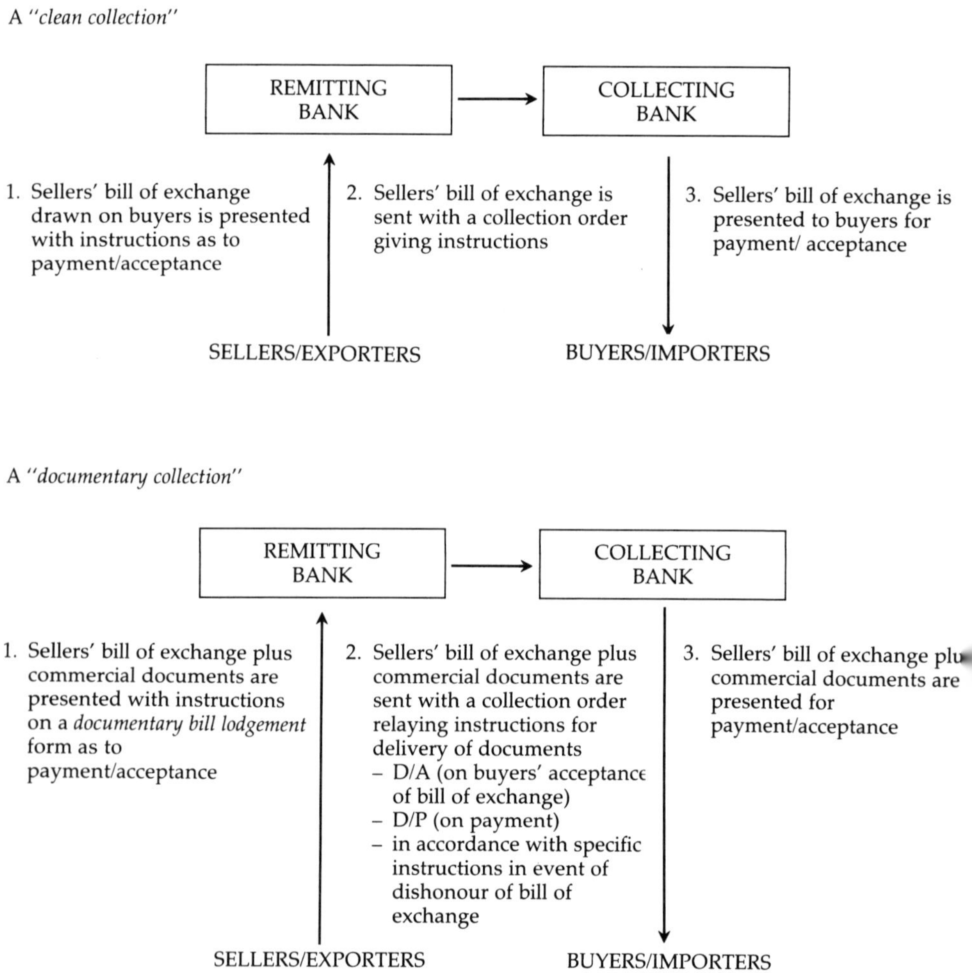

Figure 4.1 Collection arrangement

documents, assuming they are in accordance with the stipulations set out in the documentary credit, the "advising bank" will pay the price to the seller. The IB will hold the documents of title as security for the finance.

Figure 4.2 explains the stages whereby a documentary credit will be opened.

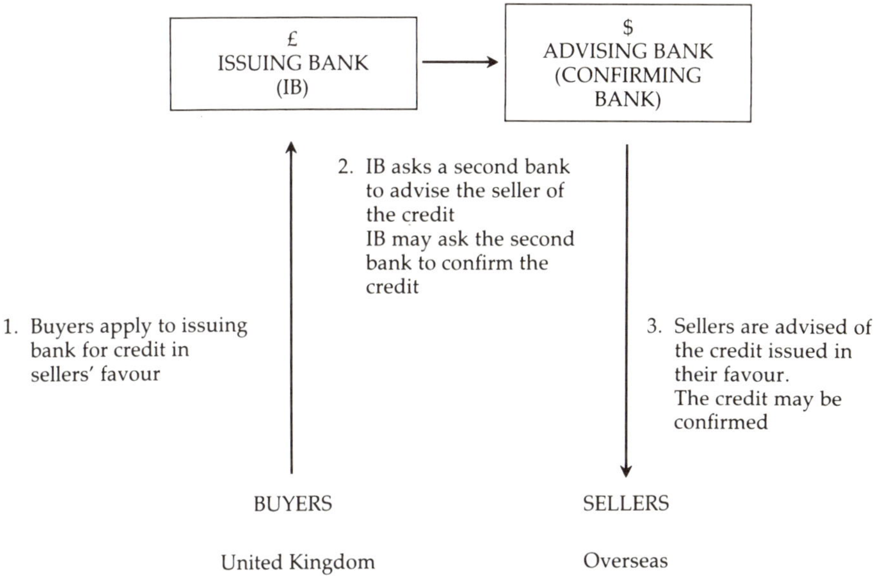

Figure 4.2 Opening a documentary credit under the Uniform Rules for Collections (1978)

When the IB is asked to open a letter of credit in this way, a detailed list of characteristics of the shipping documents will be provided to the bank. For example, the shipment period will be specified and the bank must check that the bill of lading is evidence of shipment within that period. The bank will also be concerned to ensure that any certificates of quality specified in the credit do indeed certify the correct quality.

There is a doctrine of strict compliance within which the bank must operate and if a document does not conform with the terms of the credit, the bank will reject it. Thus the advising bank making finance available to a seller on receipt of a certificate of quality signed by one expert and

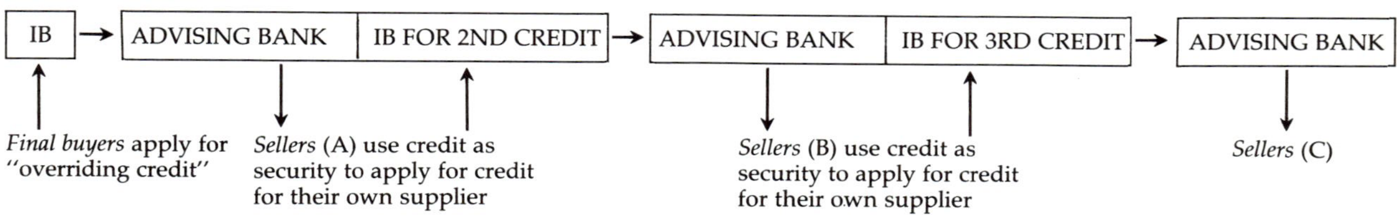

Figure 4.3 Back to back credits

not signed by "experts" as the buyer's mandate had specified, will be unable to recover from the buyer (this is because the bank has effectively exceeded the scope of its authority as the buyer's agent, by making an unauthorised payment against the wrong documents—see *Equitable Trust Company of New York v Dawson Partners Limited* [1927]).

However if the documents presented are correct, the bank must pay against them. Whilst the bank must take care to check that documents sent do indeed conform to the buyer's mandate, apart from having a duty to read those documents very closely, the bank's obligation to check small print and clauses of, for example, the bills of lading, goes no further. Indeed, even if the bank is told by the buyer that in spite of the documents being in apparent conformity, the goods themselves are not, in the absence of any defect in the documents presented and in the absence of any fraud, the bank is obliged to make payment in spite of the buyer's concern.

All documentary credits invariably contain an expiry date after which documents tendered will be returned unless the credit is renewed by the buyer.

There are a number of different types of credit falling into the category of documentary credits, these include the following.

Transferable and divisible credits

By virtue of a transferable credit, the buyer and issuing bank can agree to the seller's request to the advising bank to make the credit available to one or more beneficiaries (usually the seller's own supplier). The credit must be designated "transferable" by the issuing bank. It can be transferred once only, or in fractions of the total credit, provided that partial shipments are not excluded. (See Articles 54 and 46(e) of the UCP.)

Alternatively, the seller may assign the benefit of the credit, ie treat it as a debt subject to the presentation of documents. S. 136 Law of Property Act 1925 requires the assignment to be in writing and with written notice given to the debtor, ie the bank—see the second section of this chapter for details.

Back to back and overriding credits

Where a string of buyers are involved, one seller can use the credit opened as security in order to open a credit for the seller's own supplier.

The back bone of this chain is the "overriding credit", ie the one opened by the ultimate buyer.

Packing credits, red clause credits

Packing credits or "anticipatory credits" make finance available to a seller prior to shipment of the goods. The seller presents a document other than a transport document, stipulated by the buyer, such as a warehouse receipt. This shows the buyer that the goods are out of the seller's possession. A "red clause" inserted in the advising bank's letter of advice to the seller will inform the seller that the bank will advance part payment against the documents such as the warehouse receipt, and the remainder will be paid against transport documents.

Air waybill credit

An air waybill is a receipt for the goods showing the date of air dispatch of goods, carrier, shipper, consignee and a description of goods and freight.

The seller's air waybill is signed by the carrier and handed to the seller for delivery and this document will be required to be tendered under an air waybill letter of credit.

Revolving credits

Such a credit will be for a set maximum amount and open for a set period of months. It has the advantage to a buyer dealing regularly with a seller, that it operates automatically without the buyer having to renew the credit every time a draft presented reduces the credit below its fixed maximum amount.

Revocable/irrevocable and unconfirmed/confirmed credits

Once the seller receives notification of the credit and accepts it, the seller will want to be certain that the bank will pay. In this regard, different types of credit offer varying degrees of certainty. The least secure is the *revocable unconfirmed credit*. If revocable, the issuing bank instructed by the buyer may cancel the credit in the seller's favour at any time. The advising bank is unlikely, therefore, to confirm payment to the seller in such a case.

Greater security is offered to the seller by the *irrevocable unconfirmed credit*. If the issuing bank makes the credit irrevocable it must keep the seller's credit open. The advising bank however, is not under any duty to make payment to the seller if it does not confirm the credit.

Maximum security is available to the seller with the *irrevocable confirmed credit*. If the issuing bank makes the credit irrevocable, the advising bank is guaranteed payment and will usually confirm the credit, ie undertake to make payment to the seller on receipt of the correct documents within the required time. The seller can expect payment irrespective of any dispute which the buyer may have over the goods received under the sale contract.

Different types of credit will dictate different times and modes of payment to the seller. Payment may be *at sight* of the documents. Payment may be at the *deferred* date after their presentation, ie the maturity date of the letter of credit. Should the seller require cash before this date, the credit can be negotiated.

Non-recourse finance

Typically, this describes the situation where a finance house will accept the financial risk; the second section of this chapter may be of particular interest as to the operating of this arrangement.

The finance house will enter into two contracts, one with the buyer and one with the seller. The seller will agree with the finance house that it will pay the full price less the deposit that will have to be paid by the buyer. Usually, for security, the finance house will take delivery of specific shipping documents prior to payment being made. The finance house will very often be covered by an export credit guarantee policy (see below) and will take pains to ensure in the contract that it has no interest in the goods, but is simply involved as an investor. It will contract with the buyer and the buyer will agree to pay the finance house the purchase price and charges. When the shipping documents are presented the buyer will usually be obliged to accept bills of exchange drawn by the finance house. By this method, the finance house can elect to extend credit to the buyer for a specified period or to make provision for instalment payments.

Factoring and forfeiting

At its simplest this is a financial transaction whereby the finance house or factor assumes responsibility for collection of the purchase price from the purchaser on behalf of the seller. It is different from non-recourse finance in that shipping documents will not be passed to the factor by the seller but will go directly to the buyer.

An "open" factoring transaction comprises a contract with the seller and the factor whereby the factor will agree to purchase short-term debts due to the seller from overseas buyers. Whenever the seller then sells goods, the claim for the price will be assigned to the factor and it is disclosed to the buyer that the finance house should receive payment from the buyer. Generally the sale will be a legal assignment and accordingly notice will be given. The second section of this chapter deals with this in some detail. The advantage to the seller is that potential bad debts are eliminated, although the seller will inevitably take a discount (reflecting the risk to the factor) on the debts so assigned.

A hybrid of the open factoring transaction is the "undisclosed" factoring transaction, ie the buyer is not informed of the factoring arrangement. The seller will actually sell the goods to the factor for a discounted price and the factor, as an unnamed principal, will resell them through the seller to customers on a credit basis. The customers will pay the seller who will pass the proceeds to the factor. The risk to the factor is enhanced by this operation and for that reason the discount is likely to be more substantial.

In the case of forfeiting, the bank or finance house in the seller's country (ie the forfeiter) purchases a negotiable instrument, for example a bill of exchange, from the seller, at a discount since it is on a non-recourse basis as against the seller. For security the forefeiter will require a bank guarantee or a valorisation of the negotiable instrument from the buyers' bank, since there is no recourse to the seller.

Export credit guarantees

Before considering assignment for additional security in any transaction in further detail, the Export Credit Guarantee Department (ECGD) and the facilities offered will be briefly considered. The Export Guarantee Overseas Investment Act 1978 empowers the Secretary of State to give export guarantees. This is to encourage trade with other countries. The administration of the scheme of export credit guarantees is in the hands of the ECGD. The department charges premium rates for the insurance that it offers to enable the seller to eliminate export risks which would not be covered by their more general insurance. The ECGD is a non-profit making body, and sellers who obtain its assistance may find themselves more likely to have the confidence of financial institutions which they approach for financial assistance.

The ECGD can be approached through a branch office or through an insurance broker. A proposal form should be completed and a quotation obtained. Facilities are offered by the department on a declaration basis where an overseas buyer can obtain short-term credit (say up to six months), or supplemental credit guarantees for longer periods. The comprehensive short-term guarantee is the standard policy available and it will cover the whole overseas trade of the exporter for short-term credit, that is, up to six months. It remains in force until terminated, which can be done annually. It protects the seller from the time of shipment through to receipt of payment, although it can be extended to pre-credit risk. It is, of course, primarily to protect against the insolvency of an overseas buyer.

Full details of services provided by the ECGD and copies of the relevant policies can be obtained by contacting its headquarters at Aldermanbury House, Aldermanbury, London EC2P 2EL.

Assignments as additional security in lending transactions

Introduction

This section is designed to inform readers of the principal differences between various forms of assignment; to discuss their individual difficulties and to recommend specific steps for the avoidance of problems which often subsequently occur.

The acquisition of legal rights by way of assignment can give rise to a number of attendant problems which may be both legal and practical in nature. Therefore, when additional loan security is arranged, or agreed to be arranged, by way of assignment of legal rights or choses in action the entire enterprise must be undertaken with great caution.

In this chapter the following types of assignment are considered:

(a) *Assignments relating to insurances,* being:
- (i) the assignment of the subject-matter of an insurance policy
- (ii) the assignment of an insurance policy itself
- (iii) the assignment of the proceeds of an insurance policy.

(b) *The assignment of income, earnings and other moneys* arising from the operation of the subject-matter of a particular finance project (eg the earnings of a vessel).

Assignments relating to insurances

The assignment of the subject-matter of an insurance policy

(a) Generally, where the assured voluntarily disposes of their entire interest (usually by sale) in the subject-matter insured (ie any given asset) under an insurance policy, they are unable to present a claim under the policy over that particular subject-matter. The insurance policy lapses automatically on loss of insurable interest even without express provision to that effect existing in the insurance policy (see *Rogerson v Scottish Automobile & General Insurance Co. Ltd* [1931]).

In the absence of express or implied agreement with an insurer and an assignee, an assignment or sale of the subject-matter insured does not automatically carry with it an assignment of the policy itself—s. 15 of the Marine Insurance Act 1986.

(b) Where assureds do not dispose of their *entire* insurable interest then, of course, the policy will not automatically lapse. This is the case where the subject-matter insured is mortgaged to a third party and where an assured assigns the subject-matter absolutely but retains possession by way of security for payment. If a policy is stated to cover the interests of a buyer of the subject-matter insured, it remains in force as against that person, even though the assured may have lost the right to sue under it.

From a practical point of view, it is therefore vital to agree in express terms a contemporaneous sale of both an asset and its insurances before safely concluding that the sale of a particular asset also entails the assignment of the existing insurance policy over that asset. The existing insurance arrangements over the asset in question should also be reviewed before arranging the assignment of any insurance policy contemporaneously with the sale of its subject matter. The terms of the existing insurance policy should be checked to see if there is any express prohibition against such a contemporaneous assignment. In addition, even in the absence of such a provision, the assent of the insurer to a change of assured should be obtained. For further discussion of these additional requirements, see Chapter 5.

Assignment of the policy

Under English law, a policy of insurance as a chose in action is freely assignable, subject to compliance with three conditions:

(a) the consent of the insurer must be obtained
(b) to avoid problems of insurable interest, the assignment of the policy and its underlying subject-matter must be contemporaneous
(c) the assignment must be in proper form.

With regard to (a), the giving of consent renders the contract between the insurer and the assignee a novation as opposed to a continuation of the old policy. Consent, however, is not required in relation to the assignment of marine policies—s. 50(1) of the Marine Insurance Act 1906 (see below). Any policy provision may also provide that the separate consent of the insurer is not needed and that the policy inures for the benefit of any purchaser of the subject-matter insured.

With regard to (b), there are two situations to consider:

(a) Assignment of the subject matter of the policy before the policy itself: the policy automatically lapses once its subject matter is assigned. Therefore the assignee has no claim to make against the insurer.
(b) Assignment of the policy before assignment of the subject-matter thereof—two consequences follow:
    (i) assured cannot recover as they have assigned the policy
    (ii) assignees cannot recover since at the date of assignment of the policy they had no insurable interest. This is clearly a situation which a lender should avoid when attempting to assume the benefit of existing insurances.

    Of course, problems relating to contemporaneity do not arise where the assignor has not disposed of the entire insurable interest in the property insured. Contemporaneity is necessary in marine insurance (see below).

As to (c), the assignment of an insurance policy may be achieved either *at law* or *in equity*. The significant advantage of a legal assignment is that it permits assignees to sue the insurer in their own name without having to join the former assured as a party to the legal proceedings, and also confers upon assignees the right to give a good discharge for the policy moneys upon receiving them. Under s. 136 of the Law of Property Act 1925:

(a) the assignment must be *in writing* and *signed by the assignor*
(b) it must be *absolute* and not by way of charge only (so that, as previously mentioned, a mortgage will not divest mortgagors of their entire interest in the mortgaged property)
(c) *notice in writing* of the assignment must be given to the insurer.

An assignment not complying with these formalities may nevertheless take effect as a valid *equitable assignment* upon proof of the assignor's unequivocal intention to assign and the assignee's provision of consideration. However, in legal proceedings an equitable assignee must join the assignor as a co-plaintiff in order to bring suit. This is one of a number of disadvantages that an equitable assignment has as against a legal assignment.

From a practical point of view, therefore, in order to ensure the complete security and effectiveness of the assignment, it is vital to comply with conditions (a), (b) and (c) above right from the very start. Whilst non-compliance with particular formalities (such as the giving of notice to the insurer) can be cured after the creation of an equitable assignment, an assignee runs the risk of losing priority.

Priorities between competing assignments are determined by the date of notice of assignments to the insurer (*Dearle v Hall* (1882)). However, legal assignees cannot take priority over an equitable assignee of whose assignment they had notice and equitable assignees cannot take priority over an earlier equitable assignee of whose assignment they had notice at the date of their own assignment (*Newman v Newman* (1885)).

All assignments (whether legal or equitable) take subject to equities such as defences of the insurer which have accrued both prior to and after the assignment. These defences, such as non-disclosure of a material fact to the insurer at the time the insurance was initially placed, may be pleaded against the assignee by the insurer.

Assignment of the proceeds of a policy

Under English law, the right to recover insurance proceeds under a policy is freely assignable as a chose in action under s. 136 of the Law of Property Act 1925 or by way of equitable assignment. The following points should be noted in relation to this type of assignment:

(a) A new contract between the insurer and the assignee is not created by such an assignment. The *assignor* of the proceeds is still the assured under the policy. It therefore follows that, since there is no change of assured, the consent of the insurer to the assignment is not necessary.

(b) The assignee need not possess any insurable interest. Accordingly, a contemporaneous assignment of the subject-matter of the policy is not required. The assignee is simply the assignee of the proceeds of the policy and not of the policy itself.

(c) Separate rules apply to marine policies under English law.

(d) As where the policy itself is assigned, the assignee of the proceeds takes subject to the rights and defences of the insurer against the assured.

Special rules relating to marine insurance policies

(a) Under English law, a marine policy is assignable without formality. According to s. 50(1) of the Marine Insurance Act 1906 a marine policy is assignable unless it contains terms which expressly prohibit assignment. It should be especially noted that the consent of the insurer is not required to the assignment of a marine policy.

(b) With regard to freight and hulls, the position is governed by the standard Institute Clauses which provide that:

> No assignment of or interest in any moneys which may be or become payable hereunder is to be binding on or recognised by the Underwriters unless a dated notice of such assignment or interest signed by the assured and by the assignor in the case of subsequent assignment, is endorsed on the policy and the policy with such endorsement is produced before payment of any claim or return premium hereunder (Institute Time Clauses cl.5, Institute Voyage Clauses Hulls cl.3, Institute Time Clauses Freight cl.6, Institute Voyage Clauses Freight cl.4).

This is so except where new marine insurance is placed or where, as discussed above, the assignee is simply a mortgagee of the property insured; there must be a contemporaneous assignment of both the marine insurance policy and its subject-matter.

(c) S. 50(3) of the Marine Insurance Act 1906 states that a marine policy maybe assigned "by endorsement thereon or in other customary manner". A clear intention to assign must be shown, whatever the manner in which any given assignment is effected.

(d) Any defence available to the insurer against the assured will also prevail against the assignee (ie an assignment takes effect subject to equities).

(e) Assignees of a marine policy can sue in their own name: s. 50(2) of the Marine Insurance Act 1906.

(f) Any conduct by the assured following the assignment which would otherwise have given the insurer the right to repudiate liability, confers the same right as against the assignee (the *"Litsion Pride"* [1985]).

Summary: assignments related to insurances

(a) Where existing insurance is assumed over an asset without the placing of new insurance, a lender must ensure that such insurance does not automatically lapse as a result of the sale of the asset to the borrower. An express assignment of the existing insurance policy is therefore required which is contemporaneous with the sale of the asset (ie the subject-matter of the insurance) to the borrower. The consent of the insurer to such an assignment must also be obtained and in the case of a non-marine policy, the requisite formalities must be complied with.

(b) A lender should try to ensure that it has control over the actual insurance placing, both in terms of recommending placing brokers or sub-brokers and approving the quality of the security underwriting the risk. A lender should avoid the situation where the borrower alone arranges the insurance through poor brokers with inadequate underwriters without prior reference to the lender. Specific provision can always be made in loan documentation to the placing of insurance and a condition precedent to drawdown of the loan can be specified to the effect that insurance brokers and underwriters acceptable to the lender respectively place and bear the risk. If it subsequently becomes necessary to commence legal proceedings against either the broker (for breach of duty) or the underwriters (under the contract of insurance), a lender does not want to be faced with the prospect of expensive litigation in many different jurisdictions against underwriters of poor repute for small fractions of the total risk originally insured. It must be borne in mind that each underwriter has a distinct and separate contract with the assured and/or any subsequent assignee of the assured (such as a lender of money), notwithstanding that the same broker's slip is subscribed to.

(c) In the case of non-marine policies, a lender should ensure that the wording of the assignment unequivocally transfers to the lender either the policy itself or the proceeds to be paid under the policy. The disadvantage of the latter is that in any legal proceedings the lender must compel the assignor to sue under the policy as it cannot sue in its own name.

The assignment of income, earnings and other moneys

Forms of assignment

The assignment of income, earnings and other moneys tends to give rise to different considerations and problems. Such an assignment can take one of many forms. The direct repayment of a loan by the collection of income and the immediate application of that income (or a defined portion of that income) to outstanding loans is possible. In such cases, a lender must be placed in the position of being an absolute legal assignee. Also possible is the collection of assigned earnings in a designated escrow account to be applied against outstanding loans. In the event of default or otherwise under the loan agreement (see model on page 101—cl. 2). In this instance, the lender holds the position of an equitable assignee until its absolute entitlement to the moneys in question crystallises upon the terms contained in the loan agreement or otherwise pursuant to s. 136 of the Law of Property Act 1925. In the context of shipping finance, where a lender collects voyage freight and/or time charter hire the flow of money will obviously depend upon the state of the market and the employment situation of the mortgaged vessels. A stipulation may be required to the effect that, with the lender's consent, sums accumulating to the escrow account can be applied towards the payment of the vessel's operating expenses and any related costs (see Model Clause, page 101). The amount left in escrow, however, should never fall below the amount necessary to secure repayment instalments of the principal and/or interest.

Charterparty provision for lender's assignment of income

It is important that charterparties contain express provision for payments to be made directly to the mortgagee lender. This should be specifically checked, if possible, each time a vessel obtains new employment. Such a charterparty provision will serve a two-fold function as it will constitute notice of assignment to the charterer of the lender's position as assignee and ensure that the lender actually makes collection of voyage freight and charter hire in the first instance, albeit perhaps with limited powers of disposal until a default occurs under the loan. In the event that notice to the charterer does not take the form of a charterparty provision of this kind, then a separate written notice is necessary, followed, if possible, by an acknowledgement of the terms of notice by the charterer. For long term arrangements involving the continued operation of a vessel by one charterer, on either a voyage or time basis, and especially in the case of a bareboat charter, a tripartite agreement between the lender, the shipowner and the charterer constituting the lender as assignee of the vessel's earnings and other moneys would probably be preferable to a simple "notice system".

Advance voyage freight—a special case

In the case of advance voyage freight which is earned before commencement of the voyage, the assignee lender is in an extremely strong position. Freight which is earned on shipment or on signing bills of lading gives the person entitled to receive that freight (including an absolute assignee) an accrued right to the freight which is in itself indefeasible. Consequently, even a repudiatory breach of charter by a shipowner giving a charterer counterclaims for damages against the owner will not defeat the right of an assignee lender to be paid the freight without deduction (*Bank of Boston Connecticut v European Grain and Shipping Ltd* (the "*Dominique*") [1989]). Charterparties concluded on this basis therefore provide almost complete protection to lenders who are the assignees of earned advance freight subject, it would seem, to any fraud or misrepresentation on the part of the shipowners disentitling them to the freight in the first place.

Model clause for assignment of earnings

Earnings account

1. All Earnings of the Ship, however arising, will be credited to a deposit account with the Lender in the name of the Borrower ("the Earnings Account").
2. Without prejudice to clause 1, the Borrower undertakes regularly to credit to the Earnings Account sufficient moneys to ensure that the Borrower's obligation to pay interest, and the [ ] Repayment Instalments of $ and $ of the Final Repayment Instalment, as and when they become due, can be met by deduction from the Earnings Account and to make provision for such other sums as may be from time to time due and owing to the Lender under the Security Documents. Any shortfall, actual or anticipated, in the Earnings Account must be made good by the Borrower within thirty (30) days of the Lender's giving notice thereof.
3. Moneys from time to time standing to the credit of the Earnings Account will earn interest from day to day at the rate the Lender is prepared to pay for call deposits in Dollars at seven (7) days notice.
4. All sums from time to time standing to the credit of the Earnings Account are hereby charged, pledged and hypothecated to the Lender as security for the obligations of the Borrower to the Lender.
5. Moneys will be disbursed from the Earnings Account only to the extent that the Lender is satisfied either that they will be applied to the reasonable and necessary operating expenses of the Ship and that adequate provision has been made for such expenses and for the Borrower's actual or contingent liabilities to the Lender and to third parties.

5

The role of insurance in international commercial transactions

Introduction

It is indisputable that every commercial transaction involves an element of risk. It is this risk which insurance attempts to cover. Insurers and insurance brokers are therefore fundamental to virtually all commercial transactions and have as much financial interest in the dealings of others as the actual participants. Without the protection of insurance, most business activities would not happen. International trade illustrates this most markedly in contracts of marine insurance in respect of hulls, cargo, freight and other insurable interests.

The purpose of this chapter is not to give a comprehensive analysis of all the ramifications of marine insurance contracts (in particular, the doctrine of utmost good faith which has received intense scrutiny in recent years and which is commented upon in passing only), but to comment upon selected aspects of such contracts and to summarise the relevant law (and where necessary the wider context of insurance law generally). Most importantly, this chapter attempts to deal with and offer suggestions upon certain legal and practical difficulties which often arise in relation to contracts of marine insurance. These difficulties, which largely relate to the coordination of insurance cover with other inter-related and quickly effected transactions, have a significant effect upon the interests of all concerned, be they buyers or sellers of goods, carriers, financiers or insurance brokers and other intermediaries to such transactions.

Policy forms and documentation

Old system of forms

The document in which the contract of insurance is embodied has always been a fundamental feature in the consideration of contracts of marine insurance. S. 22 of the Marine Insurance Act 1906 provides:

> Subject to the provisions of any statute, a contract of marine insurance is inadmissible in evidence unless it is embodied in a marine policy in accordance with this Act. The policy may be executed and issued either at the time when the contract is concluded, or afterwards.

The policy document is therefore the primary evidence of the contract itself, and if no policy document exists or is placed in evidence at trial, the contract of insurance itself cannot be evidenced by any other means. To have a contract of marine insurance without a policy would be akin to Hamlet without the Prince! Legal proceedings based solely upon the contract will be ineffectual without the corresponding policy and a broker can be compelled by an assured to produce a policy at trial in an action against underwriters of the policy and to testify to all matters connected with the policy (*Hunter v Leathley* (1830)).

For most of this century, the form of policy contained in schedule 1 of the Marine Insurance Act 1906 dominated the lives of insurers and brokers alike. This form, the Lloyd's S.G. Policy, was applicable to both hull and cargo insurances. Whilst not being an obligatory part of every marine insurance placing, the form established itself in use, to be read in conjunction with the Rules for Construction (again contained in schedule 1 of the 1906 Act), the Institute Clauses as drafted by the Joint Drafting Committee of the Institute of London Underwriters and the Lloyd's Underwriters Association, and the Rules of Practice of the Association of Average Adjusters. Production of the original Lloyd's S.G. Policy was always a prerequisite to payment by underwriters.

New system of forms

It was not until 1982 that the old S.G. form of policy was abandoned. The new form is much simpler. The standard introductory wording is very brief and is followed by a policy schedule to be completed with the salient contractual information. Standard clauses can be attached, as can further endorsements and special conditions and warranties which form part of the policy. The document can be "tailor-made" to suit the particular needs of any insurance placing. The policy schedule itself will be considered in more detail below.

New Institute Clauses were drafted by the Institute of London Underwriters in co-operation with the Lloyd's Underwriters Association. These clauses do not depend upon any other document for their contractual validity. They are attached only to the marine policy (MAR) form, which is a straightforward top sheet. One main feature of the clauses is that they draw a distinction between "all risks" and "named perils". The order of the cargo clauses has been changed and the language updated, although the old titles are retained. Moreover, the provisions of extraneous documents can be incorporated into the new policy form, provided that accurate and sufficient wording is used to incorporate the pertinent provisions. The present attitude of the courts towards the incorporation of terms derived from extraneous sources is to disallow the attempted incorporation of the irrelevant or inappropriate and to require unequivocal words of incorporation. Careful thought must therefore always be given to what is strictly needed to give effect to the transaction in question. Commonplace but unnecessary provisions should not be included as part of the contractual framework simply because they have never been omitted before! Particular reference should be made to the decision of the House of Lords in *Vesta v Butcher* [1989] which, despite its reinsurance context, contains important judicial comments upon the wording and compilation of contractual documentation which are applicable to the placing of direct marine insurances.

There are many Institute Clauses, of which the following are the most important:

(a) Institute Time Clauses—Hulls (1983)
(b) Institute Voyage Clauses—Hulls (1983)
(c) Institute Cargo Clauses (A), (B) and (C) (1982)
(d) Institute Standard Conditions for Cargo Contracts (1982)
(e) Institute Time Clauses—Freight (1983)
(f) Institute Voyage Clauses—Freight (1983)

There are also various Institute War and Strike Clauses for hulls, freight and cargo on both a time and a voyage basis.

It is not the purpose of this chapter to comment in detail upon the respective provisions of each set of clauses. The purpose is rather to note the flexibility of the new form of marine insurance policy and the various elements which can be incorporated into it as appropriate, depending upon the subject-matter insured and other material factors. Freedom of contract can never be inhibited by the use of standard forms, however desirable they may be.

The slip

Whilst the policy itself remains vital to the contract of insurance, it is invariably not the first document to come into existence. S. 22 of the Marine Insurance Act 1906 itself recognises this.

Most contracts of insurance are usually first evidenced by a "slip". The slip will contain bare contractual details:

(a) the name of the assured
(b) the risk to be insured
(c) market abbreviations of the terms and conditions of the insurance and
(d) the insurers' notification of their acceptance of those terms and conditions, usually indicated by the presence of their company stamp, the initials of the actual underwriter concerned and the date of acceptance, together with the proportion of the insurance risk accepted, which is either indicated as a percentage or sum of currency.

The slip will have been prepared by the insurance brokers placing the insurance and will be circulated amongst underwriters in the marine market who will indicate thereon their acceptance of a portion of the risk. At a later stage, in the absence of a corresponding policy, the slip will assume great significance in the insurance recovery process and its precise terms, scope and accuracy will be subjected to close scrutiny by both sides in a dispute, and perhaps even by the courts or an arbitration tribunal. The observations made above concerning the incorporation of terms in policy documents apply equally to the preparation of slips.

Slips will often include a section headed "Information", containing further details about the insured business. Statements in this section have been held by the English commercial court to be representations of fact which may reasonably be relied upon by underwriters (*Highlands Insurance Co. v Continental Insurance Co.* [1987]). If statements contained in the "Information" section of a slip prove to be untrue or misleading, they may give rise to a claim for rescission of the insurance contract and/or damages by the insurers against the assured.

The broker's slip will usually provide evidence of the conclusion of the marine insurance contract, since s. 21 of the Marine Insurance Act 1906 provides that a contract of marine insurance is deemed to be concluded "when the proposal of the insured is accepted by the insurer...", notwithstanding that the issue of a policy may not have taken place at that stage.

S. 21 also expressly recognises that "for the purpose of showing when the proposal was accepted, reference may be made to the slip or covering note or other customary memorandum of the contract". It is important to remember that each of the insurers is contractually bound from the time they initial the slip. Consequently, in the absence of special provision to the contrary, the insurance cannot be cancelled or amended without each underwriter's consent. Without express stipulation in the slip, the agreement to an amendment by one underwriter does not of itself bind other underwriters named in the slip, since each underwriter has a separate contractual relationship with the assured.

Example 1
Broker A places hull and machinery insurance on a time basis in the Lloyd's marine market with underwriters X, Y and Z. X, Y and Z initially accept terms to the effect that they are on risk for 12 months as from 1 January 1990. X is "lead underwriter" in that his initials were placed first on the slip and the proportion of cover accepted by him on the slip ahead of the initials and proportions of Y and Z. Broker A then receives instructions from his assured to extend the period of risk to 18 months (ie up to 30th June 1991). Underwriter X accepts the amendment and initials an endorsement to the slip to this effect. Y and Z are not content with the amendment and do not initial the endorsement. Is X's agreement binding upon Y and Z? Clearly not.

Example 2
The slip in Example 1 above contains wording to the effect that amendments to the cover accepted by the lead underwriter bind those underwriters who follow. In this instance, the amendment to the period of cover agreed by underwriter X, the lead underwriter, binds Y and Z.

Where a particular broker only places a part of the total risk to be insured, each of the underwriters named on that broker's slip is only liable for their particular agreed proportion of the placing broker's "order" as opposed to a proportion of the total risk.

Where formal policies are not actually required, the broker's slip can be converted into a "slip policy" by attaching a standard policy wording to the slip.

The policy schedule

The standard policy schedule forming part of the new simplified policy form will usually set out the basic contractual details such as:

(a) the policy number
(b) the name of the assured
(c) the vessel
(d) the voyage or the period of insurance
(e) the subject-matter insured
(f) the agreed value (if any)
(g) the sum insured
(h) the premium and
(i) any other special conditions, warranties, clauses or endorsements.

The subject-matter insured deserves special consideration. The starting point is s. 3 of the Marine Insurance Act 1906 which provides in sub-section 1 that "subject to the provisions of this Act, every lawful marine adventure may be the subject of a contract of marine insurance". Sub-section 2 then provides that:

> In particular there is a marine adventure where:
>
> (a) any ship, goods or other moveables are exposed to maritime perils. Such property is in this Act referred to as "insurable property"
> (b) the earning or acquisition of any freight, passage money, commission, profit, or other pecuniary benefit or the security for any advances, loan or disbursements, is endangered by the exposure of insurable property to maritime perils
> (c) any liability to a third party may be incurred by the owner of, or other person interested in or responsible for, insurable property, by reason of maritime perils.

Therefore, as well as the vessel itself or the cargo carried thereon, intangible interests may form the subject-matter of the marine insurance contract, including freight and charter hire (sub-section (2)(b)). Moreover, where an owner of a vessel or of cargo incurs a liability to a third party by reason of a maritime peril, such liability may be insured against (sub-section (2)(c)). (For example, the carriers of goods may insure them up to their full value against loss or damage during the course of carriage.)

Defeasible and contingent interests

Defeasible and contingent interests in freight and cargo are also insurable (s. 7(1) of the 1906 Act). A defeasible interest is an actual interest which an assured has in the subject-matter insured but which might later come to an end. A contingent interest is an insurable interest which depends upon the occurrence of a particular event or contingency. The context of a voyage charterparty provides a good illustration of actual and contingent interests in freight. Since voyage freight is the consideration for the carriage of goods by the shipowner to their destination *in specie*, the shipowner has an actual insurable interest in the freight during the voyage. The owners of the cargo carried by the shipowner only have a contingent interest since the risk in respect of the freight is contingent upon the goods reaching their destination. On arrival, freight becomes payable to the shipowner. This contingent interest can be insured against. Similarly, shipowners can insure against the eventuality that a ship might not arrive at the port of destination thereby destroying any entitlement to voyage freight. Where freight is payable in advance or upon terms which provide that it is payable "ship and/or cargo lost or not lost", the cargo owner's interest becomes an actual interest in the freight, for as soon as the shipowner has loaded the goods on board the vessel, the freight is at the cargo owner's risk. Where a seller sells goods on a CIF basis, and where freight is at the risk of the buyer/cargo receiver the moment the goods are loaded on board the vessel, the freight is usually merged in the insured value of the cargo.

In an FOB contract, the sellers of goods may retain a contingent interest in them which can be insured since, although the risk in the goods passes to the buyers upon shipment and the sellers' ordinary insurable interest in the goods ceases at that point, if ownership reverts to the sellers together with risk, they have an actual insurable interest again. The contingency that this might occur is itself insurable. This usually occurs where the goods and/or the relative documents of title are refused or not taken up by the buyers once the goods have been shipped by the sellers.

Valued and unvalued policies

Marine insurance distinguishes between valued and unvalued policies. A valued policy is one which "specifies the agreed value of the subject-matter insured" (s. 27(2) of the 1906 Act). This agreed value is ascertained at the time the insurance is placed and may not be a vessel's real value.

S. 28 of the 1906 Act defines an unvalued policy as "a policy which does not specify the value of the subject-matter insured, but, subject to the limit of the sum insured, leaves the insurable value to be subsequently ascertained . . .".

A valued policy will contain the amount of the value of the subject-matter insured in the policy schedule. This ascertained value, to which an underwriter has agreed, cannot be reopened. According to s. 27(3) of the 1906 Act, "subject to the provisions of this Act, and in the absence of fraud, the value fixed by the policy is, as between the insurer and assured, conclusive of the insurable value of the subject intended to be insured, whether the loss be total or partial".

If there is a fraudulent over-valuation of the subject-matter insured then the entire policy may be avoided. An excessive but non-fraudulent valuation constitutes a material fact which, if not disclosed, also entitles an underwriter to avoid the policy. The amount by which an insured is indemnified for loss is ascertained by reference to the agreed valuation. This is the case whether the actual valuation has fallen or risen between the time the insurance is effected and the time a loss occurs.

In the case of unvalued policies, the insurable value of the subject-matter where there is no express stipulation in the policy is ascertained in accordance with s. 16 of the Marine Insurance Act 1906 which provides that:

> Subject to any express provision or valuation in the policy, the insurable value of the subject-matter insured must be ascertained as follows:
>
> (1) In insurance on ship, the insurable value is the value, at the commencement of the risk, of the ship, including her outfit, provisions and stores for the officers and crew, money advanced for seamen's wages, and other disbursements (if any) incurred to make the ship fit for the voyage or adventure contemplated by the policy, plus the charges of insurance upon the whole . . .

(2) In insurance on freight, whether paid in advance or otherwise, the insurable value is the gross amount of the freight at the risk of the assured, plus the charges of insurances;

(3) In insurance on goods or merchandise, the insurable value is the prime cost of the property insured, plus the expenses of and incidental to shipping and the charges of insurance upon the whole;

(4) In insurance on any other subject-matter, the insurable value is the amount at the risk of the assured when the policy attaches, plus the charges of insurance.

The policy schedule normally includes an appropriate space for the insertion of the amount insured under the policy. Of course, an insurance placing by a broker may be for less than the total insured value. The entire risk may be placed by a number of different brokers, perhaps partly in the London companies market, partly with Lloyd's underwriters and partly in the foreign market. Accordingly, a number of different policies may be issued, each recording the amount insured thereunder. This diversity in the insurance placing programme can lead to complications at the recovery stage if the underwriters on risk refuse to pay, and the assured turns to litigation. A multiplicity of jurisdictions and governing laws should be avoided in order to ease recovery should legal proceedings to collect under different issued policies become necessary.

Types of policy or insurance cover

Apart from voyage and time policies, there are other types of policy containing special features of their own. Whether they are appropriate or not depends upon the nature of the assured's business.

Floating policy

A "floating policy" is defined by s. 29(1) of the 1906 Act as "a policy which describes the insurance in general terms, and leaves the name of the ship or ships and other particulars to be defined by subsequent declaration".

This type of policy is particularly suitable for cargo insurances, so that many different shipments of cargo can be included within one policy rather than be insured separately. The name of any particular vessel is not inserted in the policy, but reference is usually made to the type of vessel on which the cargo is to be shipped. Subsequent declarations take place in relation to specific values and interests insured. These can be endorsed on the policy itself or entered into a separate schedule. They are usually initialled by the underwriters to indicate their approval. Policies are "fully declared" or "run off" when the total amount of declarations are made, which is the amount specified in the floating policy. S. 29(3) provides that declarations must be made in the order of despatch or shipment. They must, in the case of goods, comprise all consignments within the terms of the policy, and the value of the goods or other property must be stated honestly. An omission or an erroneous declaration may be rectified even after loss or arrival, provided the error was made in good faith.

Where goods are being sold and a letter of credit is required, certificates of insurance are usually issued in respect of the particular consignment sold. Certificates of insurance do not set out in full the wording of the floating policy for which they were issued but merely summarise the essential terms and elements of the insurance cover. A "CIF" buyer who receives documents including a certificate of insurance assumes that the underlying policy contains ordinary expected insurance provisions. However, such a buyer will not be bound by any special provisions or clauses which are not repeated in the certificate of insurance and of which the buyer was not otherwise aware at the time the goods were purchased. Indeed, if the buyer has not expressly agreed to the provision of a certificate of insurance instead of an actual policy, the tender of a certificate by the CIF seller of goods may be rejected. In practice, however, the issue and tender of certificates of insurance is usually both commonplace and safe. Policies are not issued quickly and certificates are therefore recognised as basic trading documents. They will be honoured by underwriters and claims adjusters provided that they set out the salient contractual terms. Of course, the presence of fraud in the compilation or presentation of a certificate will lead to its rejection.

Block policy

Individual declarations may be dispensed with and underwriters may accept a "block" declaration showing the total quantity of shipments over a specified period which are protected under a "block policy".

Open Cover

"Open covers" are similar to floating policies and an underwriter insures all shipments for certain voyages. Actual policies are issued from time to time if required, although they will usually be preceded by certificates of insurance.

The main complication with floating policies and their like is that, strictly speaking and in the absence of express agreement to the contrary, a buyer of goods is entitled to receive a policy of insurance covering only those goods which are contracted for. A "block policy" can therefore be rejected by buyers. Conversely, the issue of separate policies and certificates under an open cover does suit each individual buyer's interests, especially in the context of an immediate sub-sale of goods.

By contrast, where insurance is placed on hulls there is less flexibility about acceptable documentation and policies are invariably issued either on an individual vessel or fleet basis, as appropriate, with subsequent endorsements being made thereto if necessary.

Brokers' cover notes

When insurance has been effected, and a broker has been involved in its placing, a cover note is usually issued confirming that the risk is insured and setting out the terms agreed. If the insurance is ineffective for some reason or the details contained in the cover note are wrong to some degree then the assured may have recourse against the broker for breach of duty if a loss is suffered which cannot be recouped from the underwriters. The confirmation of cover by a broker is often of as much importance to an assignee of the insurance policy itself or of the proceeds thereof, as it is to the original assured. The provision of a letter of undertaking by a placing broker to an assignee, such as a lender of finance, creates distinct and separate contractual relations between the broker and the recipient of the letter of undertaking. Often brokers will attach a copy of the cover note to the letter of undertaking together with a draft notice of assignment which, in accordance with the terms of the undertaking, will be endorsed upon the policy or policies to be issued by the underwriters. If the insurance cover fails for some reason due to the broker's fault or if one of the specific undertakings is not honoured by the broker (such as the giving of notice of assignment to underwriters or the collection of claims moneys to the order of the assignee), the assignee may have a number of causes of action against the broker in order to recoup any loss that has been sustained.

Other aspects of assignments are dealt with under "The assignment of insurances" below. It is sufficient to state here that documentation of the kind described above is extremely important and great care should always be taken to ensure precision of language and the exact expression of all those commitments which the parties intend to enter into. An imprecise undertaking or a misleading or erroneous statement of insurance cover can cause difficulties for those subsequently attempting to pursue claims or make recovery of their losses upon the basis of written representations and agreements.

Payment of premium

The general rule for the payment of premium, in the event that there is no specific agreement to the contrary, is set out in s. 52 of the Marine Insurance Act 1906. This provides:

> Unless otherwise agreed, the duty of the assured or his agent to pay the premium, and the duty of the insurer to issue the policy to the assured or his agent, are concurrent conditions, and the insurer is not bound to issue the policy until payment or tender of the premium.

In practice, the strict pattern of events envisaged by s. 52 rarely takes place. As s. 87(1) of the 1906 Act provides:

> Where any right, duty or liability would arise under a contract for marine insurance by implication of law, it may be negatived or varied by express agreement, or by usage, if the usage be such as to bind both parties to the contract.

Statutory recognition is therefore given to established market practices concerning methods of payment which bind both parties to the contract of insurance, such as monthly or quarterly accounting between a broker and an underwriter for premiums and claims payable under the contract. Where debit or credit balances are settled in account in this way, the result will invariably be that the policy will have been issued prior to the receipt of premium by the underwriter at risk.

In theory, an assured who is unaware of market practice which permits the payment of claims in account between an underwriter and a broker, still has a right of recourse against the underwriter in respect of a particular loss even though the amount claimed for loss may previously have been settled in account between that underwriter and the broker.

This is also the case where an assignee of an insurance policy, such as a bank in the case of a hull policy or a purchaser of goods in the case of cargo, is in a position to claim insurance proceeds from underwriters. It is therefore common practice for the loss payee (being either the original assured or an assignee) to sign a payment order or authorisation stating that if underwriters make payment to the broker, in account or otherwise, then such a payment operates as a complete discharge in those underwriters' favour.

The statutory rules governing the payment of premium in relation to marine insurance contracts effected by a broker are set out in s. 53 of the Marine Insurance Act 1906. S. 53(1) provides as follows:

> Unless otherwise agreed, where a marine policy is effected on behalf of the assured by a broker, the broker is directly responsible to the insurer for the premium, and the insurer is directly responsible to the assured for the amount which may be payable in respect of losses, or in respect of returnable premium.

Consequently, where there is no specific agreement between the parties displacing the general statutory rules, the position of the assured is fully protected vis-à-vis the underwriters. The assured is not directly responsible for payment of premium but has recourse against underwriters for the payment of claims. Naturally, if a broker is authorised to collect a claim or a return premium then payment by underwriters to that broker takes the situation outside the scope of s. 53(1) and the underwriter obtains a valid discharge as against the assured or an assignee of the assured by making payment to the broker. It should be noted, however, that depending upon the knowledge of the assured, settlement in account might not amount to actual collection by a broker (*Stolos Compania S A v Ajax Insurance Co. Ltd* (the *"Admiral C"*) [1981]). The safe conclusion to draw is that express written agreement between all affected parties to particular payment methods is more reliable than assumed market practice.

Insurable interests

If purported assured do not have an insurable interest as defined by the Marine Insurance Act 1906, any insurance effected in their favour is void: see s. 4 of the Act. S. 5(1) of the 1906 Act defines an insurable interest as follows:

> ... every person has an insurable interest who is interested in a marine adventure.

Sub-section (2) continues that:

> in particular a person is interested in a marine adventure where he stands in any legal or equitable relation to the adventure or to any insurable property at risk therein, in consequence of which he may benefit by the safety or due arrival of insurable property, or may be prejudiced by its loss, or by damage thereto or by the detention thereof, or may incur liability in respect thereof.

The terms of s. 5 are wide and it is not only an owner of property who may insure it. A bailee, such as a carrier, has an insurable interest if the goods carried are damaged in transit. Charterers of vessels have an insurable interest in the freight or hire which they may have to pay. Banks have insurable interests as mortgagees of vessels. S. 12 of the Marine Insurance Act 1906 provides that in the case of advance freight, the person advancing the freight has an insurable interest, insofar as such freight is not repayable in case of loss. Consequently, those liable for such advance freight may insure their interest specifically or include it in the insured value of the cargo.

S. 14 deals specifically with the position of mortgagees and consignees and provides as follows:

> (1) Where the subject-matter insured is mortgaged, the mortgagor has an insurable interest in the full value thereof, and the mortgagee has an insurable interest in respect of any sum due or to become due under the mortgage.
> (2) A morgagee, consignee or other person having an interest in the subject-matter insured may insure on behalf and for the benefit of other persons interested as well as for his own benefit.
> (3) The owner of insurable property has an insurable interest in respect of the full value thereof, notwithstanding that some third person may have agreed, or be liable, to indemnify him in case of loss.

Even though an assured need not be interested in the subject-matter insured when the insurance is effected, an assured must be so interested at the time of the loss (s. 6(1) of the Marine Insurance Act 1906). A proviso to this is that where the subject-matter is insured "lost or not lost", assureds may recover even though they have not acquired an interest until after the loss, unless at the time of effecting the contract of insurance, they were aware of the loss and the insurer was not.

However, where an assured has no insurable interest at the time of the loss, it is not possible to acquire it by any act or election after the loss becomes known (s. 6(2) 1906 Act). These considerations can have a major impact where goods are subjected to a number of rapid sale and sub-sale contracts during their carriage from one place to another. It is therefore important to ascertain when risk and/or property pass to a particular buyer or sub-buyer in order to find out *who* has an insurable interest in the goods during transit and *when* such an interest arises. In the absence of express agreement to the contrary, until such time as property in goods is transferred to buyers (or goods are transferred into a buyer's possession or payment is made in respect of them), those goods are at the risk of the sellers. After property has been transferred to a buyer, the goods are at their risk, whether or not delivery of the goods has actually taken place (see s. 20(1) Sale of Goods Act 1979).

The buyer does, however, have an insurable interest from the moment risk passes, whether or not property also passes at the same time as risk. Often in international sale transactions, as has been explained earlier, property and risk pass at different times depending upon the precise terms agreed between the seller and the buyer. In the context of an FOB contract, risk is transferred to the buyer as soon as shipment of the goods has taken place. They will not, therefore, have an insurable interest in the goods during their transit to the vessel for shipment. Conversely, the seller will have a contingent insurable interest after shipment of the goods has taken place. Property in the goods will not pass to the buyer on shipment if, for example, the seller has reserved to themselves a right of disposal: see s. 18, rule 5(2) of the Sale of Goods Act 1979. Despite this, the buyer will have an insurable interest as risk has passed to them. The onus will therefore lie upon the buyer to arrange insurance for those goods for the duration of their carriage and s. 32(3) of the Sale of Goods Act 1979 provides that a seller of goods which are to be carried by sea must "give such notice to the buyer as may enable him to insure them during their sea transit . . ." Otherwise the goods remain at their risk during the sea transit. This provision has been held to apply to an FOB contract (*Wimble, Sons & Co. Ltd v Rosenberg & Sons* [1913]). However, in practice, strict compliance with s. 32(3) is unnecessary in the context of an FOB sale contract as the purchaser of goods will usually know when the insurance should commence given the obligation to nominate a vessel upon which the goods are to be loaded.

Where goods are sold on a CIF basis, the seller is contractually committed to providing a valid insurance policy or certificate of insurance. If they fail to do so then they expose themselves to a potential action by the buyer for the amount of the loss which the buyer is unable to recover under the policy provided by the seller.

In a CIF situation, risk passes from seller to buyer when the goods are shipped to a specified destination, even though property will not usually pass, in the absence of special agreement, until the requisite shipping documents including a policy or certificate of insurance (if provision of the latter is specially agreed), are delivered to the buyer and payment of the price is made by them against those documents. As soon as risk passes, the buyer again has an insurable interest in the goods, although since the seller has agreed to arrange the necessary insurance cover, the buyer will not actually become the assured until the policy of insurance is assigned. To have an insurable interest is one thing; to have an *insured* insurable interest is another. Moreover, this is equally the case where the buyer acquires an insurable interest through having property in or possession of the goods or through having made a payment in respect of those goods. In all cases, the relevant time to consider is the time the loss occurs, both for determining where the insurable interest resides and who the actual assured is.

Example 1

A buyer contracts to buy goods on a CIF basis. After shipment of the goods and during the course of sea carriage, those goods are damaged, but only after the seller has delivered the requisite shipping documents, including a policy or certificate of insurance on those goods which has been endorsed over, to the buyer. Clearly, the buyer has, in this instance, both an insurable interest at the time when the damage occurred, and effective insurance cover of which the buyer is the absolute assignee. Claims in respect of the damage may therefore be made by the buyer under the policy in their name and rights of recourse also exist against the carrier, as has been explained elsewhere in this book. It should also be noted in passing that the relevant underwriters will, of course, be entitled to exercise rights of subrogation encompassing any right of action or recovery which the assured is entitled to exercise against the carrier.

Example 2
Again, goods are contracted to be sold on a CIF basis. This time, the goods are damaged after shipment but *before* delivery of the shipping documents to the buyer and, in particular, before assignment of the insurance policy or endorsement of the certificate. Consequently, the buyer has an insurable interest but does not have a claim under the policy since the policy was not assigned prior to the date of the loss. The seller remains both the owner of the goods and the assured under the insurance policy at the time of the loss. The buyer is therefore left with rights against the seller under the sale contract.

Conclusion

In conclusion therefore, an assignee of an interest can recover under insurances assigned, provided the assignment was effective before the loss occurred. It is important to remember that the purchaser of goods to whom the policy of insurance in respect thereof is assigned can claim under that policy if the assignment took place before the goods were damaged or lost at sea. The swift and efficient assignment of interests is therefore a necessary part of maximising protection for buyers and sub-buyers and reducing the level of risk in complex transactions. One method of circumventing the problem is to have insurance arranged for the benefit of a named assured seller of goods and all subsequent buyers and sub-buyers, whether named or not at the time of the insurance placing. Established and reputable traders will often declare, if known, the names of buyers and sub-buyers before placing an open cover, and request individual certificates of insurance each made out in the appropriate name for subsequent transfer during the course of the sales transactions. It is even common practice for blank certificates to be issued in advance to a well-known trader who later endorses them over to individual buyers. Nevertheless, there are many instances where an assignment has not been perfected prior to the occurrence of a loss. This and other matters which arise in relation to assignments are considered immediately below.

The assignment of insurances

As briefly stated above, the assignment (ie transfer) of insurable commercial interests can give rise to many difficulties if certain basic ground rules are not observed. This is the case whatever the subject-matter of the insurance. The purpose of this section is to highlight those ground rules and to focus on potential difficulties which can always be avoided.

An important distinction must be drawn between the following types of assignment:

(a) an assignment of the subject-matter of an insurance policy
(b) an assignment of the insurance policy itself
(c) an assignment of the proceeds of an insurance policy.

Each of these will be explained in turn below, and the special position of marine policies of insurance discussed last of all.

The assignment of the subject-matter of an insurance policy

Generally, where an assured voluntarily disposes of the entire interest (usually by sale) in the subject-matter insured (ie any given asset) under an insurance policy, the assured is unable to present a claim under the policy over that particular subject-matter. An insurance policy lapses automatically when an assured sells or otherwise loses the insurable interest even without express provision to that effect existing in the insurance policy (*Rogerson v Scottish Automobile & General Insurance Co. Ltd* [1931]). However, in the absence of express or implied agreement with an insurer and an assignee, an assignment or sale of the subject-matter insured does not automatically carry with it an assignment of the policy itself (s. 15 of the Marine Insurance Act 1906).

Where an assured does not dispose of the *entire* insurable interest then, of course, the policy will not automatically lapse. This is the case where the subject-matter insured, such as a vessel, is mortgaged to a third party and where an assured assigns the subject-matter absolutely, as in the case of goods, but retains possession as security for payment. A retention of title clause in a sale of contract also has this effect.

If a policy is stated to cover the interests of a buyer of the subject-matter insured, it remains in force against that person, even though the assured may have lost the right to sue under it.

From a practical point of view, it is therefore vital to agree in express terms a contemporaneous sale of both an asset and its insurances before safely concluding that the sale of a particular asset also entails the assignment of the existing insurance policy over that asset. To assume otherwise may lead to insuperable difficulties such as a lack of insurance at a later stage and, in particular, at the time of loss. A CIF sale contract, if performed as intended, conquers the problem of contemporaneity with the simultaneous transfer of both property in goods and insurance cover over goods (usually achieved by delivery of the bill of lading, and assignment of the insurance policy or an insurance certificate respectively).

The existing insurance arrangements over the asset in question should also be reviewed before assigning an insurance policy contemporaneously with the sale of its subject-matter. The terms of the existing insurance policy should be checked to see if there is any express prohibition against such a contemporaneous assignment. In addition, in a non-marine context, even in the absence of such a provision, the assent of the insurer to a change of assured should be obtained.

Assignment of the policy

Under English law, a non-marine policy of insurance as a chose in action is freely assignable subject to compliance with three conditions:

(a) the consent of the insurer must be obtained
(b) to avoid problems relating to the lack of an insurable interest or the lapse of a policy, the assignment of the policy and its underlying subject-matter must be contemporaneous
(c) the assignment must be in a proper form.

With regard to (a) the giving of consent renders the contract between the insurer and the assignee a novation as opposed to a continuation of the old policy. Consent, however, is not required in relation to the assignment of marine policies—see s. 50(1) of the Marine Insurance Act 1906 (see below). Any policy provision may also provide that the separate consent of the insurer is not needed and that the policy comes into effect for the benefit of any purchaser of the subject-matter insured. This is particularly appropriate in the context of a chain of rapid sales and sub-sales.

With regard to (b), there are two situations to consider:

(a) the assignment of the subject-matter of the policy before assignment of the policy itself: where the policy automatically lapses once its subject-matter is assigned and the assignee of the subject-matter therefore has no claim to make against the insurer.
(b) the assignment of the policy before assignment of the subject-matter thereof: where two consequences follow—

(i) the assured cannot recover as they have divested themselves of the policy by way of assignment
(ii) the assignee cannot recover since at the date of assignment of the policy they had no insurable interest. This is clearly a situation which any assignee should avoid when attempting to assume the benefit of existing insurances.

Of course, problems relating to contemporaneity do not arise where, as mentioned in the context of the assignment of the subject-matter of a policy, the assignor has not disposed of the entire insurable interest in the property insured.

It should also be noted at this stage (although it is implicit in the above discussion) that contemporaneity is also necessary in the context of marine insurance as will be explained below.

Insofar as (c) is concerned, the assignment of an insurance policy may be achieved either *at law* or *in equity*. The significant advantage of a legal assignment is that it permits the assignee to sue the insurer in their own name without having to join the original assured as a party to the legal proceedings and also confers upon the assignee the right to give a good discharge for the policy moneys upon receiving them. Under s. 136 of the Law of Property Act 1925, certain formalities are specified which, if complied with, render an assignment fully effective at law. The formalities are as follows:

(a) the assignment must be *in writing* and must be *signed by the assignor*
(b) it must be *absolute* and not by way of charge only (so that, as previously mentioned, a mortgage will not divest a mortgagor of the entire insurable interest in the mortgaged property. Likewise, the mere transfer of physical possession of goods by an owner of those goods to a third party will not effect a legal assignment.)
(c) *notice in writing* of the assignment must be given to the insurer.

An assignment not complying with these formalities may nevertheless take effect as a valid *equitable* assignment upon proof of the assignor's unequivocal intention to assign and the assignee's provision of consideration. However, in legal proceedings an equitable assignee must join the assignor as a co-plaintiff in order to bring suit. This is one of a number of disadvantages that an equitable assignment has when compared with a legal assignment.

From a practical point of view, therefore, in order to ensure the complete security and effectiveness of the assignment, it is vital to comply with conditions (a), (b) and (c) above right from the very start. Whilst non-compliance with particular formalities (such as the giving of notice to the insurer) can be cured after the creation of an equitable assignment, an assignee runs the risk of losing priority as priorities between competing assignments are determined by the dates of the notices of those assignments to the insurer (*Dearle v Hall* (1882)). The first in time prevails. However, the legal assignee cannot take priority over an equitable assignee of whose assignment they had notice at the date of their own assignment, and an equitable assignee cannot take priority over an earlier equitable assignee of whose assignment they had notice at the date of their own assignment (*Newman v Newman* (1885)).

All assignments (whether legal or equitable) take subject to equities such as defences of the insurer which have accrued both prior to and after the assignment. These defences, such as non-disclosure by the assured of a material fact to the insurer at the time the insurance was initially placed, may be pleaded against the assignee by the insurer. The fundamental principle of utmost good faith in all insurance contracts cannot be circumvented by assignment in so far as infringements of that principle by the original assured are concerned. Likewise, given the existence of a new contract between the assignee of an insurance policy and the insurer, reciprocal duties of utmost good faith arise between and fall upon such an assignee and the insurer.

Assignment of the proceeds of a policy

Under English law, the right to recover insurance proceeds under a policy is freely assignable as a chose in action (ie a non-tangible legal right) under s. 136 of the Law of Property Act 1925 or by way of equitable assignment. The following points should be noted in relation to this type of assignment:

(a) A new contract between the insurer and the assignee is not created by such an assignment. The *assignor* of the proceeds is still the assured under the policy. It therefore follows that since there is no change in the identity of the assured, the consent of the insurer to the assignment is not necessary. It should also be noted that according to the Court of Appeal, a duty of utmost good faith is not owed by an insurer to an assignee of the proceeds of an insurance policy for the reason that the latter is not the assured

(*The Bank of Nova Scotia v Hellenic Mutual War Risks Association (Bermuda) Ltd* (the *"Good Luck"*) [1989]). It follows from this that the assignee of the proceeds is likewise unburdened by the constraints of utmost good faith in this situation.

(b) The assignee need not possess any insurable interest. Accordingly, a contemporaneous assignment of the subject-matter of the policy is not required. The assignee is simply the assignee of the proceeds of the policy and not of the policy itself.

(c) As where the policy itself is assigned, all claims of the assignee of the proceeds take subject to the rights and defences of the insurer against the assured.

(d) The proceeds of a policy are incapable of forming the subject-matter of a lien asserted by a charterer of a vessel in respect of moneys paid in advance since such proceeds do not represent the insured vessel itself or constitute the fruits of that vessel for the purpose of tracing a claim. The proceeds of a policy are payable solely in consideration of the payment of premiums (the *"Lancaster"* [1980]).

(e) Separate rules do apply to the proceeds of marine policies under English law as will become apparent from the discussion which follows.

Special rules relating to the assignment of marine insurance policies

Under English law, a marine policy is assignable without formality and without compliance with s. 136 of the Law of Property Act 1925. According to s. 15(1) of the Marine Insurance Act 1906 a marine policy is assignable unless it contains terms which expressly prohibit assignment. Most contracts are assignable since changes of ownership do not generally affect the risk of loss or damage. Such is the case with cargo and goods in transit. The position is probably different in respect of hull and freight since if ownership of the vessel changes, the risk will be materially affected thereby. As previously stated, CIF contracts in fact provide that sellers are to assign to buyers an effective policy of insurance or a certificate of insurance.

It should be especially noted that the consent of the insurer is not required to the assignment of a marine policy. With regard to freight and hulls, the position as governed by the standard Institute Clauses is that:

> No assignment of or interest in any moneys which may be or become payable hereunder is to be binding on or recognised by the Underwriters unless a dated notice of such assignment or interest signed by the assured and by the assignor in the case of subsequent assignment, is endorsed on the policy and the policy with such endorsement is produced before payment of any claim or return premium hereunder (Institute Time Clauses cl.5, Institute Voyage Clauses (Hulls) cl.3, Institute Time Clauses (Freight) cl.6, Institute Voyage Clauses (Freight) cl.4).

Except where new marine insurance is placed or where, as discussed above, the assignee is simply a mortgagee of the property insured, there must be a contemporaneous assignment of both the marine insurance policy and its subject-matter in order to avoid the consequences discussed above.

S. 50(3) of the Marine Insurance Act 1906 states that a marine policy may be assigned "by endorsement thereon or in other customary manner". A clear intention to assign must be shown, whatever the manner in which any given assignment is effected. A purported assignment is not effective if it cannot be shown that there was an intention to transfer the benefits of and rights under the policy to the person to whom it was delivered.

An assignee of a marine policy can sue in their own name (s. 50(2) of the Marine Insurance Act 1906). However, assignees can only sue underwriters in their own name if the whole beneficial interest has been passed to them. If part of the beneficial interest remains with the assignor, then the assignee cannot sue under the policy without joining the assignor as a co-plaintiff. In such circumstances, the assignee is an equitable assignee only. If the assignment is simply of a right to sue on the policy and not an assignment of the policy itself, the position is the same.

S. 51 of the 1906 Act provides that:

> Where the assured has parted with or lost his interest in the subject-matter insured, and has not, before or at the time of so doing, expressly or impliedly agreed to assign the policy, any subsequent assignment of the policy is inoperative:
>
> Provided that nothing in this Section affects the assignment of the policy after loss.

As stated in a wider context earlier, an assignment of a hull policy not resulting in the automatic termination of insurance occurs where a mortgagee is assigned such a policy as part of the security in respect of a loan given for the purchase of a vessel by the assignor/mortgagor, or where the owner of goods retains possession of them as security for payment of their sale price.

S. 50(2) continues to provide that a defendant is "entitled to make any defence arising out of the contract of insurance which he would have been entitled to make if the action had been brought in the name of the person by or on behalf of whom the policy was effected". Consequently, an assignment of a policy only transfers to the assignee those rights possessed by the assignor and no other rights. The assignee is in no better position than the assignor, so that fraud or concealment on the part of the assignor at the time the insurance was placed, or the deliberate cause of a loss by the assured, would prevent an assignee, such as a consignee of cargo or mortgagee of a vessel, from successfully claiming under the policy assigned. A marine assignment therefore takes subject to equities like any other assignment.

Any conduct by the assured (such as breach of a policy term) following the assignment which would otherwise have given the insurer the right to repudiate liability confers the same right as against the assignee (the *"Litsion Pride"* [1985]).

Summary

(a) Where existing insurance is assumed over an asset without the placing of new insurance, an assignee must ensure that such insurance does not automatically lapse as a result of the sale of the asset itself. An express assignment of the existing insurance policy is therefore required which is contemporaneous with the sale of the asset (ie the subject-matter of the insurance). In the case of non-marine policies, the consent of the insurer to such assignment must also be obtained and the requisite formalities complied with. In the case of marine policies governed by the Institute Clauses, only notice of assignment to the underwriters is usually required in addition to the element of contemporaneity referred to above.

(b) Where new insurance is to be placed the benefit of which is to be assigned immediately to an assignee, it should be ensured that there is control over the actual insurance placing both in terms of recommending placing brokers/sub-brokers and the approval of the quality of the security underwriting the risk. A lender in particular should avoid the situation where a borrower alone arranges the insurance through poor brokers with poor underwriters without prior reference to the lender. Specific provision can always be made in loan documentation to the placing of insurance and a condition precedent to drawdown of the loan can be specified to the effect that insurance brokers and underwriters acceptable to the lender respectively place and bear the risk. If it subsequently becomes necessary to commence legal proceedings against either the broker (for breach of duty) or the underwriters (under the contract of insurance), one does not want to be faced with the prospect of expensive litigation in many different jurisdictions against underwriters of poor repute for small fractions of the total risk originally insured. It must be borne in mind that each underwriter has a distinct and separate contract with the assured and/or any subsequent assignee of the assured (such as a lender of money), notwithstanding that the same broker's slip is subscribed to.

(c) In the case of non-marine policies, a lender should ensure that the wording of the assignment unequivocally transfers to the lender either the policy itself or the proceeds to be paid under the policy. The disadvantage of the latter is that in any legal proceedings the lender must compel the assignor to sue under the policy as it cannot sue in its own name.

Sale and sub-sale contract—the insurance element

It is a common provision in CIF sale contracts that the relevant policy of insurance should cover the invoice value plus a stated percentage. In a chain of sale contracts, therefore, it is perhaps insufficient to pass on in a resale the insurance policy provided by the immediate supplier of the goods to be resold as such a policy might not satisfy the terms of resale as to the amount to be insured.

If there is no express term in the resale contract as to the amount of insurance, it will probably be satisfactory to provide a policy in which the goods are valued at less than their invoice price. However, such a course would be open to objection by a buyer as the fundamental principle in CIF sales is that the amount of insurance must protect the reasonable value of the goods. The insured value must be sufficient to cover the market value of the goods at the date of shipment (see Sassoon: *CIF and FOB Contracts*, second edition, paragraph 135).

In a rising market, a policy for less than invoice price may be a good tender to buyers down the chain if there is no contractual provision preventing this from being a valid tender. However, where there is a specific clause providing for the amount to be covered by insurance, such a clause must be adhered to otherwise the risk will arise that the documents might be rejected by the CIF buyer. Where there is no such contractual provision, then it is probably safe to pass on a policy for less than the invoice price in a rising market.

"Top-up" insurances are common in CIF resale chains and sometimes take the form of an endorsement upon the existing policy stating that such insurance is "effected on increased value ... and not on cargo itself". This renders the "top-up" insurance an "honour" policy since there is no insurable interest. Strictly speaking, such a policy is legally unenforceable but may nevetheless be honoured by underwriters, and is binding upon them if there is a "PPI" clause in the slip or on the endorsement.

In a CIF resale chain an intermediate buyer or seller might never have an insurable interest at the time of loss; indeed they might never have an interest at all. In theory, it is possible that they might have an interest in insuring their profit, even though the goods never pass through their hands. Such an insurable interest is legally enforceable. Where the insurance is on "increased value" ("IV"), the intention of the intermediate buyers/sellers is not to recover a loss of profit but to receive the price of the goods and the proceeds of the "increased value" policy. However, it was held in *Strass v Spillers & Bakers* [1911] that a buyer has no right to benefit under a seller's "increased value" cover. It was also stated that there was probably no insurable interest under such a cover. In *Landauer v Asser* [1905], it was stated that a CIF seller did not have an insurable interest in a policy taken out for an amount greater than the invoice price to the buyer. Nevertheless a seller's "IV" policy provides a wider form of protection than a legally enforceable insurance in respect of loss of profits, although an "IV" policy is binding in honour only.

6

The international carriage of goods by road in Europe— the CMR regime

Introduction

International road haulage in Europe is largely governed by the Convention for the International Carriage of Goods by Road which was signed in Geneva in 1956. In 1965 the United Kingdom Parliament passed the Carriage of Goods by Road Act which adopted the Convention as part of United Kingdom law, although the Act actually only came into force in October 1967.

The CMR Convention (as the 1956 Convention is most generally known—from its French title: Convention Relative au Contrat de Transport International de Marchandises par Route) was born out of a general post-war resolve to encourage international trade by road and the recognition that this could only flourish within a common legal framework.

The scope of the Convention in law and in context

The Convention has 51 separate articles in eight chapters. At the end of this chapter is a schedule of the countries presently party to it.

The Convention states that it shall only:

> . . . apply to every contract for the carriage of goods by road in vehicles for reward, when the place of taking over of the goods and the place designated for delivery, as specified in the contract, are situated in two different countries of which at least one is a contracting country, irrespective of the place of residence and the nationality of the parties.

"Vehicles" means motor vehicles (and trailers etc). The Convention applies to carriage by state organisations but excludes postal, funeral or furniture removal services.

Example 1

Thus a qualifying contract for carriage from London to Paris would be included but not where separate contracts were entered into by the sender for the parts:

(a) from London to Dover
(b) for the sea crossing and
(c) from Calais to Paris (in which case the taking over of the goods and delivery of the goods under the two road carriage contracts would have occurred within the same country).

Example 2

Similarly, a qualifying contract to carry goods from Zurich to London would be within the Convention but if there were three *separate* contracts, say,

(a) from Zurich to Calais,
(b) for the sea crossing and
(c) from Dover to London,

only the first of these would be governed by the Convention.

The Convention's concentration upon the contract for international carriage creates difficulties. Whilst the Convention would apply to such a contract even if the goods never crossed the border of the country of shipment, there are problems where freight forwarders or sub-contractors are involved. Furthermore, although the Convention specifies certain formalities (concerning, for example, CMR "consignment notes") it also confirms that the absence of such documents shall not prejudice its application to a relevant contract. Consequently, it is often far from easy to tell who is party to a CMR contract and who is not.

Freight forwarders may be involved in this. They would have a contract of agency with their principal, the shipper, but they do not (generally) accept liability for the shipment themselves (as carriers or otherwise). However a freight forwarder may be hard to distinguish from a CMR carrier and a CMR carrier may seek to avoid liability by claiming to be a freight forwarder. The problem may become even more obscure when various parties are involved and the Convention concept of "successive carriers" has to be considered. (These complexities will be explored in some detail later.)

The Convention—content and application

Structure

The Convention's eight chapters are divided into logical sections as follows:

(a) *Chapter I (Articles 1 and 2)—Scope of application:*
This defines the contracts to which the Convention applies and the intended dovetailing of this with other conventions related to carriage by air, sea, rail, etc.

(b) *Chapter II (Article 3)—Persons for whom the carrier is responsible:*
This expressly makes the carrier responsible for the acts and omissions of its employees and agents.

(c) *Chapter III (Articles 4–16)—Conclusion and performance of the contract of carriage:*
This is concerned with explaining the contractual documentation, the carriers' obligations on taking over the goods, the right of carriers to make "reservations" with regard to the goods and the formal aspects of shipping and delivery.

(d) *Chapter IV (Articles 17–29)—Liability of the carrier:*
This defines situations where carriers may be liable or can avoid liability for loss, damage or delay to the goods, the position with regard to "dangerous goods" and the limits of monetary liability and interest.

(e) *Chapter V (Articles 30–33)—Claims and actions:*
This deals with time limits governing claims and jurisdictions where claims against carriers may be pursued.

(f) *Chapter VI (Articles 34–39)—Provisions relating to carriage performed by "successive carriers":*
This concerns the position where more than one road carrier performs the same contract and defines which of those carriers are liable and may be sued.

(g) *Chapter VII (Article 41)—Nullity of stipulations contrary to the Convention:*
This formally provides for the supremacy of the provisions of Convention over contract terms.

(h) *Chapter VIII (Articles 42–51):*
This concerns relations between the Convention countries and the coming into force of the Convention and is not discussed.

Documentation and initial responsibilities

The consignment note

The key clause in respect of formal documentation is Article 4 which states:

> The contract of carriage shall be confirmed by the making out of a consignment note. The absence, irregularity or loss of the consignment note shall not affect the existence or the validity of the contract of carriage which shall remain subject to the provisions of this Convention.

The consignment note is not a document of title (unlike a bill of lading) but is merely:

> *Article 9*
> . . . prima facie evidence of the making of the contract of carriage, the conditions of the contract and the receipt of the goods by the carrier.

So, the consignment note is neither necessary to the existence of a Convention-governed contract nor conclusive as to its terms (including even the parties).

No particular form is prescribed for the consignment note (although the standard form developed by the International Road Transport Union has largely been adopted). Where issued, multiple copies are required because the first copy is to be "handed to the sender", the second copy is required to accompany the goods and the third is "retained by the carrier" (Article 5). The Convention assumes that the consignment note will be issued by the carrier although it does not expressly state that this is required, nor when it is to be drawn up.

The consignment note is required to contain certain information (Article 6) including the identity of the carrier, the place and date of taking over of the goods, the place for delivery and the name and address of the consignee. The sender is responsible for any expenses, loss or damage suffered by the carrier from inaccurate or inadequate information concerning customs instructions, gross weight, numbers of packages and their marks and numbers, etc (Article 7): Otherwise "irregularities"in the consignment note are excused by Article 4.

Although, by Article 4, a consignment note is not essential, it does have importance. A consignment note may provide evidence in a dispute, particularly where more than one possible carrier is involved, or there are arguments as to the role of various persons and whether or not they are actually parties to the Convention contract at all. Further, if no consignment note is issued, the carrier will be unable to make reservations in it, will be assumed to have received the goods in good condition and, in the absence of an applicable defence, will be required to deliver them in the same good condition. Also the sender's right to dispose of the goods during the carriage depends upon an amendment of an existing consignment note. Additionally, although not necessary to the existence of the contract, the consignment note is needed if the sender of the goods wishes to make a declaration of their value to override the Convention's compensation limitations. Lastly, a consignment note may be necessary to establish a successive carrier relationship. These issues will be explored.

Taking over the goods—reservations

On taking over the goods carriers should check, so far as possible, both the accuracy of any consignment note and also, whether or not there is a consignment note, the apparent condition of the goods. If there is no reasonable means of checking the statements, carriers should enter any reservations in the consignment note concerning the apparent condition of the goods together with the grounds for such reservations. These reservations do not bind the senders unless they expressly agree to be bound by them in the consignment note. If there are no specific reservations, the accuracy of the consignment note with regard to package numbers and marks together with the apparent good condition of packaging is assumed, unless the contrary can subsequently be proven by the carriers (Articles 8 and 9).

Obviously, in many circumstances it will be extremely difficult or impossible for carriers to inspect the goods, for instance if an already fully stuffed container is received. Consequently, they should take care to make proper reservations and include these on all the copy consignment notes (to show they were made at the time of taking over the goods). Failure to take proper precautions will lead to the carriers having to prove that the condition of the goods on taking over was not as stated, which may be difficult (Article 9).

Sender's liabilities—packing and formalities

Senders may be liable to the carriers to an unlimited extent for damages or expenses as a result of defective packing of the goods, but only if the defect was not apparent or known to the carriers when they took over the goods and they made no appropriate reservations. Obviously, this must be seen in the context of the carriers' obligations both to check the goods and to make reservations (Article 10).

Senders are also obliged to deal with customs formalities by providing relevant documents to carriers and any other information necessary. Except in the case of a negligent or wrongful act of the carriers, senders will be liable for any damage caused by inaccuracies in the documents. This liability is unlimited in contrast to the carriers' liability for loss or misuse of the documents, which is limited as in the case of loss of the goods (Article 11).

Performance of the contract—delivery and disposal

The rest of Chapter III relates to the performance of the contract after taking over the goods and initial formalities (or lack of them).

Change of destination and rights of disposal

During carriage, senders are entitled to change the destination of the goods or may dispose of them generally as they wish. However, this right ends when either the consignment note is handed to a consignee or if that consignee exercises the right to require delivery of the goods once they have arrived at the designated destination. The senders' right of disposal is subject to production of the first copy of the consignment note containing the new instructions to the carriers and indemnifying them against acting in accordance with those instructions. Also, the instructions must be possible, they may not interfere with the normal working of the carriers' business and the instructions may not require the division of the consignment (Articles 12 and 13).

It follows that these senders' rights of disposal cannot be exercised without the existence of a consignment note. Additionally, they are subject to somehow fitting in with the carriers' business undertaking and, failing this, the carriers are not bound to obey the instructions (even though the senders are required to indemnify them). On the other hand, the senders may insert in the consignment note, at the time of drawing it up, that the consignees shall have immediate rights of disposal, in which case the senders' rights are immediately surrendered (Article 12).

Consignees acquire a right to the goods either when they receive a copy of the consignment note or the goods arrive at the place designated for delivery. They may require delivery to another consignee (but this successor has no similar right) (Article 13).

Delivery

Once the goods have arrived at the destination, the consignees are entitled to demand delivery against a receipt (not necessarily the copy of the consignment note which, realistically, they might not have for some time). If this right is not exercised the consignees will lose it if the senders order an alternative disposal under Article 12 discussed above. However, if the goods do not arrive (after the period allowed for under Article 19), the consignees are entitled to enforce against the carriers any rights arising under the contract, but in so doing the consignees will be themselves liable for any charges due on the consignment note or, should these be disputed, for security (Article 13).

Concurrent rights

Although Articles 12 and 13 are clearly intended to establish which party has rights over the goods at any particular time, some court decisions have held consignees and senders to have concurrent rights of action. This is not upheld in all jurisdictions and would seem to be against the intention behind the articles. Further, Article 13 does not expressly allow for the consignees to have rights of action in respect of damage to goods, as opposed to delay and loss, although, not unreasonably, the consignees' rights of action in such circumstances have been upheld.

Impossibility of and variation in performance

If, *before* the goods arrive at the destination, it becomes impossible to carry out the contract in accordance with the consignment note, the carriers must seek instructions from the person entitled to the goods. If these cannot be obtained within a reasonable time and if carriage can be carried out under differing conditions, the carriers may take such steps as are considered to be in the best interests of the person entitled to the goods. However, it is clear that the carriers must seek instructions first otherwise they may face a claim from the person entitled to the goods, although, if performance can still be achieved, any damages may be slight (Article 14).

If, *after* arrival at the destination, it is not possible to deliver the goods, the carriers again must seek instructions from the *senders*. If the consignees refuse the goods, the senders may dispose of them but if, prior to the carriers' receipt of such instructions from the senders, the consignees change their mind and require delivery, the carriers are bound to obey, subject to the consignees providing the necessary receipt (Article 15). Where such a problem arises with respect to a successor consignee nominated by the first consignee, the roles of sender and consignee are effectively taken by, respectively, the first and second consignees.

In seeking and obeying instructions under Articles 14 and 15, carriers are probably entitled to recover reasonable costs unless these were incurred as a result of their own neglect or wrongful act (Article 16). The carriers would normally endorse these charges on the consignment note and the consignees would pay them or put up security in respect of them under Article 13(2) before delivery is effected.

If it becomes impossible to deliver the goods, as contemplated in Articles 14 and 15, the carriers may unload them, at which point the carriage will be deemed to be at an end, although the carriers must still, at least technically, hold the goods on behalf of the person entitled to dispose of them. This responsibility may be delegated and further cause of liability avoided provided the delegatee was selected with reasonable care. Any charges accumulating against the goods are required to be paid before they are released (Article 16).

If the goods are perishable or if their condition warrants it, the carriers may sell them without awaiting instructions and may act in a similar fashion where instructions, once sought, are not received within a reasonable period. The carriers may also require the sale of the goods if storage expenses "would be out of all proportion to the value of the goods". The proceeds of such a sale (after deduction of expenses) shall be held at the disposal of the person entitled to dispose of the goods (Article 16).

Summary

Articles 12 and 13 may be engaged in changing economic circumstances and allow senders and consignees limited rights to divert goods to other destinations. Generally carriers are protected in the face of difficulties by Articles 14–16 as long as they seek instructions on how to escape problems and a reasonable time elapses for those instructions to arrive. If circumstances are drastically changing and it is reasonable to dispose of the goods, and to do so without awaiting instructions, the carriers may take the necessary steps to sell the goods in order to salvage the best from unfortunate circumstances. However, irrespective of whether the goods are perishable or their condition warrants sale, or storage expenses would be out of proportion to the value of the goods, a carrier may sell the goods, in these and other cases, if he has not received, within a reasonable period, instructions not to sell "which he may reasonably be required to carry out". It is not clear what "reasonable" means in this context when the carrier is dealing with the other party's goods and instructions, although the demands of the carrier's continuing commercial operation should be taken into account (Article 12(v)(b)).

Liability, defences and compensation

Basic obligation

The basic liability of carriers is defined in Article 17 as:

> 1. the Carrier shall be liable for the total or partial loss of the goods and for the damage thereto occurring between the time when he takes over the goods and the time of delivery, as well as for any delay in delivery.

Damage

Damage means physical injury to the goods and is distinct from delay and loss of the goods.

Delay

In the absence of any applicable defence, carriers are liable for delay in delivery. "Delay" is defined as being either when the goods are not delivered within the time limit agreed or, failing such an agreed time limit, where the duration of the carriage, in all the circumstances of the case (including making up a complete load) one exceeds what it would be reasonable to allow a diligent carrier (Article 19). The Convention does not require that any time limit need be stated in the consignment note or even written down. Neither does it provide for circumstances where delivery is impossible. However, insofar as they are applicable, the defences available under Article 17 include protection where delay is a result of "circumstances which the carrier could not avoid and the consequences of which he was unable to prevent".

Loss

At a point mere delay becomes presumed loss. "Loss" is deemed to have occurred 30 days after an agreed time limit has expired or in the absence of such agreement, 60 days from when the carrier took over the goods, after which non-delivery "shall be *conclusive* evidence of the loss of the goods and the person entitled to make a claim may thereupon treat them as lost" (Article 20(i)).

Whilst helpful to the sender and consignee in resolving an uncertain situation, this provision can cause obvious problems to carriers. For instance, they could be ensnarled by bureaucracy at a border post without there being any fault on the part of the carriers or senders or, perhaps following a dispute or accident, they may have been held by a particular country's authorities. The goods in such circumstances are clearly not lost in any real sense, although they may undoubtedly be delayed. Apart from possibly leaving the carriers with an unwanted cargo, if the senders claim for a constructive total loss on the basis of this clause, the entitlement is to damages on the general basis provided for loss, whereas mere delay is compensated less generously (Article 23—see later). This is obviously extremely significant and if claimants can establish constructive total loss it places them in a strong position to re-negotiate with the carriers to obtain the goods in due course, but at some cost to the carriers and unwarranted benefit to the senders or consignees. Further, the right to consider such delays as having caused a constructive loss is only vested in cargo interests, not the carrier.

Recovery of "lost" goods

A party compensated for such a constructive loss may request the carriers to provide notification in writing if the goods are recovered within a year of the payment of compensation. If they are recovered, within 30 days of being notified, the person (who is entitled to the goods) may require that they be delivered against payment of the charges due on the consignment note but subject to all compensation paid being refunded less only any charges included. This is without prejudice to a continuing right to claim for delay although, as mentioned, a simple claim for delay has only limited value. Obviously, whether a person entitled to the goods adopts this strategy will depend upon whether there is a special reason for wishing to have these particular goods. It may be that, for one reason or another, the goods are worth more than the compensation (which, it will be seen later, is limited). If the persons entitled to the goods do not make the initial request to be notified if they should become available or, having made the request and being notified, fail to give notice within 30 days that the goods should be delivered to them, the carriers may deal with the goods "in accordance with the law of the place where the goods are situated". Subject to local law, this presumably means carriers can deal with the goods as they wish (including selling them on the spot or re-exporting them for their benefit).

Defences

The basic obligation is qualified by the available defences (Article 17) which relieve carriers of liability if the "loss, damage or delay" was caused by:

(a) the wrongful act or neglect of the claimant
(b) the instructions of the claimant (except as the result of the wrongful act or neglect of the carrier)
(c) inherent vice
(d) circumstances which the carriers could not avoid and consequences which they could not prevent.

Further, carriers are relieved of liability for "loss or damage" (but not expressly delay) if it is caused by:

(e) the use of open unsheeted vehicles when their use has been expressly agreed and specified in the consignment note

(f) the lack of or the defective condition of packing in relation to goods likely to be damaged or wasted if not properly packed
(g) the handling, loading, stowage or unloading of the goods by the sender or consignee or those acting on their behalf
(h) the "nature" of certain goods which particularly exposes them to partial loss or damage "especially through breakage, rust, decay, desiccation, leakage, normal wastage, or the action of moth or vermin"
(i) insufficiency or inadequacy of marks or numbers and
(j) the carriage of livestock.

If, in the circumstances of the case, the loss or damage "could" be attributed to one or more of the causes (e) to (j) it is "presumed" that it is so caused. The claimant is then bound to refute the presumption to establish a claim. Carriers have the burden of proof with regard to causes (a) to (d) (Article 18).

Defective vehicle

No relief from liability is granted by reason of the carriers using a defective vehicle (Article 17). However, operating a defective vehicle is not a ground for liability unless this contributed to the damage.

The basic position is that, if carriers fail to deliver the goods or they are delayed, or the consignment is partially lost or damaged, the carriers will be *prima facie* liable for the loss unless they can rely on one or more of the defences. Article 17(2) relieves carriers of liability where the "claimant" has caused the loss, damage or delay by a wrongful act or neglect. Unfortunately, if the claimant is the consignee and the wrongful act or neglect was the senders', the carriers would not appear to be relieved of initial liability to the consignee or, in the reverse situation, to the senders).

Clearly, the room for argument over Article 17 is considerable. This is particularly the case when considering which side is liable for a "wrongful act or neglect". Much may depend on the relevant parties relative expertise and knowledge and, in the case of carriers, whether or not, following their mandatory inspection of the load (per Article 8) reservations were made.

Refrigerated vehicles

Article 18(4) provides separately for the specific case of refrigerated vehicles. With regard to these, the carrier is not entitled to rely on the exception "the nature of certain kinds of goods which particularly exposes them to total or partial loss or to damage" . . . unless he proves all proper steps with respect to the choice, maintenance and use of such equipment were taken and that he complied with any special instructions . . .".

Cash on delivery

Carriers are also liable to obey a requirement to collect a "cash on delivery" charge required of the consignee by the sender where it is so directed. If the carriers fail to do so, they will be liable to compensate the sender (Article 21).

With regard to this, it is important that the sender makes the obligation expressly known to the carrier and that the direction should be unambiguous. By Article 6(2)(c) the consignment note is required, where applicable, to state the amount of "cash on delivery" charges to be recovered. Nevertheless, as Article 4 provides that "the absence, irregularity, or loss of the consignment note shall not affect the existence or validity of the contract of carriage" it seems logical that it is not necessary to have a consignment note in order to impose the cash-on-delivery obligations upon the carrier. Even if there is an existing consignment note, it is likely that incorporation of the cash-on-delivery terms is still not necessary to make them valid as long as they have been notified in unambiguous terms to the carrier and are part of the contract of carriage. The consignment note is (by Article 4) not definitive of the terms of the contract of carriage although the wise sender will always use it where possible.

Dangerous goods

Article 22 concerns "goods of a dangerous nature to the carrier". Nowhere in the convention is "dangerous" defined and whilst some goods will be obviously dangerous, others will be less clearly so, particularly where the danger (of whatever sort) might arise from the way the goods are carried or looked after by the carrier.

Article 10 makes senders generally liable for defective packing of all goods unless the defect was apparent or known to the carriers and they made no reservations concerning it. However, apart from packing, by Article 22 (1) senders are obliged to inform carriers of the exact nature of the danger and indicate if necessary the precautions to be taken. If this information is not inserted in the consignment note, the senders or consignees may still prove that the carriers knew of the exact nature of the danger. Where goods of a dangerous nature are loaded and discovered by the carriers who did not know they were dangerous, they may at any time unload the goods and destroy them or render them harmless without compensation and the senders are liable for all related expenses and for any losses. This should be a powerful incentive to the sender to give proper warning.

Although the carriers are entitled to exact information and, in the absence of this, are entitled to destroy the cargo, it would appear appropriate to apply a qualification of reasonableness both with regard to the information required to be supplied and the action of the carriers, with regard to the goods.

The European Agreement concerning the Carriage of Dangerous Goods is applicable to every international contract for the carriage of goods by road. This also fails to define "dangerous" in specific terms but lists in its appendices goods which are considered to be dangerous for the purpose of the Agreement. The Convention does not make reference to the Agreement but it seems reasonable that its lists of goods should be used at least as a guide in interpreting and applying Article 22.

It is thought, goods that are dangerous merely because of the way they are carried (for example a loose load of timber) would not be considered to be dangerous in the context of Article 22. However, it is possible that goods could be inherently dangerous and that the danger would only arise if they were improperly carried. For instance, a loose load of bananas would not be inherently dangerous but a loosely stowed load of explosives, even though properly packed, might be. It is an interesting question whether the senders should warn the carriers of the special need to fulfil their normal obligations and of the particularly dangerous potential consequences if they should fail to do so even if, had they stowed properly, no danger would have resulted.

Compensation and limitation of liability—shortage and loss

Compensation is payable by a liable carrier for the total or partial loss of the goods, to be calculated by reference to the value of the goods "at the place and time at which they were accepted for carriage"; that is, not the destination nor, where any particular loss occurred, *en route*. The value in question is to be fixed according to the commodity exchange price or, failing this, the market price, or the "normal value of goods of the same kind and quality" at the place at which they were accepted for carriage (Article 23).

Compensation under the Convention is limited. Originally, the limitation figure was expressed in gold francs but the law in the United Kingdom has been amended by the Carriage by Air and Road Act 1979 such that Article 23 (3) now reads:

> Compensation shall not however, exceed 8.33 units of account per kg of gross weight short.

This reference to units of account is a reference to the SDR (Special Drawing Rights) defined by the International Monetary Fund, and although the number of SDRs is fixed, the value of these depends upon the relative values of a number of currencies. Consequently, the daily value of an SDR is reported in the newspapers, usually along with currency values. Many countries (though not all) now refer to SDRs.

Practically speaking, the sales invoice will usually be referred to as evidence of the value of the goods "by reference" to which compensation is to be calculated but it is not conclusive that this should define the level of compensation.

In addition to the sums recoverable under Article 23(1) to (3), the claimant is entitled to a refund of customs duties and other charges incurred in respect of the carriage of the goods "in case of total loss and in proportion to the loss sustained in case of partial loss". The paragraph ends by stating that "but no further damages shall be payable". Whilst an exact term like "customs duties" is open to varying interpretations in different jurisdictions, it does not include Value Added Tax which, in Britain, happens to be collected by H.M. Customs and Excise. At the same time, the House of Lords held in *James Buchanan & Co. Limited v Babco Forwarding and Shipping (UK) Limited* [1978] that excise duties are within the scope of "charges incurred in respect of the carriage" because they arose "in consequence of" or "as a result of" the carriage. It is also probable that preparatory packing and related pre-shipment costs are also recoverable, notwithstanding that in the case referred to above, the court concentrated on costs incurred as a result of (rather than prior to) the carriage (Article 23(4)).

Delay

Article 23(5) limits damages for delay (as opposed to loss or shortage) to a maximum of the carriage charges, referred to before, and this loss must be proven to be recoverable.

There is no suggestion here that the refund of customs duties or other charges as contemplated in Article 23(4) is available as additional compensation in the case of mere delay. The level of carriage charges can only be exceeded in damages if either Articles 26 or 29 apply (see later).

Damage

Article 25 has regard to damage claims and states that:

> In case of damage, the carrier shall be liable for the amount by which the goods have diminished in value, calculated by the reference to the value of the goods fixed in accordance with Article 23, paragraphs 1, 2 and 4.

(Provided that, by Article 25(2), compensation shall not exceed the amount payable in case of total loss and, in the event of only partial damage, the amount payable in case of the loss of the part affected.)

It is first to be noted that Article 23(3) contains limitation provisions by reference to weight and is not expressly incorporated into Article 25. Nevertheless, because the total compensation is limited to the amount payable in the case of loss, the effect is to include by implication Article 23(3), at least with regard to the maximum figure recoverable, although it is less clear how this applies to part damage. That Article 25 (2) refers to the "part affected" suggests that compensation may be payable for more than the damaged part's weight, if this can be justified to show that a larger part is affected. An obvious example would be where there is partial damage to a machine which may render the whole unit useless and compensation based on the weight of the damaged part would hardly be compensation at all.

Surcharge—additional compensation

Additional compensation may be bought by the payment of a surcharge. Under Article 24, against such a surcharge and upon declaring in the consignment note a value for the goods exceeding the limit laid down in Article 23, the higher value shall be substituted for the limitation figure. This surcharge is not fixed but is one that is "to be agreed upon" between the sender and the carrier.

Surcharge—special interest delivery

Against payment of a surcharge to be agreed, the sender may "fix the amount of a special interest delivery" in the case of loss or damage or any agreed time limit being exceeded, by entering the fixed amount in the consignment note. Compensation may then be due up to this new amount, provided liability is established (Article 26).

The difference between Articles 24 and 26 is that the former only applies to raising the maximum limitation figure without dismissing the other basis of calculation in Article 23, whereas Article 26 allows for compensation to be calculated, in accordance with the declared "special interest" "independently of the compensation provided for in Articles 23, 24 and 25".

Interest on claims and currency

The Convention entitles the claimant to a modest five per cent per annum interest on compensation accruing from the date on which the claim was sent in writing to the carrier, or from the commencement of legal proceedings if no such written claim was made (Article 27). Obviously, bearing in mind recent history, five per cent interest is a more attractive proposition in Switzerland or West Germany than it would be in say the United Kingdom or Poland where this rate of interest provides no incentive on the part of a defendant to settle the claim earlier rather than later.

Article 27(2) provides that, where a claim is pursued in one jurisdiction but is expressed in another currency, conversion into the currency of the country of jurisdiction is to occur on the day and at the place of the payment of compensation. Consequently, there is no advantage in the claimant selecting a jurisdiction on the basis of relative interest rates or currency strengths as they relate to a specific claim.

Extra-contractual claims

The Convention provides a regime for contracts but Article 28 deals with extra-contractual claims. It provides that, where these occur in respect of alleged loss, damage or delay arising out of a contract of carriage subject to the Convention:

> the carrier may avail himself of the provisions of this Convention which exclude his liability or which fix or limit the compensation due.

Thus by law, the carrier's liability in tort (in England) or in delict (on the Continent) is limited to the contractual level of liability. Furthermore, in England, this provision would also relate to the relationship of bailor and bailee in respect of the goods. Article 28 (ii) extends the protection granted in paragraph (1) to "the person for whom the carrier is responsible under the terms of Article 3".

Wilful misconduct

Although the Convention and the Articles discussed above limit the compensation available, the right of their carriers to take advantage of the limitation provisions either on their own behalf or on behalf of those persons whose services they make use of, is lost if damage (including loss) is sustained and it was caused by the "wilful misconduct or by such default on his part as, in accordance with the court or tribunal seised of the case, is considered as equivalent to wilful misconduct" (Article 29).

In England, liability is usually assured if negligence can be established and there is little certainty in discussing concepts such as "gross negligence". However, it is clear from the general provisions of the Convention that more than mere negligence is required to establish "wilful misconduct" and so break the normal limitation provisions in the Convention. Wilfulness implies deliberate misconduct or, at least, recklessness in the sense of appreciating the danger but not caring to do anything about it. Negligence would only be an unreasonable failure to appreciate the danger or failure to exercise proper care with regard to it. Obviously there will be marginal cases where it will be difficult to decide which is the proper concept to apply best to particular circumstances.

It is also worth noting that the carriers' liability for other persons' "wilful misconduct" only applies insofar as those persons are acting within the scope of their employment.

In the recent English case of *Texas Instruments v Nason Europe* (1991) the Commercial Court upheld the concept of wilful misconduct being subjective. The individual concerned should have appreciated that there was a particular risk and have either intentionally or recklessly disregarded it in order for wilful misconduct to be established. However, the Court also suggested that where an employee was aware of particular risk in relation to his conduct (for example a driver parking a trailer overnight in a car park where he realises it was vulnerable to theft) but his employer did not appreciate the danger and still ordered the employee to act in a way that endangered the goods, the employer would not be responsible for wilful misconduct, should loss result as a consequence of these instructions. This rather odd view perhaps suggests that the employer should prefer not to be advised of any particular danger which the goods in his or her care may be subject to or, if so advised, he or she should not particularly try to appreciate the risk. This appears a little unreasonable where the employer's own employee is perfectly capable of appreciating a danger.

Combined transport

Where carriage under a Convention contract is not performed entirely by road, it is necessary to consider the implications of Article 2 which deals with combined methods of transport, and paragraph (1) which provides:

> Where the vehicle containing the goods is carried over part of the journey by sea, rail, inland waterways or air and, except where the provisions of Article 14 are applicable [which relate to impossibility of performance], the goods are not unloaded from the vehicle, this Convention shall nevertheless apply to the whole of the carriage. Provided that to the extent that it is proved that any loss, damage or delay in delivery of the goods which occurs during the carriage by the other means of transport was not caused by an act or omission of the carrier by road, but by some event which could only have occurred in the course of and by reason of the carriage by that other means of transport, the liability of the carrier by road shall be determined not by this Convention but in the manner in which the liability of the carrier by the other means of transport would have been determined if the contract of carriage of goods alone would have been made by the sender with the carrier by the other means of transport in accordance with the conditions prescribed by law for the carriage of goods by that means of transport. If, however, there are no such prescribed conditions, the liability of the carrier by road shall be determined by this Convention.

Obviously, all contracts for the international carriage of goods by road that begin or end in the United Kingdom must involve some other means of transport and this will continue until a road tunnel is completed between the United Kingdom and the Continent.

Where goods are unloaded from a vehicle (eg a container is sent by rail or goods on a trailer are unloaded into a ship) then the Convention shall not apply to that part of the carriage. It also appears that if a vehicle is loaded, say on a ship, but a container needs to be unloaded from the vehicle (say, to fit on the ship), similarly, the contract will be taken outside the Convention. However, in the light of Article 14, unless it has been expressly or impliedly agreed by the person entitled to dispose of the goods in accordance with Article 12 that such unloading should take place, it is possible that the English courts at least would not accept that the carrier was entitled to avoid the provisions of the Convention in favour of something less stringent. As a logical reflection of this, it may be reasonable to consider that, should the persons entitled to dispose of the goods suffer loss by an unauthorised change in the performance of the contract (by, say, such unloading) then they ought to be entitled to recover against the carrier for all losses.

The proviso in Article 2(1) is designed to ensure that carriers have similar obligations to senders or consignees to those that are owed to them under the separate contract that they will have entered into with regard to the other means of transport. If achieved, this protects carriers but to the detriment or advantage of the senders or consignees, depending upon the relative advantages or disadvantages of the relevant means of transport as these are determined by the law. Before this applies, it is necessary to establish that the loss, damage or delay occurred:

(a) during the carriage by the other means of transport
(b) that this was not the result of an act or omission by the road carrier and
(c) that there are prescribed by law conditions applicable to the other means of transport which govern liability.

In the absence of any of these factors, liability will remain determinable under the terms of the Convention. This applies whether or not the road carrier is also the carrier by the other means of transport, provided that the conditions as described are met—-per Article 2(2).

The burden of proof in respect of shifting the standard of obligation from one convention to another probably falls upon the party who wishes to rely upon the shift.

It is not uncommon for damage to goods carried on a trailer to be due to poor stowage. Notwithstanding that a stowage method might suffice for carriage by road, where it is anticipated that carriage will include a sea voyage, it is reasonable to infer that a failure to stow properly for this part of the journey is an omission on the part of the road carriers which should prevent them from relying upon, say, the Hague-Visby Rules applicable to certain carriages by sea. However, this example rather assumes that the Hague-Visby Rules as referred to could be "conditions prescribed by law for the carriage of goods by that means of transport" (and, respectively, the Warsaw Convention for carriage by air and the CIM—the international convention on the carriage of goods by rail—for goods carried by rail). However, the Hague-Visby Rules are not necessarily prescribed by law in all contracts for the carriage of goods by sea and indeed, even where they do apply, the obligations of the sea carriers can be increased by their consent so that, in effect, enhanced obligations can apply. Furthermore, it is quite open and not unusual, particularly on the North Sea, for non-negotiable waybills to govern the terms of the contract by sea and the Hague-Visby Rules do not necessarily apply to these depending upon different national laws. The result of this is that the applicability of Article 2, insofar as it apparently applies terms outside the CMR Convention, must be treated with care. Close examination of the relevant alternative conventions must be regarded but, in the absence of their applicability, the CMR Convention will apply.

Successive carriers

Goods being carried under a Convention contract between sender and consignee may be taken over and carried by more than one carrier. Where different forms of transport are used, the provisions of Article 2 relating to combined transport may apply. Where two or more road carriers are used, the provisions of Chapter VI relating to "successive carriers" need to be considered.

Article 34 in Chapter VI of the Convention prescribes that:

> If carriage governed by single contract is performed by successive road carriers, each of them shall be responsible for the performance of the whole operation, the second carrier and each succeeding carrier becoming a party to the contract of carriage under the terms of the consignment note, by reason of his acceptance of the goods and the consignment note.

Although more than one apparent road carrier may be involved to some extent or other in the carriage of the goods, some or all of these may not necessarily be evident "successive carriers". A number of different situations must be distinguished.

Single contract

The successive carriage must be a continuance of the carriage under the same contract. Consequently, if a sender engages a freight forwarder as agent to conclude a contract of carriage which is within the Convention, the forwarder will not be a CMR carrier. Consequently, the carrier engaged by the forwarder will be a first, not successive, CMR carrier (which is important when considering rights of action) and the sender's separate contract with the forwarder will not be governed by the Convention but by relevant national law. Where forwarders are used as agents, they act on behalf of the sender so that the sender effectively contracts with the engaged CMR carriers as principal under a direct contract with that CMR carrier.

Alternatively, an engaged CMR carrier may sub-contract all or part of the carriage to another carrier or carriers. The first CMR carrier will remain liable throughout under the Convention. However, the second and any subsequent sub-contractors' liabilities may, depending upon the contractual arrangements, be governed by the CMR Convention as successive carriers, or some or all of them may be sub-contractors on other contractual terms governed by domestic law. It may often be a difficult question to decide whether or not a possible contractual relationship is in fact the correct one, or whether or not an apparent carrier (or non-apparent carrier) is a successive carrier under the Convention.

What is clear is that carriers under the Convention need not physically carry the goods themselves. It is enough that they "accept" the goods under the contract, which they may do either themselves or through a sub-contractor delegated to take that responsibility. Similarly, engaged successive carriers or sub-contractors may also delegate the whole or part of the particular carriage which they are contracted to do. Conversely, a carrier may be a successive carrier even if performing only a short part of the carriage within the borders of one country, provided that the agreement being performed is a Convention contract and the qualifications of being a successive carrier are otherwise met.

Where a person involved in the carriage is neither a carrier nor a successive carrier, he or she is not a party to a Convention contract and may not be sued by the sender under the terms of that contract. Such a person will, however, be able to benefit from the limited defences available under the Convention to persons used by the CMR carrier in the performance of their obligations.

Consignment note

Article 4 provides that the absence of a consignment note or any irregularity in that consignment note, will not affect the basic applicability of the Convention to a relevant contract of carriage. On the other hand, Article 34 states that any second and each succeeding carrier becomes a party to the contract of carriage under the terms of the consignment note "... by reason of his acceptance of the goods and the consignment note". It is, therefore, important to decide how this requirement of a consignment note squares with Article 4.

The apparent need for the would-be successive carrier to accept the consignment note is reinforced by the consequential provisions contained in Article 35, which require that the successive carrier should give the preceding carrier a dated and signed receipt for the goods and that "He shall enter his name and address on the second copy of the consignment note. Where applicable he shall enter on the second copy of the consignment note and on the receipt reservations of the kind provided for in Article 8, para. 2".

There is English and Continental authority for the view that the provisions of Article 4 (relating as they do to the formation of the contract) do not override the requirement for a consignment note to be accepted under Article 34 should "the consignment note" to be accepted actually exist. What is not so clear is whether or not the total absence of a consignment note prevents a successive carriage taking place.

There is a logic in making a successive carriage dependent upon acceptance of the consignment note. In the absence of such a consignment note, the potential successive carrier would not necessarily be privy to the information that the consignment note should contain, nor even necessarily be aware that the carriage is subject to the Convention at all. If carriers are not given this information, it appears reasonable for them to deal with the preceding carrier on a sub-contracting basis on terms that that sub-contractor is familiar with.

If no consignment note was issued when the goods were taken over by the first carrier, and the first carrier wishes to engage a succeeding carrier under the terms of the Convention, it may be necessary to issue a consignment note for the purposes of ensuring that the successive carrier is bound under the Convention.

Although Article 35 requires that successive carriers insert their names on the consignment note, it would appear that their obligation and their failure to comply with it should not affect their status as successive carriers.

It is also not entirely clear what accepting the consignment note entails. If the consignment note travels with the goods and the goods are accepted by a sub-contractor for part of the carriage, it would appear unreasonable always to assume that that sub-contractor has become a successive carrier. Consequently, it appears reasonable to take the view that physically taking the consignment note must be accompanied by a definite intention to accept it, and by implication, the obligations that this entails. Whereas sub-contractors appear to sub-contract under their own terms whilst carrying a consignment note, this "acceptance" of the consignment note may only be physical but not intended to establish relations on the basis of the consignment note, the carriage of which may be merely a convenience for the actual CMR carrier.

It is important to note, at all times, that where successive carriers are involved, they are performing obligations under the same single contract for the international carriage of goods by road. It is possible for a carrier under the Convention to sub-contract part of the carriage under a different limited contract without involving the sub-contractor as a successive carrier.

Sub-contractors

From the above it follows that where a carrier sub-contracts or a sub-contractor sub-contracts part or all of the carriage under a different contract, then the Convention does not apply to that particular sub-contract unless this too is governed by the Convention as a separate contract in its own right, and the party having responsibility under the Convention retains it. Unfortunately, it is sometimes difficult to decide whether or not there has in fact been a separate contract or a successive carriage under the same contract, particularly because, although Article 34 refers to the terms of and acceptance of the consignment note, the presence or absence of the consignment note does not affect the basic contract being governed by the Convention. Consequently, it is not clearly necessary to the existence of a successive carriage, which may exist in the absence of any consignment note (but see later).

Physical carriage

It is not essential that a carrier (successive or otherwise) under the CMR Convention physically carries the goods at all. It is possible to be a carrier and to contract the entire carriage out to one or more other parties who, depending on the circumstances, will either be successive carriers or independent sub-contractors. The situation will be different where the sender enters separate contracts. Carriers under these agreements will obviously not be carriers under the same contract and none of the separate carriers will be successive carriers unless a contract is Convention-governed and more than one carrier successively undertakes the obligations of that contract.

Successive carriers' responsibilities

Each successive carrier is responsible to cargo interests for the performance of the "whole operation" which is to say the entire contract in question (Article 34). They are therefore potentially liable to be sued by any cargo interest with that right (subject to Article 36—see later) and would be entitled, where relevant, to obtain compensation from other carriers (under Article 37) as indeed those other carriers would be entitled to claim compensation from them. Although all successive carriers may be liable to cargo interests in theory, Article 36 prescribes that (except in the case of a counterclaim or raised set-off) legal proceedings may be brought only against the first carrier, the last successive carrier, or the carrier who was performing the portion of the carriage during which the event causing the loss, damage or delay occurred (or all or any of these at the same time). In each case where there is liability to cargo interests between successive carriers, "the carrier responsible for the loss or damage shall be solely liable for the compensation whether paid by himself or by another carrier" (except where there is joint liability, in which case apportionment of liability of payment is required in accordance with Article 37) and except where the carriers agree to vary the procedures under Articles 37 and 38 as is their entitlement under Article 40.

By Article 35(2), the provisions of Article 9 are to apply to the relations of successive carriers which is to say a consignment note is only *prima facie* evidence of the making of the contract and, if no specific reservations are made by a succeeding carrier, it is presumed in the absence of contrary proof that the goods and packaging appeared in good condition when the succeeding carrier took them over and also that the number of packages and marks (etc) corresponded with the consignment note statement (if there is one).

Insolvent carrier

If a carrier is insolvent, any compensation due from and unpaid by that party shall be divided amongst the other carriers in proportion to the share due from them (Article 38). This will apply both with regard to claims from cargo interests and, succeeding such, between successive carriers where appropriate. Dispute between successive carriers shall not be entitled to question the validity of the payment required under Articles 37 and 38 if such has been determined by judicial authority (which may include arbitration by Article 33) and after the potentially disputing carrier had been given due notice of the proceedings and afforded the opportunity of making an appearance (Article 39). Any claim by one carrier against another under these provisions may be made only in the jurisdiction in which the carrier from whom a contribution is sought is ordinarily resident or has its principal place of business or its branch or agency through which the particular contract was made. In the English case, *Cummins Engine Co. Limited v Davis Freight Forwarding (Hull) Limited* [1981] it was held that the "carriers concerned" referred only to carriers from whom a contribution was claimed, not merely one of the successive carriers.

The period of limitation for beginning actions between carriers is governed by the provisions of Article 32 (see later) which period is to begin on the date of the final judicial decision fixing the amount of compensation payable under the provisions of the convention or, failing such a decision, the actual date of payment. Arbitration may also be agreed (Article 33—see later).

Claims and actions

The rules governing the procedure for pursuing claims under the Convention are contained in Chapter V (Articles 30–33).

Claims for damage

Under Article 30, taking delivery is *prima facie* evidence of receipt of the goods in the condition described in the consignment note (should there be one) unless the goods are inspected on delivery and reservations are notified to the carrier giving a general indication of the loss or damage claimed. Such reservations should be given not later than the time of delivery in the case of apparent loss or damage, or within seven days of delivery (excluding Sundays and public holidays) in respect of non-apparent loss or damage. In the latter case, such reservations should be communicated in writing.

It should be noted that, subject to the paragraph below, if the goods were not checked on arrival, a failure to comply with the requirements as regards reservations only leads to a *prima facie* assumption that the goods were received in the condition described in the consignment note. Such a contention can be rebutted by adequate evidence which, at least in English law, it would probably be necessary to produce in any event to win an action. However, this limited advantage will be more important in other jurisdictions and therefore any reservations should be made and should be as specific as is reasonable in the circumstances (given the limited amount of time available). Also, although it is only required that reservations be in writing in the case of non-apparent damage, it is obviously prudent for a consignee to confirm any reservation or complaint in writing should it be likely to be necessary to rely on it at a later date. Such a written complaint also has significance with regard to time limits for beginning claims (see later).

If the consignee inspects the goods with the carrier on delivery, evidence contradicting the result of the findings of the checking is only admissible in the case of non-apparent damage or loss and provided that the consignee gives the relevant written reservations within the seven days referred to in Article 30(1) (Article 30(2)).

Claims for delay

The Convention prohibits compensation for delay in delivery unless a reservation has been sent in writing to the carrier within 21 days from the time that the goods were ultimately placed at the disposal of the consignee (Article 30(3)). This amounts to an absolute bar on a claim unless the narrow time-limit is complied with.

Jurisdiction

Legal proceedings arising out of the contract of carriage may be begun in any court or tribunal in a contracting country as is designated by agreement between the parties and "in addition" (meaning in practice alternatively) "in the courts or tribunals of the country within whose territory either the defendant is ordinarily resident or has his principal place of business or the branch or agency through which the Contract of Carriage was made or the place where the goods were taken over by the carrier or the place designated for their delivery is situated and in no other courts or tribunals".

It is apparent that if the claimant pursues a claim in one of the alternative jurisdictions (other than agreed), this need not be in a contracting country to the Convention to qualify. For example, where damage occurs to goods being carried from London to Moscow, the claimant may bring an action in the Soviet Union. Nonetheless, oddly Article 31(3) only provides that such a judgment will be enforceable (by virtue of the Convention) in other contracting states if such a judgment was, in the first place, "entered by a court or by a tribunal of a contracting country".

Whilst an action as contemplated by Article 31 is pending, by Article 31(2) no new action may be begun between the same parties on the same grounds unless the judgment of the court or tribunal before which the first action was brought is not enforceable in the country in which the fresh proceedings are brought. This may be necessary where the action is begun or enforcement is necessary in a country not party to the Convention or, if the problem is not identified before judgment, it will allow a second set of proceedings to be begun in a jurisdiction which meets the qualifications described and which may ultimately succeed in giving the claimant a remedy.

It is worth noting that the jurisdiction provisions have nothing at all to do with the place where the damage might have occurred to the goods and indeed such a place would be excluded from hearing the case unless any other of the jurisdiction qualifications were met.

Security for costs

As Article 31(3) essentially provides that judgments in one Convention country will be enforceable in other Convention countries, Article 31(5) excludes a right to security for costs "in proceedings arising out of carriage under the Convention from nationals of contracting countries resident or having their place of business in one of those countries" irrespective of whether the claim is between carriers or against a carrier by cargo interests. This appears to be the case notwithstanding the possible impecuniosity of any claimant and in respect of any of the other grounds on which it will be normal to seek security for costs in United Kingdom jurisdictions or otherwise. However, if an action is pursued in a non-Convention jurisdiction, that jurisdiction's rules with regard to security for costs will remain.

Time-bar

As under the Hague-Visby Rules for the carriage of goods by sea, the period of limitation for bringing an action under the CMR Convention is (generally) one year. However, under Article 32, it is prescribed that this period shall be three years in the case of wilful misconduct and, in either case, the period of limitation shall begin to run:

(a) in a case of partial loss, damage or delay in delivery, from the date of delivery
(b) in the case of total loss, from the 30th day after the expiry of the agreed time-limit or, where there is no agreed time-limit, from the sixtieth day from the date on which the goods were taken over by the carrier, and
(c) in all other cases, on the expiry of a period of three months after the making of the contract of carriage. The day on which the period of limitation begins to run shall not be included in the period.

Note, however, the necessity to express early reservations following delayed delivery to avoid the consequential bar on proceedings.

Notwithstanding the limitations dates referred to above, by Article 32(2) the one year limitation period shall be suspended if and from when a written claim is delivered and for the period until and if such a written claim is rejected by the carriers in writing and they return the documents attached to the claim. On the other hand, if part of the claim is admitted, the limitation period shall run again but only in respect of the balance of the claim in dispute. (Further claims and rejections to the contrary will not affect the limitation period.)

Notwithstanding this, by Article 32(iii) the parties are entitled to agree to extend the limitation period provided this is not in conflict with the law where the claim is heard.

Arbitration

Article 33 states that the contract of carriage may provide for arbitration as long as "the clause conferring competence on the tribunal provides that the tribunal shall apply this Convention". Unless there is this express contractual provision, a reference to arbitration and even the agreement to pursue such arbitration will have no effect and may trap the claimant by causing a failure effectively to begin proceedings as the limitation period continues to run out.

If arbitration is pursued, enforcement will depend on the 1958 New York Convention on the Recognition and Enforcement of Foreign Arbitral Awards. Only Yugoslavia and Luxembourg, of the states contracting to the CMR Convention are not also parties to the New York Convention. However, many other countries not parties to the CMR Convention are parties to the New York Convention which may assist in other circumstances.

Derogation from the provisions of the Convention

Chapter 7 (Article 41) provides that subject to the provisions of Article 40 (discussed above) any contractual term that would directly or indirectly derogate from the provisions of the Convention shall be null and void. However, other provisions of the contract will remain valid. Also any term diverting the benefit of insurance in favour of the carrier or any clause shifting the burden of proof shall be of no effect.

The parties may thus agree their own terms as to the contract of carriage. However, these may not conflict with the Convention where such conflict would weaken its provisions. This is clearly an essential provision unless the Convention is allowed to be negotiated out of contracts by stronger parties.

Comment

The Convention is an almost comprehensive guide to European international road transport and the relations between carriers and senders/receivers. It remains quite a triumph, and it is of great assistance to all involved to know that goods are carried under "CMR Terms". This not only makes disputes easier to resolve but assists in keeping insurance costs down. However, there are difficulties in applying the Convention (for example distinguishing sub-contractors from carriers) there are inevitable consequences of the complexity of the transport business (the application to successive carriers) or casualness, or pressure of work on carriers and drivers (the desire for consignment notes but the uncertain consequences of their absence). It is a testament to the Convention that it mostly seems to work and that it tries to cope with these problems in a realistic and not too legalistic way. However, where there are disputes, these can be complicated (with many different parties whose roles are often unclear) and correspondingly difficult and thus expensive to unravel and resolve.

Schedule of countries party to the CMR Convention

Austria, Belgium, Bulgaria, Czechoslovakia, Denmark, Finland, France, Germany, Greece, Hungary, Italy, Luxembourg, Netherlands, Norway, Poland, Portugal, Romania, Spain, Sweden, Switzerland, UK, USSR, Yugoslavia.

C.F.

7

Carriage of goods by sea

Introduction

There may be a large number of parties involved in the carriage of a cargo by sea and as a result the legal relationships between them are often complex. This chapter seeks to outline the structure of those legal relationships and how they arise, focusing particularly on the position of the importer to or exporter from Great Britain.

An importer or exporter is likely to be involved in one of three types of carriage by sea contracts. The type of contract used will depend upon the quantity and nature of the cargo. The first type of contract is where the whole vessel is engaged under a voyage charter to carry the cargo from the loading port to the discharge port. Typically this will be for the carriage of a full load of bulk cargo such as oil, grains, coal, fishmeal, etc. The second type of contract is used where a smaller quantity is to be carried. The contract will often be with, or arranged by, a liner operator who operates a scheduled service on a set route. The contract will be on the terms of a bill of lading, normally the liner operator's standard form. The third alternative is really a miscellaneous category which includes a variety of contracts tailored to specific needs. One common arrangement is a long-term contract for the carriage of a certain number of shipments per year, known as a contract of affreightment. This is sometimes used by a large scale importer or exporter of bulk cargo such as a power company importing coal. It is not considered further in this book.

The majority of contracts for the carriage of goods by sea fall into the second category and this chapter will concentrate on carriage under bills of lading. Carriage under charterparties, and the consequences where charterparties are interposed between the shipper or consignee and the vessel owner, are considered under the heading "Carriage under charterparties" below.

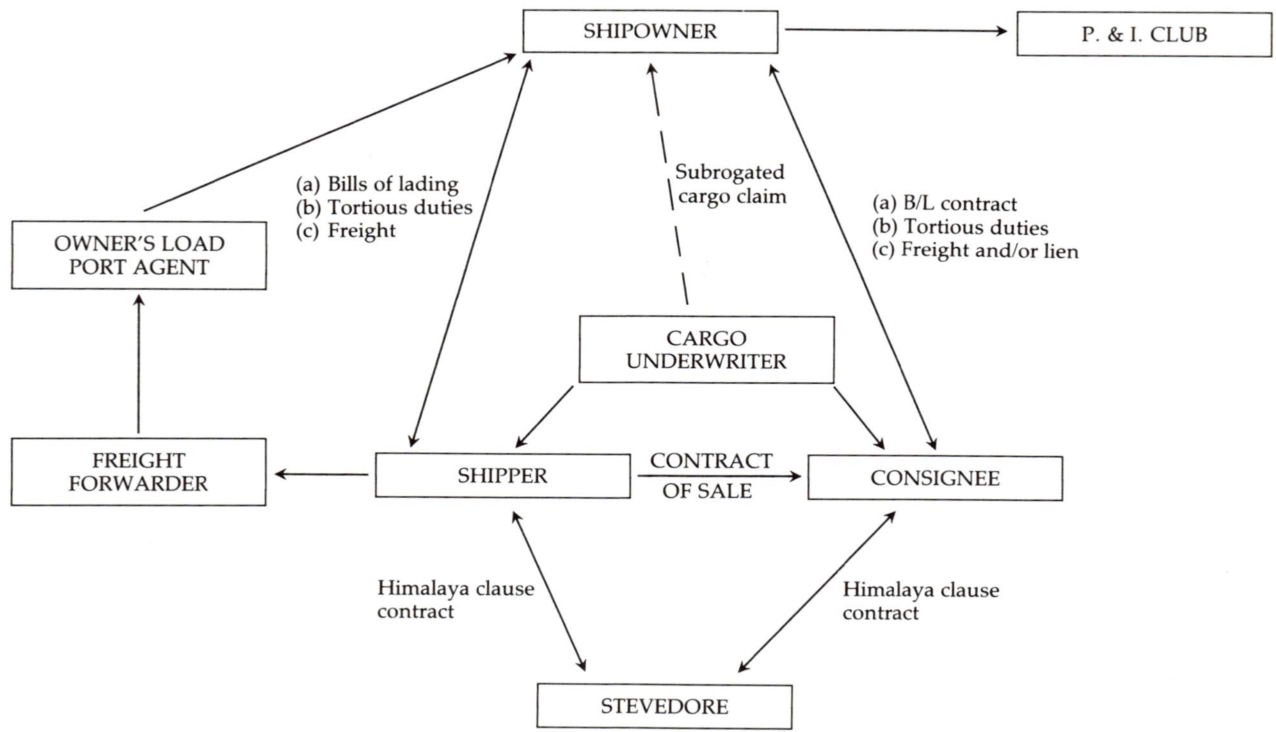

Figure 7.1 Carriage of goods

Carriage under contracts contained in or evidenced by bills of lading

Figure 7.1 illustrates the various parties that are involved in a typical carriage of goods by a liner operator. In the example, the shipper has not chartered the vessel and the liner operator is the shipowner. The situation where the shipper is also the charterer is considered later (page 183), as is the situation where the liner operator is a charterer and entering the bill of lading contract as agent for the owner of the vessel. For the moment we shall assume the liner operator is the shipowner.

Booking and consignment

Shippers wishing to arrange shipment will generally instruct freight forwarders who are normally their agents. A freight forwarder's responsibility is to find out what vessels will be available to carry the cargo and to book it aboard with the shipowner's agent. The freight forwarder will often arrange for the goods to be collected (and perhaps properly packed) and delivered to the vessel or the owner's agents. One important role of the freight forwarder is to attend to the documentation. On delivery of the goods to the vessel's side or to the owner's agent, the forwarder will give written instructions about shipment. These instructions should contain a description of the goods, their condition and the quantity. The freight forwarder will also deliver to the owner's agents a set of draft bills of lading.

The role of the shipowner's agents is to advertise that space aboard the vessel is available and to book cargo to fill it. The agents will normally also be responsible for checking the cargo and sometimes for arranging loading. On receipt of the goods they will issue a receipt setting out the details of the goods. Since Article III rule 3 of the Hague and Hague-Visby rules provide that the carrier must, on demand, issue a bill of lading showing the shipper's identification marks, the number of packages, the weight or quantity of the cargo and its apparent order and condition, the receipt will also normally contain this information. This receipt is usually called a mate's receipt (which derives from the old practice that the mate issued this document when the goods were received on board) although local custom may dictate otherwise. Such a receipt is normally an acknowledgement by vessel owners that they hold the goods on behalf of the shippers and that the goods are in accordance with the description, although they may prove to the contrary. If the receipt has no qualification as to the order and condition of the goods, it is a "clean" receipt and if it has a qualification it is a "claused receipt". Clausing may be achieved by expressly stating a defect in the condition (for example "rusty"), or may merely negate the implied representation of good order and condition by stating "said to be in good order and condition". The latter may be appropriate where there is no simple means of inspection, for example when the goods are in a container not packed by the carrier. The significance of the description in the bill of lading is considered further on page 178.

The contract of carriage and the bill of lading

It can be a difficult question to identify precisely when the contract of carriage between the shippers and shipowners has been concluded and what its terms are. In most cases these questions do not have practical importance. Once the goods are shipped the shipowners' agents or the master will sign sets of bills of lading which will be in the shipowners' standard form with a description of the goods as on the mate's or other receipt. It is customary to issue a set of three original bills of lading. This is discussed under the heading "Functions of the bill of lading".

The bill of lading and sometimes the mate's receipt are the strongest evidence of the terms of the contract between shippers and shipowners. Usually the contract will be concluded before shipment and, thus, before any bill of lading is issued, but the shippers will generally be taken to have assented to the terms of the owners' standard bill of lading. The contract is probably made at the latest at the time the goods are received for shipment by the shipowners or their agents. Often the form of receipt will refer to the standard terms in the bill of lading. The bill which is issued is not conclusive and if the shippers can show that some other terms were agreed prior to the issue of the bill of lading, or that they were unaware of unusual or exceptional terms in the bill of lading, they may be able to establish a contract in different terms.

Through bills of lading

As we have seen, whilst the contract is usually concluded before the issue of the bill of lading and the bill is only evidence of its terms, in practice in the vast majority of cases the bill will fix the scope of the contract and the responsibilities of the carrier. Historically shipowners only undertook to transport the cargo from alongside the vessel at the load port to alongside at the discharge port. Normally modern carriers will undertake further responsibility, the scope of which will be determined by the bill of lading.

It is now common, particularly in container transport, to issue a bill of lading which governs not merely a single ocean voyage but covers more than one such voyage with transshipment on to another carrier's vessel, or includes other stages of transport by land or air. Such a bill is called a "through bill of lading". Because of the myriad of possible combinations it is difficult to lay down general rules.

One important question is whether the shipowner contracts as a principal for all stages of the voyage or just for the ocean voyage. This will depend on whether for the non-ocean legs the shipowner or liner operator purports to contract as principal or merely as agent for the on-carrier. Usually through bills of lading will make it clear that the shipowner is only an agent for the on-carriers although the freight paid to the liner operator is for the entire voyage. Each on-carrier will issue a bill of lading for its portion of the carriage, but it is usually provided that the goods are to be delivered only upon presentation of the original through bill of lading.

The position of through bills as documents of title and under the Bills of Lading Act 1855 is considered on page 170.

The function of bills of lading

There are three primary functions of bills of lading. The first, the bill as evidence of the contract of carriage, has been considered. It is also a confirmation of receipt of the goods, and a document of title.

Bill of lading as a receipt and confirmation of shipment

The mate's receipt, which is given on delivery of the goods to the shipowner or agent, is a confirmation of receipt of the goods and also evidence of their condition. The bill of lading will contain the same information and if it is a "shipped" bill of lading it will confirm that the goods have been shipped on board.

If the bill of lading is issued before shipment it will be a "received for shipment" bill, which merely confirms that the shipowners have the goods in their custody. Article III rule 3 of both the Hague and Hague-Visby Rules requires that shippers can demand bills of lading once the goods are in the shipowners' custody. However, once they have been shipped shippers can demand shipped bills of lading. If a received for shipment bill of lading has been issued it must be surrendered to obtain a shipped bill or the received bill can be endorsed with the shipment date. The significance of the difference is that a received for shipment bill is not generally acceptable under a CIF contract, nor is it normally sufficient to ensure payment under a letter of credit since the bill would not confirm that the goods were "on board".

The representations in the bill of lading that the goods have been shipped and as to the quantity and apparent order and condition of the goods on shipment are of importance in the context of cargo claims and are considered on page 178.

It will usually be a requirement under both CIF contracts and letters of credit that the bills be clean bills. The reason is that both the bank and the buyer want to be sure that the cargo is in good condition on shipment. Less reputable shipowners will occasionally be prevailed upon to issue clean bills to shippers when the cargo is not in good order and condition or is shortloaded, in exchange for an indemnity for any loss that they may suffer. This is a very unsound practice and may in some cases be so tainted with fraud that the indemnity is unenforceable. Shipowners who indulge in such conduct do so at their peril. They are not merely likely to face a cargo claim, since the inaccurate bill of lading is *prima facie* evidence of the order quantity and condition of the goods, but may face a claim for tortious misrepresentation from buyers.

The bill of lading as a document of title

The law has adopted ancient mercantile custom in holding a bill of lading to be a document of title. In this context there are two consequences. The first is that holders of the bills of lading are entitled to call for delivery of the goods. So long as shipowners deliver the goods to the holders of any one of the set of original bills of lading they will not be held liable if that person does not have the best title to the goods.

The second principle, which probably was a consequence of the first, is that the bill of lading is a symbol representing the goods, so that it is a quasi-negotiable document. Most bills of lading forms will have a space for the consignee's name and generally state that the cargo is to be delivered to that party. There will normally also be a space headed "notify party". This is the person who will be warned of the arrival of the vessel by the shipowners' agent at the discharge port. If shippers wish bills to be negotiable they will insert the name of the consignee in the notify party box and insert "to order" in the consignee box. Shippers may then endorse the bill to the consignee, or any other person they wish, by signing the bill and writing "to deliver to the order of" that consignee or person. This is normally done on the back. If the bill is then delivered to the consignee it may, depending on the terms of the contract of sale, pass title to that party. Alternatively, if the bill is marked to order and shippers merely sign in blank (which means the endorsement does not name the endorsee), or if it was originally marked "to bearer", it is a bearer bill and physical delivery of it with the intent to transfer title to the cargo will do so.

This characteristic of the bill of lading is similar to the bill of exchange. However, it differs in that, unlike a bill of exchange, by transfer of title under a bill of lading transferors cannot give better title than they had. A transfer cannot cure a defect in title.

There are usually three original bills of lading signed by or on behalf of the shipowners. The mode in which they are transferred to the consignees will depend on the nature of the transaction. If the shipment was of goods sold on an FOB basis then the bills will be issued with the buyers named as consignees and forwarded to them by air mail or courier. If the goods were sold on a CIF basis the bills of lading are normally endorsed in blank by the shippers and tendered with the other documents required under the letter of credit (usually the sale invoice and the insurance documents). The shippers will pass these to their bank, the collecting bank, which will tender them under a letter of credit to the consignees' bank, the paying bank. On payment from one bank to another they will transfer the documents. In theory the documents will then be passed on to the consignees by the time the goods arrive at the port of discharge so that they can take delivery.

In practice it is not uncommon, particularly in less developed countries, for the bills of lading to be delayed in the banking system until long after the consignees want delivery. In most jurisdictions, whilst shipowners cannot be required to deliver goods without production of the original bills, they may be prepared to do so if an appropriate indemnity is provided, backed by a bank guarantee if necessary. If shipowners are then sued by the true owners of the goods or the due holder of the bill of lading, they may reclaim any sums they have to pay under the indemnity. Such an indemnity would probably be unenforceable on the grounds of fraud if the shipowners did not honestly believe the person taking delivery was entitled to do so. If the original bills are not available, the only alternative for shipowners, who will not want their vessel delayed, is to leave the cargo with an agent with clear instructions not to release it without production of original bills.

The Bills of Lading Act 1855 and the parties to the contract

When the contract of carriage evidenced by the bill of lading comes into existence it will generally be between the shipper and the shipowner. Often, because of the negotiability of the bill of lading, the title to the cargo will have passed when the bill and other shipping documents are negotiated before the cargo is delivered.

This will happen if title to the goods has passed to the consignee or endorsee of the bill of lading upon or by reason of the consignment or endorsement.

The general rule, therefore, is that the bill of lading holder will have title to sue the carrier if the cargo has been damaged in transit. However, there are exceptions to this general rule. One of the exceptions is that if title, under the contract of sale, has passed when the goods are shipped, and not when the bill of lading is negotiated, then the bill of lading holder may not have title to sue the carrier. Another exception arises where there is an undivided bulk cargo. Title to part of the bulk cargo cannot pass until the cargo has been discharged and the various parcels allocated to a particular contract. If the bill of lading has been negotiated before this happens, the bill of lading holder may not have title to sue for shortage or damage.

Where the Act applies the consignor or endorser ceases to be a party to the bill of lading contract so that they can no longer claim under it for, say, damage to the cargo, nor can the shipowner claim against them under it, for example, for freight (see page 172). A contract may be implied between a consignee and the shipowner if the consignee takes delivery of the goods upon presentation of the original bills of lading.

The rights of the shipowner

The primary right of shipowners is to freight. This is the money that is payable to carriers in return for carrying the goods. At common law (which will apply in the absence of any express term of the contract to the contrary) freight is only earned and payable once the goods are delivered at the port of discharge. If they are lost before delivery nothing is payable. Freight is generally calculated according to the size or weight of the cargo. It may sometimes be a "lump-sum freight" where shippers have the use of the whole or a specified part of the vessel. If lump sum freight is agreed it does not matter how much cargo is loaded, the freight will be the same fixed sum. The maximum cargo will be limited by safety and stability considerations because shipowners are entitled to refuse to load more than is prudent.

The bill of lading will usually modify the common law position that freight is not earned until delivery so that it is "deemed earned on shipment" or "deemed earned on signing bills of lading". This is called advance freight and is payable even if the vessel or the goods or both are lost shortly after the event specified, whether shipment or signing of the bills of lading. Freight would not be payable if the cause of the loss was a breach of contract by the carrier which was not within an exemption to liability. If the bill merely states that freight is payable (as opposed to earned) "on shipment" or "on signing bills of lading" then, whilst it must be paid at that time, it is returnable in full if the cargo is not delivered at the port of discharge.

To whom is freight payable?

Freight is normally payable to carriers under the contract of carriage but this is not always so. In practice shippers will normally pay agents who arrange the shipment and they will pass it on. This rarely presents a problem for shippers. However, the position can be more complex where the goods are carried on a chartered vessel. If the vessel is chartered, the carriers under the bill of lading contract may be the vessel owners or the charterers—commonly where they are a liner operator. This is considered further on page 183. Generally the bill of lading freight on goods carried on a chartered vessel will be payable to the charterers who will pay whatever freight or hire is due under the charterparty to the owners. Where the charterers are the carriers under the bill of lading, the bill will stipulate the freight and it will be payable under it. Where the owners are the carriers under the bill of lading, the freight will be agreed and paid between the charterers and the shippers separately. In such circumstances the bill of lading will often provide "freight payable as per charterparty". This will not allow the shipowners to claim freight from the shippers or consignees but may give them a lien "over the cargo" for the freight due under the charterparty from the charterers, allowing them to retain possession of the cargo until they have been paid. This is discussed below.

By whom is freight payable?

If freight prepaid bills of lading are to be issued, then shippers will generally have to pay the freight to obtain the original bills of lading. Such bills are often required under letters of credit for CIF contracts. If the contract of sale between shippers and consignees provides that the latter are to pay the freight, then either they will pay the freight or "freight collect" bills of lading will be issued. Under such bills of lading shipowners need not deliver the cargo until they have been paid the freight and so whether or not the consignees are liable to the carriers in the sense that they could be sued, they will, in practice, have to pay the freight to get delivery of the cargo. It is not uncommon for a charterparty to provide for two sets of bills of lading to be issued. The first are freight collect and the second, freight prepaid, are only to be issued once freight has been paid. Charterers will undertake to surrender the first set and given an indemnity for any losses that shipowners may suffer if they fail to do so.

The right of shipowners to demand payment of freight before giving delivery of the cargo is called a "lien". The possession of the goods gives shipowners security for freight. At common law they only have a lien where freight is earned upon delivery at the port of discharge, not where it is deemed earned earlier. The lien will often be extended by the terms of the bill of lading to cover deemed earned freight and sums due from a charterer to the shipowner, such as demurrage, charterparty freight or salvage. The lien is lost once the shipowner gives up possession of the cargo.

In England under the Merchant Shipping Acts 1894 to 1984, where cargo is shipped into the United Kingdom shipowners may discharge the goods into a warehouse and preserve the lien by giving appropriate notice to the warehouse. The warehouse will hold the goods and may not release them until the consignees pay a deposit in the same amount as that claimed under the lien. The right to this deposit can then be decided by litigation. Many other jurisdictions (particularly in the Commonwealth) have similar provisions which are designed to save time and cost to both shipowners and consignees whilst preserving their rights to be decided in due course.

Consignees may be liable for freight if they are party to the bill of lading contract by virtue of having taken title to the cargo by reason of the consignment of the goods or endorsement of the bill of lading under the Bills of Lading Act 1855. The old common law rules which evolved before 1855 may also make consignees liable if they undertake expressly or implicitly to pay the freight. This may create a separate contract on the terms of the bill of lading between shipowners and consignees if the consignees actually take delivery upon presentation of original bills of lading.

General average

Under common law, where shipowners incur expense or make a sacrifice either of cargo or the vessel (whether all or part) to avert a danger which threatens the safety of the ship and all the cargo (often called "the adventure"), complex rights to apportion the expenditure or sacrifice amongst shipowners, charterers and cargo arise. For example, if part of the cargo catches fire and must be jettisoned to save the vessel and the remaining cargo, the loss is not borne solely by the owners of the jettisoned cargo but may be apportioned between all those interested in the voyage *pro rata* according to the value of their interest. Similarly, if the vessel gets into difficulty and needs to be towed or salvaged to get out of danger, the cost of that is apportioned between those interested in the adventure. It is insufficient if only part of the adventure, for example the cargo, is in peril.

Once general average is declared by shipowners, they will normally instruct an "average adjuster" to prepare a general average adjustment setting out full details of the incident and calculating all the contributions. The rules governing contribution are complex, which is why a specialist average adjuster is instructed. There are two points of importance to cargo interests. The first is that shipowners may only claim general average if the reason the vessel was in danger was not a breach of contract. The second is that it will be the cargo interest who has title at the time of the expenditure or sacrifice that will be liable to pay the general average contribution. This may be the consignees or the shippers, which will depend upon the terms of their contract of sale. However, in practice this does not often cause difficulties because the shipowners have a lien over the cargo for general average contributions and need not release it until security is received. Cargo interests' insurance will normally cover such contributions and the underwriters will generally be prepared to put up a "general average bond" to provide the shipowners with security and allow delivery of the cargo.

Unsafe cargo

Where cargo is unsafe in that it causes damage to the vessel or other cargo, shippers are generally liable to recompense for damage unless they gave notice of the dangerous nature of the cargo before it was delivered to the carriers. This will apply even where the lack of safety arises, not from the nature of the cargo alone, but from the way it is stowed. The liability arises from common law but a term to this effect is probably implied into a bill of lading so that such liability may pass on to a consignee or endorsee of the bill of lading who falls within s. 1 of the Bills of Lading Act 1855.

Shipowners or carriers will generally also have a remedy against charterers since a term will normally be implied into the charterparty that the charterers will not load an unsafe cargo. They will be liable for the costs of discharging it and reloading in a safe manner if this is necessary and is carried out to render the cargo safe.

Claims against the shipowner by cargo interests

The common law position

The most common claims are for cargo damage or shortage, where it is alleged that less was discharged than loaded. At common law carriers are under an absolute obligation to provide a seaworthy vessel at the start of the voyage. The obligation of seaworthiness is very wide and requires that the vessel be fit for the particular voyage carrying the particular cargo in question in the conditions likely to be encountered. It also extends to the vessel's function as a carrier so that it must be fit to carry the particular cargo safely on the voyage.

The second important implied obligation upon the carriers is that the vessel will commence and carry out the voyage with reasonable *diligent* dispatch. This requires carriers to take care to complete the voyage as quickly as is reasonable. They will be liable for delay if they fail to do so.

The third important implied obligation is that carriers must carry out the voyage without unreasonable deviation. They must take the usual or customary route from the port of loading to the port of discharge unless they have a justifiable reason not to. Such a reason may be to save life or to assist a vessel in distress. The usual or customary route is taken to be the most direct geographical route unless it is shown to be otherwise.

These obligations are, in the vast majority of cases, modified by express contractual terms in the bill of lading or by the application of statute law incorporating the Hague or Hague-Visby Rules. In practice this old common law does not merit detailed examination but is relevant since the express contractual terms and statutes operate by modifying the common law position.

The right to bring a claim

Generally there are at least two parties involved on the cargo side, the shippers and the consignees. There may be many more. In some markets, such as oil trading, where the cargo is shipped on a CIF basis, there may be a chain of sale contracts with ten or more parties. It is a vexed problem to sort out which party or parties have the right to bring claims. To the lawyer the party or parties who can bring a good claim have "title to sue". This involves showing not merely that they have a cause of action (perhaps because they had a contract with the shipowners) but also that they have suffered a substantial loss. The difficulties are not merely academic but have great practical significance because for most cargo claims legal proceedings must be commenced on behalf of the correct party within one year of discharge or the claim is time barred. If it is only realised after one year who is the correct party, then whatever the merits of the claim the carrier is free from all liability. A claim may be brought for breach of contract, in tort or both.

As has been explained above, the bill of lading will generally provide evidence of the contract of carriage. The parties to that contract will be the carrier and the shipper unless the contract has been transferred to a subsequent holder of the bill of lading within the terms of the Bills of Lading Act 1855. It is not sufficient to be the holder of the bill; that holder must have taken title by reason of the consignment of the goods or by endorsement of the bill to him or her. If the holder has not taken title to the cargo or did so at some other time, that person falls outside the Act and will generally have no claim in contract. As mentioned above, consignees who fall outside the Act may be able to rely upon an implied contract where they present the bills of lading to the carrier and are given delivery. Charterers may have a contractual claim under the charterparty if either they have an interest in the goods or they are exposed to a claim by cargo interests. Their claim will normally fall under the charterparty rather than the bill of lading (see page 183).

To bring a claim in contract it is merely necessary to establish the contract and breach of it. However, to recover anything more than nominal damages it is necessary to show a loss. There has been a flurry of recent case law on this question but it will generally be sufficient for claimants to show that they had title to the goods or the right to possession of them. It is not generally necessary to show that they had the risk of loss under the sale contract.

Carriers will owe a duty of care by virtue of their possession of the goods. They are said to be a bailee of the goods. The duties they owe are called tortious duties and they are obliged to take reasonable care in the carriage and custody of the goods. These duties arise outside any contract but will almost always be varied by the contract. To bring a claim in tort the claimants must establish that at the time the tort was committed (for example the negligent act or delivery to the wrong person) they either had title to the cargo or the right to possession as against the carriers. The holder of the bill of lading will normally have the right to possession.

The Hague and Hague-Visby Rules

In the early part of this century it was thought in many countries that it was important for international trade to be governed by regulating the relationship between carriers and cargo interests which would be similar in whatever country the claim was brought. The rules were agreed in 1921 between delegates from a number of countries. The agreement is known as the Hague Convention. The rules became known as the Hague Rules. These rules only deal with carriage covered by bill of lading contracts and will apply if either the contract expressly says so or a statute, applicable in the jursidiction where the proceedings are brought, provides that they are to apply. This book can only deal with English law and so only considers the current English statute, but there is a discussion of the problems arising where claims are brought in other jurisdictions in Chapter 10.

The 1924 Carriage of Goods by Sea Act incorporated the Hague Rules to all contracts for the carriage of goods from the United Kingdom. In 1977, the 1971 Carriage of Goods by Sea Act came into force and repealed the 1924 Act. In 1968 some of the countries which were parties to the Hague Convention agreed that it should be amended in material respects and so signed the Brussels Protocol. The 1971 Carriage of Goods by Sea Act put into effect those amendments and applies the amended rules known as the Hague-Visby Rules. The earlier Act was repealed and so the English courts will not apply the Hague Rules unless they are expressly incorporated and the 1971 Act is inapplicable. The main cases in which this Act applies the Hague-Visby Rules as a matter of law to bill of lading contracts and irrespective of the express terms of the contract are:

(a) where shipment is from a port in the United Kingdom
(b) where shipment is from, or the bill of lading is issued in, a state which is a party to the Brussels Protocol
(c) where the contract provides that it is to be governed by the legislation of any state giving effect to the rules.

The rules will not apply as a matter of law in the following cases:

(a) where shipment was not out of a state party to the Brussels Protocol even if it is a party to the original Hague Convention
(b) to shipments not covered by a bill of lading unless the contract expressly states they are to apply
(c) to carriage of live animals or carriage of deck cargo where the bill expressly states that the carriage is to be on deck. Where there is merely a liberty to carry on deck the carrier may load on deck but the rules still apply.

Shipments into the United Kingdom will only be subject to the Hague-Visby Rules if the shipment was from (or the bill of lading was issued in) a state which is a party to the Brussels Protocol or the bill expressly applies the rules or legislation giving effect to the rules. It is doubtful that it is sufficient that the bill is subject to English law. At the end of this chapter is a schedule setting out the states which are parties to the Brussels Protocol and those which are only party to the Hague Convention.

Where the rules apply as a matter of law, shipowners may not reduce their liability and any provision attempting to do so will be struck out. This includes a clause purporting to make the contract subject to another law or jurisdiction with lower limits of liability (see page 185).

A clause in a bill of lading which incorporates either the Hague or Hague-Visby Rules is often called a clause paramount. It may incorporate legislation giving effect to either set of rules (such as the United Kingdom Carriage of Goods by Sea Act 1924) or the American Carriage of Goods by Sea Act 1936) or it may directly incorporate the set of rules. These clauses are very common and most bills of lading will incorporate all or at least some of the rules.

The scheme of liability under the Hague-Visby Rules

The rules are set out in ten articles with numerous sub-rules in each article. Article III sets out the general responsibility of the carrier and Article IV sets out the exceptions to the carrier's liability.

Under Article III, the carrier is to exercise due diligence to make the ship seaworthy and make the holds fit and safe for the carriage of goods. The carrier must also properly and carefully load, stow, carry and discharge the goods.

When the obligations commence and when they cease can be a difficult question. Carriers are responsible for loading but when that responsibility commences will be determined by the express terms of the contract and custom at the port. The same applies to discharging. Carriers may be responsible for collecting the goods from the warehouse or merely from the time when the goods cross the ship's rail. Similarly they may be responsible for delivery of the goods to the consignee's premises or merely for putting them on the quay. The rule merely requires that they be responsible for loading, discharging and the ocean voyage. Under a through bill, the ocean carrier may be responsible for carriage on land and this may be subject to the Hague-Visby Rules.

Article IV provides the exceptions upon which the carrier can rely, provided it has exercised due diligence to make the ship seaworthy as it is bound to do under Article III. There are seventeen exceptions listed, the most important of which are those which exempt the carrier from liability if there has been neglect on the part of the master in the navigation or management of the ship; perils of the sea; inherent defect or vice of the goods carried; and any cause arising without the actual fault of the carrier.

The bill of lading description of the cargo

The description is of great importance if a cargo claim for damage or short delivery is brought since it will normally be the basis of the claimant's case.

The information on the bill of lading will probably be provided by the shipper, but the carrier should check it and the information should not be inserted in the bill if there are reasonable grounds for doubting its accuracy.

If the information supplied by the shippers is not accurate, Article III rule 5 gives the carrier a right of indemnity for any losses suffered as a result of the inaccuracy, such as a cargo claim.

(a) *Common law estoppel*
This is where a clean bill of lading is issued. The carrier is estopped or precluded from alleging, as against an endorsee of the bill, that the goods were not in apparent good order and condition on shipment. This estoppel does not apply to statements as to quantity because it was held in a case 150 years ago that the master or other agent of the carrier has no authority to issue a bill for goods that have not been shipped.

(b) *The Hague-Visby Rules, Article III rule 4*
The bill of lading will be *prima facie* evidence that the goods were received by the carrier in accordance with the description. It is for the carrier to show that they were not. Where the bill is in the hands of a third party the description is conclusive and the carrier cannot adduce contrary evidence unless the third party knew that the description was inaccurate when the bill was transferred. Both limbs of Article III rule 4 will apply, where, as bills almost invariably do, it is stated that the goods were shipped in apparent good order and condition. An endorsement such as "condition unknown" will not prevent the application of the rule.

In practice where carriers have reservations about the apparent condition and order of the goods they must delete the representation that the goods were shipped in apparent good order and condition or they will be unable to dispute this with a consignee. Otherwise they would be left seeking an indemnity from the shippers under Article III rule 5 or against a charterer if they signed the bills on the carrier's behalf.

Article IV rule 5: package damage claim limitation

This rule provides a formula so that the amount the carrier is liable for in connection with cargo damage claims can be calculated. There is express reference to containers, so that the number of packages or units listed on the bill of lading as packed in a container shall be the number of packages or units of account for the purposes of limitation.

The unit of account is called the SDR (special drawing right) and the value of an SDR in currency is published regularly in such papers as *Lloyd's List*, and the *Financial Times*.

The claimants may be able to recover more than these limits if the carrier has agreed to this in the contract, or if a higher figure has been notified by the shipper before shipment and the figure is declared on the bill. If a higher value is declared, the freight will be higher since the carrier's responsibility is greater. By rule 5(e) carriers cannot limit their liability to a sum less than that provided for in the rule.

The limits will not apply if the damage was caused deliberately or recklessly by the carrier. It probably must be the carrier rather than a servant who acts deliberately or recklessly, so that a claim arising from crew pilferage would still be subject to the limits.

The time-bar

Article III rule 6 gives carriers an absolute defence to any claim "in respect of the goods" unless suit has been brought within one year of delivery or, if the consignment is lost, on the date when they should have been delivered. Suit includes an arbitration which may often be necessary if the cargo claimant is the charterer and the claim is brought under the charterparty. If the claim can be brought in arbitration either because it is under a charterparty or the bill of lading has an arbitration clause, it may be possible to bring a claim after one year if undue hardship can be shown under s. 27 of the Arbitration Act 1950, so that the court may give leave.

The parties may agree to extend time but it is very important to ensure that the extension is confirmed in writing by someone with authority to do so on behalf of the carriers.

The position of carriers' servants, agents and sub-contractors

Article IV rules (2), (3) and (4) give servants or agents the same protection and limits of liability as carriers. The total amount that can be recovered from carriers, their servants and agents cannot in aggregate exceed the limit. As for carriers, the limits do not apply if the loss or damage was caused deliberately or recklessly by their servants or agents.

Independent contractors fall outside these provisions but can be protected by provision in the bill of lading. Such a clause will expressly state that independent contractors are to have the same protection as carriers. These clauses are called "Himalaya" clauses after the name of the vessel in one of the first cases to consider such a clause. The Privy Council held in 1980 that such a clause was effective because a separate contract came into being between the independent contractor and cargo interests. The case involved stevedores who clearly fall outside the Article IV but the line between an agent and an independent contractor can be a hard one to draw.

The role of insurers in cargo claims

The vast majority of shipowners and most time charterers who issue bills of lading with themselves as carriers have liability insurance which covers cargo claims. This is normally by membership of mutual insurance associations commonly known as protection and indemnity associations or, in short, P and I clubs. Since, subject to a deduction, the clubs will pay for most cargo claims brought against their members, they will be involved in the handling of the claim, appointing lawyers and surveyors and overseeing the claim generally. The principle on which such clubs were run originally in the 19th century was that each member would pay a share of the estimated losses at the start of the year and at the end of each year they would all share the excess or shortfall. The position is now more complex, with intricate schemes of reinsurance. Each owner's contributions (known as calls) will not be equal and are determined by a consideration of the claims record of their vessel or fleet, so that even if the deduction is small they retain a strong interest in minimising claims.

On the cargo side, where there is a damage or loss claim the insured will first look to the underwriter. The underwriter will have to take a decision on whether to pay the claim reasonably promptly because of the one year time bar. Once the claim has been paid to the insured the underwriters may claim against the carriers by virtue of their rights of subrogation. In practice, the majority of cargo claims are brought by underwriters although they must do so in the name of the insured. This can frequently cause difficulties for underwriters in ensuring that proceedings are commenced within the time bar in the name of a party with title to sue. Underwriters will often instruct a recovery agent who specialises in handling claims, instructing lawyers and surveyors. The recovery agent's remuneration is a percentage of the recovery.

Carriage under charterparties

The types of charterparty

A charter is the contract between the charterers and the owners for the hire of the vessel. The document which contains the terms of the contract is called the charterparty. Broadly there are three main categories of charter although there are various hybrids combining the features of more than one category.

The first category is bare boat charters (also called demise charters) whereby the owners of a vessel hire it out with all its equipment for a fixed period of time. Payment is called hire and is made per month or other convenient period. The charterers will put their own crew on board and operate the vessel as if it were their own. This form of charter is often merely a vehicle for financing the operation or acquisition of the vessel by the charterers and can be roughly analogous to a hire purchase agreement if it has a purchase option. The shippers of goods are not normally concerned about such charterers since, for most purposes, the bare boat charterers are treated as being the registered owners.

The second category is that of time charters. The charterers will hire the vessel and crew for a fixed period of time, paying hire based purely on the time the vessel is chartered. The fuel used is paid for by the charterers, who are entitled to direct the vessel wherever they wish, subject to any contractual trading limits and questions of safety. The time charterers may sub-charter to others, when for the purposes of the sub-charter they are called the disponent owners. Alternatively they may be a liner operator who, rather than using their own vessels for the service, have chartered in a vessel. For this reason time charterparties often give the charterers liberty to paint the line's mark or symbol on the vessel. This chapter does not consider the details of time charters except insofar as they affect carriage under a sub-voyage charter or a bill of lading.

The third category of charter is that of voyage charterers. Here the owners agree that the vessel and crew will perform a specific voyage from one or more load ports to one or more discharge ports. Sometimes the charterers have options as to the load and discharge ports. The charterers will provide when and where the vessel has to be ready to commence loading. Normally the owners are given a range of days (called laydays) within which the vessel must arrive at or off the load port; if it is late the charterers may cancel the charter.

The charterers' payment for the use of the vessel for the transport of goods is called freight and is either calculated according to the weight of cargo loaded, or it is a fixed figure known as lump sum freight. The charterparty will either provide that the charterers should load a certain quantity of cargo or, more usually, that they will load full cargo, subject to trim and safety factors. If less is loaded the owners will have a claim in damages for the freight that they have not earned (thus called dead freight).

In negotiating the freight provision in the charterparty the owners will consider how long the voyage should last and how long loading and discharge should take. The former is within their control but the latter is not, so the charterparty will provide the number of days that loading and discharge should take. This period is called the laytime. If loading or discharge takes longer than the laytime, the owners are entitled to damages at a figure per day, fixed by the charterparty and called demurrage. If less than the laytime is used the charterers receive money back, calculated in the same way and known as despatch. Often the daily despatch rate is half the demurrage rate. There are very complex legal rules for deciding when laytime commences to run and when it is suspended. Often non-working days, periods of rain and strikes are excluded from laytime, so that such periods are effectively for owners' accounts.

There are many different standard form charterparties used for a variety of trades and purposes. They are almost invariably amended or added to to suit the needs of the parties. The charterparties should state the law which is to govern the contract and will commonly provide for arbitration in a particular jurisdiction or place. Under English law the relations between owners and charterers are almost exclusively governed by the common law and so, unlike carriage under bills of lading, it is not normally necessary to be concerned with statutes. It is open to the parties to agree whatever terms they wish, although usual practice will dictate that the agreement has certain customary features.

The shipper as charterer

Where a shipper (whether an exporter under a CIF contract or an importer under an FOB contract) wishes to ship a large cargo, typically a bulk consignment, it will often be cheaper to charter a vessel of the appropriate size to carry the whole shipment.

The usual form of contract will be a voyage charterparty. This is illustrated by Figure 7.2 which shows the relationships between the parties where there is a time charter and a voyage charter under it. Bills of lading will be issued in the usual way. They may be issued by the carriers or an agent, or the charterparty may provide that the charterers can issue bills on the carriers' behalf. The relationship between the shippers/charterers and the carriers will remain governed by the charterparty, and the bill of lading will not be evidence of the contract of carriage between them. However, as usual it will be a receipt for the goods and a document of title. A cargo claim brought by the charterers must therefore be brought under the charterparty. The Hague and Hague-Visby Rules will not apply to such a claim unless the charterparty expressly incorporates them. This is sometimes done. If it is not, the common law will govern the claim, subject to any express terms and exceptions in the charterparty. Where the charterers/shippers transfer the bill of lading either to an endorsee who takes title to the goods by reason of this endorsement, or a consignee who takes title by reason of the consignment, under the Bills of Lading Act 1855 a contract comes into being between the endorsee or consignee and the carriers on the terms of the bill of lading. There are conceptual difficulties as to how this can happen but the courts have adopted a pragmatic approach to reach this sensible result.

Who is the carrier under the bills of lading?

In the discussion above the carrier was the owner of the vessel. Where there is a charterparty this is not always the case. In particular it is common for liner operators to time charter vessels for the liner service, perhaps when one of their own fleet is unavailable. Liner operators will normally use their own standard form of ("house") bill of lading. The bills may provide that the carrier is the liner operator. If so then the liner operator will be the carrier under the contract and for the purpose of the Hague-Visby Rules. Generally any claim would have to be brought against this party. It may be possible to bring a claim against the owners of the vessel for negligence in tort or for breach of the duties owed as bailees of the cargo. Sometimes such a claim is brought because it may be easier to get security for the claim against the owners, rather than the charterers, by arresting the vessel.

The liner operator may not wish to be the carrier under the contract and may insert a "demise" or "identity of carrier" clause into the bill.

This clause usually states that if the ship is not owned or demise chartered by the line issuing the bill, then the contract takes effect with the owner of the vessel or demise charterer as principal, with the line only acting as an agent. Such a clause is effective under English law.

Sometimes the bill of lading does not make it clear who the carriers are and it can be very difficult to identify them. If the bill is signed by the master, or by the charterer as the master's authorised agent (usually an express power under the charterparty), the contract is with the owner.

Indemnity from charterers to shipowners

Where charterers issue the bills of lading, whether under a voyage or time charter, owners will normally have an express or implied indemnity from the charterers if they are exposed to a greater liability under the bills than under the charterparty. For example, if the charterers issue through bills of lading this may expose the owners to liability for loss or damage to the cargo other than on the ocean leg. This indemnity is express in most time charters, under which it is more common than under voyage charters for the charterers to be authorised to issue bills of lading on the owners' behalf.

Jurisdiction and applicable law for claims

Thus far the discussion has assumed that the contracts are governed by English law and that the legal issues would be litigated upon in the English courts or in English arbitration. For claims under charterparties, the forum where claims may be brought and the applicable law are usually provided for by requiring claims to be brought in arbitration in a particular place. This will generally fix the applicable law as that of the place of the arbitration. Many, though not all, courts around the world will decline to hear claims where the contract provides for arbitration elsewhere and stay proceedings in favour of the arbitration.

Claims under bills of lading are more difficult. Often there is no jurisdiction or choice of law clause. The main circumstances in which the English courts can hear claims are:

(a) where the contract is governed by English law
(b) there was a breach of contract in England
(c) the defendant is based in England or has a place of business there, or
(d) a tort has been committed there.

They can also hear claims where proceedings have been served on a vessel in the same ownership as a defendant carrier whilst it is in territorial waters. Even if the courts can exercise jurisdiction, they will not do so if those of another country are clearly more appropriate.

In many countries, as in England, it is possible to arrest a vessel in the same ownership as the carriers' ship. It will only be released if the owners or the P and I club provide security for the claim. Such an arrest will often allow the local courts to try the substantive case.

The courts in some countries will not recognise either a clause attempting to require all claims to be brought in a particular country or that the contract be governed by a particular law.

It is not possible to draft a bill of lading to take account of the law of all the countries where claims may be made. It is, however, possible to see whether the countries have adopted the Hague or Hague-Visby Rules and therefore to consider in what circumstances the courts of those countries will apply the rules. We have already seen when the courts of a party to the Brussels Protocol will apply the Hague-Visby Rules.

Carriers may face claims in a variety of jurisdictions. The claimants are likely to attempt to bring against the carriers a claim in:

(a) the place of shipment
(b) the place of delivery
(c) the place of residence of the carriers
(d) a place where they can arrest a vessel owned by the carriers.

In general the Hague Rules only apply if the country is a party to the Hague Convention but not the Brussels Protocol, and either the contract expressly incorporates the rules or shipment was out of that country or another also party to the Hague Convention but not the Brussels Protocol. It is because of the uncertainty about when the rules will apply by statute in the form where a claim is brought that the clause paramount is commonly inserted in bills of lading.

Schedule

States which are parties to the Hague Convention or the Brussels Protocol.

(a) The Hague Convention and the Hague Rules

Algeria
Angola
Argentina
Australia
Bahamas
Barbados
Belgium
Bolivia
Cameroon
Cape Verde Islands
Cuba
Cyprus
Denmark
Dominican Republic
Ecuador
Egypt
Fiji
Finland
France
Gambia
Ghana
Goa
Grenada
Guinea Bissau
Guyana
Hungary
Iran
Ireland
Israel
Ivory Coast
Jamaica
Japan
Kenya
Kiribati
Kuwait
Lebanon
Malagasy Republic
Malaya
Malaysia
Mauritius
Monaco
Mozambique
Nauru
Nigeria
Norway
Palestine
Papua New Guinea
Paraguay
Peru
Poland
Portugal
Romania
Sabah
Saint Lucia
São Tome and Principe
Sarawak
Senegal
Seychelles
Sierra Leone
Singapore
Solomon Islands
Somalia
Spain
Sri Lanka
Sweden
Switzerland
Syria
Tanzania
Timor
Tonga
Trinidad and Tobago
Turkey
Tuvalu
USA
West Germany
Yugoslavia
Zaire

(b) The Brussels Protocol and the Hague-Visby Rules

Belgium
Bermuda
Denmark
East Germany
Ecuador
Egypt
Finland
France
Hong Kong
Italy
Lebanon
Netherlands
Norway
Poland
Singapore
Spain
Sri Lanka
Sweden
Switzerland
Syria
Tonga
United Kingdom
West Germany

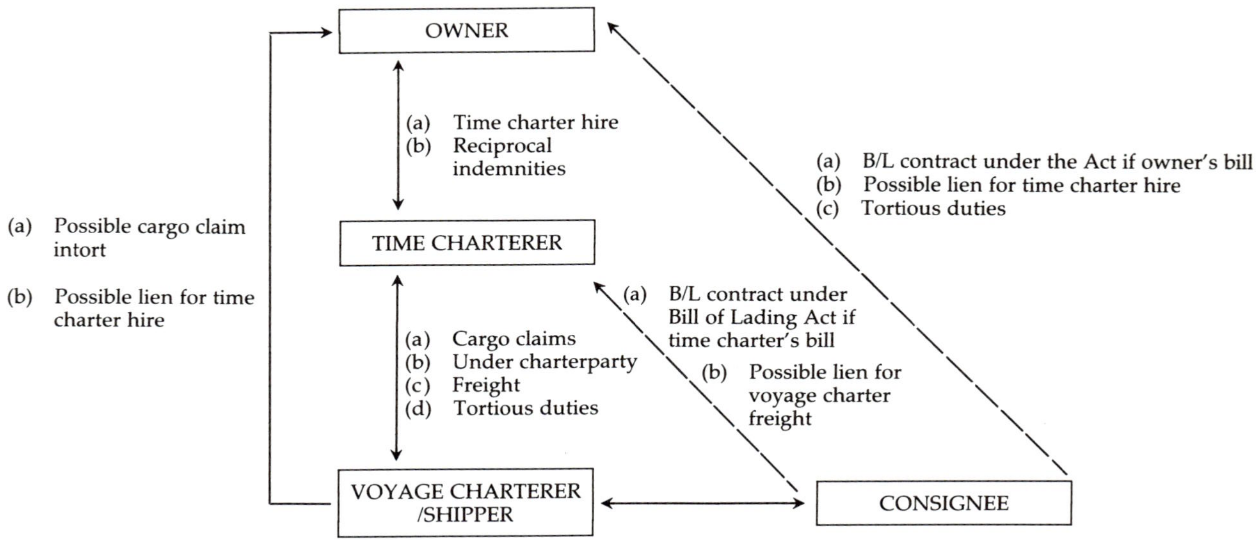

Figure 7.2 Position under voyage charterparty

8

Performance of a contract

Introduction

This chapter deals with the performance of the contract by both sides when the time comes for the goods to be handed over and paid for. Thus the chapter starts with the obligations of sellers and buyers in respect of delivery of the goods, namely the handing over of the goods themselves and what happens if problems arise at this stage. It then deals with the quantity of the goods to be handed over and also questions of title. This covers problems which may arise if the sellers have no right to sell the goods. This is to some extent connected with the transfer of ownership or title which is dealt with under the heading of "property". At what stage do the buyers become the owners of the goods and at what stage does this ownership pass from the sellers to the buyers? Closely connected with this is the question of risk. That is, if the goods are lost or damaged, who bears the responsibility to pay for them—the sellers or the buyers? This has importance in connection with the question of insurance.

The next section deals with frustration: circumstances in which the contract comes to an end as a result of extraneous events which occur after the contract has been agreed, and which prevent the contract from being carried out. Finally, there are short sections on the acceptance of the goods by the buyers and their obligation to pay for them.

Delivery of goods

The sellers of goods must deliver them to the buyers and the buyers must accept and pay for them, as set out in the contract of sale. This is laid down by s. 27 of the Sale of Goods Act 1979. Delivery means the transfer of possession of the goods and does not mean transfer of title to the goods or ownership. The passing of title or ownership is called the passing of property *in* the goods. The transfer of possession of the goods usually involves the physical transfer of possession, but delivery can also be given by the transfer of documents which represent the goods, as in a CIF contract.

The sellers and the buyers are free to agree whatever they like, in their contract, concerning the time at which delivery is to take place and the time at which payment is to occur.

Buyers should be aware that if they accept late delivery they will only be able to sue sellers for damages for breach of a warranty and not condition. If a seller telephones the buyer and asks for approval for late delivery, and the buyer agrees, the right to insist upon delivery within the original time will have been waived.

If a seller is in breach of the contract term as to delivery, this does not necessarily constitute a repudiation of the contract which the buyer can accept as bringing the agreement to an end. This is especially so in the context of instalment contracts. In such contracts the sellers agree to deliver the goods in separate instalments or parcels over a period of time. If they do not deliver one of the instalments on time or do not deliver it at all, the buyers will not be able to treat this breach as putting an end to the contract. Breaches of instalment contracts are a matter of fact and degree and each case must be looked at separately in order to determine whether the buyers can terminate the contract.

There are some breaches in connection with delivery which do amount to a breach of condition. If the sellers fail to deliver the goods at all this will be breach of condition. The general rule, also, is that if the sellers do not comply with the time of delivery set out in the contract, they may also be in breach of condition. In commercial contracts time clauses are usually treated as being very important, and a breach of such a clause will usually entitle the buyers to terminate the agreement. However it must be emphasised that this is the general rule and it gives way to any express wording in the contract.

If the sellers are in breach of a condition by not complying with the delivery clauses in the contract, the acceptance of the repudiation by the buyers brings the contract to an end. The buyers do not take delivery and can sue for damages.

The delivery of the goods by the sellers to the buyers can take many forms. The sellers can simply transfer the physical possession of the goods to the buyers, and this is perhaps the most usual method.

The terms of the contract may provide that the sellers are authorised or required to send the goods to the buyers and if this is the case delivery of the goods by the sellers to an independent carrier for carriage to the buyers will amount to delivery to the buyers themselves (s. 32(1) of the Sale of Goods Act 1979).

In these circumstances the contract made by the sellers with the carriers must be reasonable (s. 32(2) of the Sale of Goods Act 1979) and the sellers are under no duty to insure the goods for transit risks unless the contract says so or it is customary in that particular trade for a seller to do so. If sea carriage is involved, the sellers should give notice to the buyers in sufficient time to enable the latter to insure the goods for transit damage (s. 32(3) of the Sale of Goods Act 1979).

Quantity

If the sellers fail to deliver the exact quantity, the buyers can reject a tender of short delivery. If, however, the buyers accept a short delivery, the goods must be paid for. Otherwise the buyers are entitled to reject short delivery and either sue the sellers for damages or for the return of the purchase price. If the contract is one for delivery by instalments, a short delivery in one instalment will not entitle the buyers to terminate the whole contract.

If the sellers deliver too much, the buyers can reject the goods or accept and pay for them.

In cases both of short delivery and over delivery, the amount under or over must not be so small that it makes no real difference.

In some contracts sellers insert an exemption clause which is intended to restrict the right of the buyers to reject. These clauses are strictly interpreted and may fall foul of the Unfair Contract Terms Act 1977.

Buyers are also entitled to reject goods which have been mixed in with other items.

Sellers are not entitled to deliver goods by instalments unless this has been agreed between the parties. The usual rule is that a breach of contract involving an instalment must be considered in the light of the contract as a whole. In deciding whether a non-acceptance by a buyer of an instalment, or a failure by a seller to deliver an instalment or delivery of a defective instalment, entitles the innocent party to terminate the contract, the breach must go to the root of the contract. This will depend upon the facts of the particular case. The question to be asked is what proportion of goods out of the whole contract has been affected and is the problem likely to happen again? If the breaches are not sufficiently serious to enable the buyer to terminate the contract, then future instalments must be accepted. A buyer can reject an instalment, but the contract will continue and future instalments will have to be accepted.

In these contracts, payment is usually made against delivery of an instalment. If a buyer has a right to sue for damages for non-delivery of an instalment, the measure will be the difference between the contract price and the market price when the instalment was to be delivered.

Title

There is an implied condition that sellers have the right to sell the goods or will have this right when the property or ownership in the goods is passed to the buyers. This is a strict liability and if there is a breach the buyers may treat the contract as at an end and sue the sellers for damages (s. 12(1) of the Sale of Goods Act 1979).

If buyers accept goods then the right of rejection is lost and they are not entitled to terminate the contract, but have the remedy of suing for damages (s. 11(4) of the Sale of Goods Act 1979).

There is also an implied warranty that goods are free from any charge or incumbrance when sold, unless the buyers have been told about these in advance (s. 12(2) (a) of the Sale of Goods Act 1979).

There is also an implied warranty that the buyers are entitled to quiet possession of the goods. This means that no-one else is legally entitled to seize goods in the hands of the buyers and also that if the buyers deal with the goods in any way there will be no infringement of a patent or similar right (s. 12(2) (b) of the Sale of Goods Act 1979). The buyers' remedy for breaches of these warranties is to sue for damages.

Sellers cannot exclude s. 12 of the Sale of Goods Act 1979 by the terms of the contract. This is laid down by the Unfair Contract Terms Act 1977. However the Unfair Contract Terms Act 1977 does not apply to contracts for the international sale of goods.

Property

Property in the goods means ownership or title. When property passes from the seller to the buyer, the seller is transferring ownership of the goods to the buyer. The general rule is that property passes when the parties intend it to pass and this may be expressed in terms in the contract. If the contract does not cover, expressly, the passing of property, then the guidelines laid down in the Sale of Goods Act 1979 must be applied.

The terms of the contract must be examined, together with the conduct of the parties and all the surrounding circumstances.

As far as specific goods are concerned, property passes to the buyer when the contract is made, even though delivery and payment may be later (s. 18 of the Sale of Goods Act 1979).

Specific goods means goods which are identified and agreed on at the time the contract of sale is made.

If the sellers are to put the goods into a state fit for delivery, property does not pass until this has been done and notice has been given to the buyers that it has been completed. This rule also applies if the sellers have to weigh or measure the goods in order to work out the price. In this case property does not pass until the weighing or measuring has been done and the buyers have been told the result.

As far as unascertained goods are concerned they must first become ascertained and then the property will pass when the parties intend this to happen. The simplest example of unascertained goods is a part or parcel of the bulk cargo which has not yet been separated from the bulk.

In the case of a sale from the bulk cargo, the part or parcel must be separated from the bulk, for example on discharge, before the parcel can become ascertained and before property can pass.

Usually property also does not pass unless and until the goods have been unconditionally appropriated to the contract. This means that the goods have been selected and can be identified, for example by separation from a larger bulk. The sellers and buyers must be able to point to goods and state that they belong to that contract rather than any other. If the sellers and buyers can do this, the goods have been appropriated to the contract.

Sellers may reserve the right of disposal of the goods until payment has been received. That means that if payment is not received, they are free to sell the goods elsewhere. If sellers do reserve this right of disposal, the goods have not been appropriated unconditionally to the contract.

As far as future goods are concerned (that is goods which will come into existence in the future) property will pass when they have been manufactured and appropriated to the contract with the agreement of the buyers. Once again the important element is the intention of the parties and the terms of the contract.

If sellers deliver goods to the buyers or to a carrier for carriage to the buyers, and do not reserve a right of disposal, those goods will be treated as being unconditionally appropriated to the contract. This applies to goods which have been ascertained and not to goods which form part of a larger bulk.

The most common case of sellers reserving the right of disposal concerns the time of payment. They will often reserve the right of disposal until payment has been made. If sellers do reserve their rights in this way, then property does not pass until payment has been made.

Risk

The general rule is that goods are at the sellers' risk until the property has passed to the buyers, and when property has passed the goods are then at the buyers' risk whether or not they have been delivered to them (s. 20(1) of the Sale of Goods Act 1979).

This rule applies unless the parties agree otherwise in their contract. Such an agreement can be set out by the express wording of the contract, by custom of the trade or by a course of business trading over a period of time.

The importance of risk and whether it is borne by the sellers or the buyers is in the realms of insurance. If a party has an insurable risk they can insure that risk irrespective of whether they own the goods or not.

If delivery has been delayed through the fault of the buyers or the sellers, the goods will be at the risk of the party at fault should loss or damage occur as a result of the delay (s. 20(2) of the Sale of Goods Act 1979).

If property passes to the buyers when the sellers deliver the goods to a carrier, the usual rule is that risk will pass at the same time.

Frustration

The contract may be frustrated when, after it has been made and the ownership of the goods is still with the sellers, the contract becomes incapable of being performed, or performance, if it took place, would be of a radically different kind from that contemplated by the parties at the time the contract was made. This situation must also come about through no fault of one side or the other.

Questions of frustration usually arise in connection with contracts for the sale of specific goods and are rarely met in connection with the sale of unascertained goods. This is because in a sale of unascertained goods, the sellers usually have to find the goods from any source. If one source breaks down then the sellers must find another. However, even in contracts for the sale of unascertained goods a frustrating event may occur, such as the passing of legislation dealing with the goods in question (for example a prohibition on export from a country which is the only source of the goods, or the outbreak of war). If a contract becomes more expensive to perform because of change of circumstances, this in itself will not amount to frustration.

In the case of frustration, the Law Reform (Frustrated Contracts) Act 1943 will apply, although not to specific goods which have perished.

The Act provides that any money paid by one side or the other before frustration occurs is recoverable by the party who has paid it. Money which is due to be paid will no longer be payable. If one side is to repay money to the other, the court may allow that side to deduct expenses which have been incurred before the contract became frustrated.

If one side has obtained a valuable benefit, before the contract became frustrated, as a result of something which has been done by the other side, the value of the benefit may be recoverable.

It is possible for a seller and a buyer to contemplate that frustration might take place and agree specific terms to cover what happens in these circumstances. If the parties have decided to do this, then what they have agreed must be put into effect.

The most difficult problems arise when sellers have many contracts and there is a trade embargo or prohibition, and the sellers' source of goods is restricted. The courts have not yet decided whether the sellers, in these circumstances, are to fulfil in full as many contracts as they can, leaving other buyers unsatisfied, and claim frustration in respect of those contracts, or whether they are obliged to deliver a lesser quantity of goods to each buyer.

Acceptance

Acceptance takes place when the buyers inform the sellers that the goods have been accepted or when the goods are delivered to the buyers and they carry out any act in connection with the goods which is inconsistent with the sellers' ownership or keep the goods without telling the sellers that they have been rejected (s. 35 of the Sale of Goods Act 1979).

Acceptance of the goods is obviously very closely connected with taking delivery. The time when the buyers accept the goods will usually be when they have been delivered by the sellers. For example, buyers may indicate non-acceptance of the goods by refusing to take delivery of them. In the same way, by taking delivery of the goods buyers may be regarded as having accepted them and lost any right to reject the goods for breach of condition of the contract.

Payment

The obligation is upon the buyers to pay for the goods and this is usually set out in the contract. It is therefore important to examine the contract first to see what terms govern the obligation to pay, namely how and when. Usually, delivery of the goods and payment for them are concurrent conditions (s. 28 of the Sale of Goods Act 1979). If the buyers offer a reduction in the price,.the sellers may be able to accept this lower sum on account and sue for the balance up to the full price. The sellers will not be able to do so if there is an extra factor involved which provides some kind of benefit to them, for example if a reduction in the price is offered and payment is to be made earlier than would be the case with the full price. If the sellers then accept a reduction at this earlier time, they may not be able subsequently to sue for the balance.

If the buyers fail to pay, the sellers may treat the contract as at an end. This will be the case if the time of payment is of the essence of the contract. The sellers may also treat the contract as at an end if the buyers state that they are not going to pay for the goods at all.

As far as the kind of payment is concerned, this will usually be set out in the contract. If the contract is silent on the point, the buyers must pay the price in cash at the time and place set out in the contract. As far as the time of payment is concerned, again this is usually set out in the contract. Clauses in the contract as to time of payment are not of the essence of the contract, unless this appears to be the case from the agreement itself (s. 10(1) of the Sale of Goods Act 1979). This means that if time is not of the essence, and the buyers do not make payment in time, the sellers cannot treat the contract as at an end and sell the goods to someone else. However, if the buyers state that they are not going to pay at all, then the sellers can treat this as a repudiation and terminate the contract. S. 48(3) of the Sale of Goods Act 1979 provides that if sellers are not paid and the goods are perishable, or where sellers tell the buyers that they are going to resell, and the buyers do not pay within a reasonable time, the sellers are entitled to sell the goods elsewhere. In these circumstances the contract will come to an end.

A contract very often grants to the buyers a period of credit. In these circumstances obviously the buyers are not bound to pay until the period of credit has expired. During this period, the sellers must still carry out their own obligations under the contract and deliver the goods. If the buyers become insolvent, the sellers, being unpaid, have a right to stop delivery of the goods to the buyers and to sell the goods elsewhere.

9

When things go wrong—remedies

Introduction

When a problem arises, it is important that the parties know what action they may *themselves* take with impunity to protect their position, and where it is necessary to get assistance from the court. The distinction is particularly important when third parties are involved. We shall examine the difficulties that can arise from both a buyer's and a seller's point of view. The discussion assumes "classic" contracts, although we shall consider briefly, at the end of this section, some fairly standard provisions in sale and purchase contracts that may be of assistance *when things go wrong*.

The seller

What can go wrong for the seller? At least three things may occur:

(a) there may be a fear that the price will not be paid, ie there is a rumour of insolvency
(b) the price is not paid when it should have been, or is not paid in full and/or the buyer becomes bankrupt.
(c) the buyer refuses to accept the goods.

There are two types of remedy—real and personal. The distinction is that *real* remedies are those that may be exercised straight away without special permission against the goods themselves (self-help) and are therefore very useful indeed. Personal remedies are those against the buyer and not the goods and must always be pursued through the courts (unless a voluntary settlement is made)—therefore they are of less immediate use. They are slower, could be more expensive to exercise, although certain interim measures may be available to safeguard the position. (These are discussed at the end of this section.) They are very often all that is available to a seller who has been slow to act or seek advice.

The available remedies contained in the Sale of Goods Act 1979 are:

(a) the unpaid seller's lien
(b) a right of stoppage in transit and
(c) a right of resale.

The unpaid seller's lien

We consider below the statutory lien available at common law. The parties may specifically agree to extend the ambit of the lien by agreement, but such extensions are not within the scope of this section.

Sale of Goods Act 1979

39(1). Subject to this and any other Act, notwithstanding that the property in the goods may have passed to the buyer, the unpaid seller of goods, as such, has by implication of law—

(a) a lien on the goods or right to retain them for the price while he is in possession of them.

In the absence of any agreement to the contrary, sellers who *should* have been paid but have not received their due, may exercise a *lien* on the goods. In other words they may retain them as against the purchasers, until paid, so long as they have "possession" of them.

A number of considerations arise from this.

Who is an unpaid seller?

The meaning of "unpaid" is defined by s. 38 of the Sale of Goods Act 1979:

(1) The seller of goods is an unpaid seller within the meaning of this Act
   (a) When the whole of the price has not been paid or tendered;
   (b) When a bill of exchange or other negotiable instrument has been received as a conditional payment, and the condition on which it was received has not been fulfilled by reason of the dishonour of the instrument or otherwise.

Sellers may, therefore, be unpaid where they have received a partial payment, or where they have sold on credit and, therefore, payment has by agreement been deferred, always provided that the credit period has expired.

The Act further goes on to define "seller" to include the agent of the seller.

When is a seller "in possession" of the goods?

In broad terms sellers are in possession of the goods if they maintain a sufficient degree of *control* over them so as to retain the lien. Whilst there is no satisfactory definition of "possession" in this context, it probably extends to physical control of the goods by the sellers or their agent or servant, unless the sellers have somehow agreed to waive "possession", eg by expressly or impliedly holding the goods to the purchasers' order.

Sale on credit

When can sellers on credit exercise a lien? Generally speaking, if the sellers have granted credit they are assumed to have waived the right to lien. There are two statutory exceptions in s. 41(c) of the Act, namely where the credit period has expired or the purchasers have become insolvent (see next section for consideration of "insolvent").

The right of sellers to exercise a lien for the price does not in itself entitle them to sell the goods; it simply entitles them to *retain* them until they have been paid. It is unlikely that if storage charges are incurred by the proper exercise of the lien, that the lien can extend to such charges. If the buyers are slow in making payment, the lien notwithstanding, then the sellers can take steps to obtain the court's leave to sell the goods. This is dealt with below.

A lien can be exercised over all or part of the goods for all or part of the price. It can only attach to the goods which are the subject-matter of the sale contract; not to any other goods unless express provision is made for this in the sale contract.

Example 1

Shady Company receives a regular monthly order from Dubious Company for varying amounts of soft drinks, for which a separate order is placed each month. Shady Company is required to pay COD. It fails to pay for the March consignment. Has Dubious Company a lien on the April shipment? Strictly speaking no, as the goods for which a lien could be exercised were the previous shipment and possession was relinquished before the lien could be exercised. Shady Company is not in breach and Dubious Company is not an unpaid seller in respect of the April shipment. Dubious Company should have negotiated a change in the payment provisions for the April consignment, requiring cash up front. The only alternative would be for Dubious Company to argue that there was only *one* contract for a sale in instalments and thus a lien is available over other goods, the subject-matter of the one contract. On the facts, however, this looks unlikely.

Loss of entitlement to lien

The lien can be lost in the four ways set out below:

(a) payment of the price in full or tender of the price in full is made
(b) the goods are delivered up by the sellers to a third party for delivery to the purchasers without reservation of a right of disposal
(c) when the buyers or their agents lawfully obtain the goods
(d) by waiving the lien (ie representation by the sellers that they will not insist upon the lien).

(The latter three categories are governed by s. 43 of the Sale of Goods Act 1979.)

Example 2
Very Big Company sells tractors to Mega Company on payment terms of 50 per cent in advance, the balance payable on right and true delivery.

(a) Mega Company pays the 50 per cent advance, thus tendering the portion of the price required to prevent Very

Big Company being an unpaid seller and thus losing the right to lien.

(b) Mega Company omits to make any payment but Very Big Company voluntarily delivers the goods to Mega Company's own barge for shipment, possession then passing to Mega Company and depriving Very Big Company of the right and ability to lien.

(c) Mega Company fails to pay the advance. However, Very Big Company, which has an urgent and unexpected requirement for the tractors, asks Mega Company if it may use them for a 24 hour period. Mega Company agrees. This may well constitute waiver as Very Big Company is representing to Mega Company that it requires *permission* to retain the tractors which is inconsistent with insistence upon lien.

A typical notice of lien which an unpaid seller might give would be in the following format:

Dear Purchaser,

In accordance with our agreement contained in our written contract reference XYZ, £5000 was due by close of business yesterday as payment for the motor tractor, which is presently in the possession of our agents at Portsmouth pending delivery to the vessel "Sieve" nominated by yourselves. Take notice that we are exercising a lien over the goods until such time as this payment is made in full to our bank account with Townbank, 36, Toy Street, Trumpington, A/C No. 007. We have notified our agents accordingly that the vehicle is not to be loaded on board your nominated vessel, and that all loss arising by reason of delay in delivery to the vessel is to be for your account.

cc Agents

Note that the above notice is in very general terms and makes certain assumptions. In certain circumstances a simple notification such as this will be appropriate. However, sellers concerned to protect their position would be well advised to seek legal advice if their contract or the circumstances are at all complicated.

The unpaid seller's right of stoppage in transit

S. 39(1)(b) of the Sale of Goods Act 1979 explains this right:

> (1) Subject to this and any other Act, notwithstanding that the property in the goods may have passed to the buyer, the unpaid seller of goods, as such, has by implication of law—. . .
>
> (b) in case of the insolvency of the buyer, a right of stopping the goods in transit after he has parted with the possession of them.

S. 44 provides further:

> Subject to this Act, when the buyer of goods becomes insolvent, the unpaid seller who has parted with the possession of the goods has the right of stopping them in transit, that is to say, he may resume possession of the goods as long as they are in course of transit, and may retain them until payment or tender of the price.

The prerequisites of the exercise of this right are as follows.

(a) the sellers must be *unpaid*, the same considerations apply as above
(b) the goods must not have gone into the possession of the purchasers and *must still be in transit*, although the sellers will inevitably have parted with possession of the goods, or else they would simply exercise the unpaid sellers' lien
(c) the buyers must be "insolvent".

When are the goods in transit?

Goods are in transit when they have passed out of the possession of the sellers into that of the carriers but have not yet reached the possession of the buyers. Actual *motion* does not seem to be required. If the carriers are the sellers' own agents, then the sellers have retained possession and may simply exercise a lien over the goods. The right of stoppage will only need to arise when the carriers are an independent contractor. There is sometimes difficulty in establishing when "transit" actually ceases. There can, moreover, be difficulties at times in establishing whether, *through the carriers*, the goods have passed into the possession of the buyers.

For example, what if the goods are shipped on board a vessel chartered by the purchasers? If the ship has been chartered by the purchasers on a time charter or voyage charter basis, in other words if the master and crew are not the servants or agents of the purchasers but are only contractually bound to them and are truly middlemen, then the goods will not have passed into the possession of the purchasers upon shipment. If the vessel is owned by the buyers, or is demise chartered to them, however, and is crewed by their employees, then possession will have passed to them and no stoppage order will be heeded.

What is meant by "insolvency"?

S. 61(4) of the Sale of Goods Act 1979 provides:

> A person is deemed to be insolvent within the meaning of this Act if he has either ceased to pay his debts in the ordinary course of business, or he cannot pay his debts as they become due, whether he has committed an act of bankruptcy or not.

According to the provisions of the Act, therefore, insolvency is not to be given a technical meaning; it is sufficient that it can be established that debts are not being paid in the ordinary course of business for the sellers to exercise a right of stoppage in transit.

Practical steps to be taken

Once the sellers have ascertained that they are in a position to exercise the right of stoppage in transit, they should, without delay, give notice to the carriers that such a right is being exercised and that delivery of the goods to the buyers in disregard of that right may amount to conversion. Consideration must, therefore, be given to the carriers' position when they receive such a notice. The carriers may be contractually bound to the purchasers to deliver the goods without delay and may find themselves in the invidious position of being required by the purchasers to make delivery of the goods against, perhaps, a bill of lading, and being advised by the sellers that such delivery will be made at their own peril because of the exercise of a right of stoppage in transit.

A number of practical points arise.

(a) The carriers may have a lien on the goods for freight due and this will take priority over any right purportedly exercised by the sellers.
(b) The sellers, in giving notice of the right of stoppage, must take care to ensure that the exercise of the right is communicated to the

person who has the day to day control of the goods in the time available. For example, if the sellers notify the Liberian shipowning company's office in Monrovia of the exercise of the right as against goods on board its vessel, they must ensure that there is sufficient time for the principal/owner to notify the master of the vessel of the exercise of the right prior to the vessel's arrival at the discharge port. If insufficient time is given, the master and, therefore, the carriers, will not be criticised for handing over the goods in ignorance of the notification.

Assuming that the carriers do not wish to exercise a lien for freight, and that proper notice has been given in time, they may be compelled to make a rapid decision upon arrival at the discharge port as to what to do with the goods. They may have commitments to other cargo interests and have a tight timetable to adhere to. By the same token they will not wish to incur substantial discharging and warehousing costs by offloading and storing the goods ashore. Carriers who ignore a notice of lien, however, may be liable to the sellers in conversion. The carriers are obliged to deliver the goods to the sellers' order although, by the same token, they may generally look to the sellers for unpaid freight charges.

It is a sellers' duty to ensure that the exercise of the right does not cause hardship to the carriers. They must assume responsibility for the goods and do so without delay. If the sellers do prevaricate and loss and damage are suffered by the carriers, the sellers will be obliged to reimburse them. If the stoppage prevents the carriers from completing a larger contracted voyage, the sellers are still liable to them for outstanding freight for the entire original voyage.

A typical notice exercising the right of stoppage in transit might be in the following form:

Telex to Lifeboy Inc. of Monrovia, owners of the vessel "Sieve".
cc Master of the vessel "Sieve" c/o managing agents Lifeboy Associates of Piraeus.
cc Purchaser.

We are the sellers of the three motorised caravans presently loaded on board your vessel. The purchasers, Calamity Inc., have failed to pay the price due on shipment for those goods, and are understood to have ceased to pay their debts as they become due in the ordinary course of business. For that reason please take notice that we require you to retain the goods to our order and not to effect delivery of them to the purchasers or to anyone on their behalf. We do of course undertake to indemnify you for any loss you may suffer by reason of our instructions in this regard and will advise you of the arrangements that we are making for the goods without delay.

Note that particular care should be taken by sellers giving such notice that it is accurate. In particular, because it is publishing to a third party details of believed "insolvency" of the purchasers, care must be taken to ensure that there are grounds for the belief so that the likelihood of a defamation action is avoided. Because of the involvement of the interests of third parties and the potentially serious repercussions from the giving of such notification, any sellers with any doubt as to their position are advised to contact a solicitor without delay.

The unpaid seller's right of resale

Unpaid sellers, who have exercised a right of lien or of stoppage in transit, may have a right of resale of the goods and convey good title to those goods to the new buyers, as against the original purchasers. It should be noted, however, that a contract of sale is not rescinded by the mere exercise of a right of lien or stoppage in transit. Indeed, these are precautionary measures available to the sellers, the exercise of which may encourage the buyers to make payment.

There are four circumstances when the unpaid sellers may acquire the right of resale as against the buyers.

(a) If the obligation to deliver has not, at the relevant time, become an obligation to deliver any *specific* item. This should be fairly self-apparent: if there is a contract for the sale of grain and at the relevant time the grain notionally earmarked by the sellers for despatch to the buyers is required elsewhere, the sellers may indeed despatch it elsewhere and find an alternative parcel of grain for the buyers when the time arises.

(b) If the buyers repudiate the contract, the sellers may accept that repudiation as bringing the contract to an end and, so long as possession has not passed to the purchasers, may resell the goods and claim damages for any loss, if appropriate.

(c) In the contract the sellers may reserve a right of resale, in which case s. 48(4) of the Sale of Goods Act 1979 will entitle them to sell the goods. S. 48(4) provides that where the sellers resell in the exercise of an express power of resale in the contract, then that in itself causes the original contract of sale to be rescinded.

(d) Finally, the unpaid sellers have a right of resale if the goods are perishable and/or if they give *notice* to the buyers that they intend to resell, in spite of which the buyers still fail to pay the price due.

This final provision is most likely to cause difficulties.

S. 48(3) of the Sale of Goods Act 1979 provides:

> Where the goods are of a perishable nature, or where the unpaid seller gives notice to the buyer of his intention to resell, and the buyer does not within a reasonable time pay or tender the price, the unpaid seller may resell the goods and recover from the original buyer damages for any loss occasioned by his breach of contract.

The effect of a resale under s. 48(3) is potentially different from a resale under s. 48(4) (above) in that such a sale under s. 48(4) *automatically* results in the sale contract being rescinded, whereas the Act is silent in the case of a resale under s. 48(3). The practical effect of this is important if a right of resale is exercised where property has passed to the buyers (eg a simple sale where, upon agreement, property passes, in spite of which no price is tendered (contrary to agreement) and the goods, for example eggs, are perishable).

On a strict interpretation of the Act, it might be assumed that any resale by the sellers would be on behalf of the buyers. In fact this is unlikely. A request for the price should (it is said) have the effect of making payment of the price essential and continued failure would be a repudiation of the contract by the buyers. The property thus reverts to the sellers, who then sell on their own account.

A typical notice by a seller of an intention to exercise a right of resale might be in a format similar to this:

> Dear Purchaser,
>
> As you know, we have directed the Master of the SS "Sieve" to redeliver the consignment of eggs which were sold to you to our order at Tilbury. This direction was given when you failed to pay the price due upon shipment, and our attention was drawn by X to the fact that you are failing to meet your debts as they fall due. The cargo is perishable, and accordingly we give notice that unless we receive payment of the contract price in full in our bank account with the Friendly Bank, Moorchurch Street, London, by close of business on

14th September, we shall offer the goods for resale on the open market and claim damages from you for any loss occasioned by your breach of contract.

Note once again that extreme caution should be exercised by sellers before giving notice of intention to resell. In particular, they should be certain that they are entitled to give such notice and, if in doubt, should seek the advice of a solicitor.

Specific performance

Application for specific performance is usually a remedy sought by a dissatisfied buyer of goods. It is effectively the other side of the coin from a seller's action for the price. There are, however, certain cases where sellers may be able to obtain an injunction to prevent buyers from breaking their contractual obligations so as to make the remedy of specific performance available to the sellers also. There are restricted circumstances where such relief would be appropriate, and the only legal authority concerns exclusive purchasing agreements.

Damages and action for the price

In addition to any real remedy that the sellers may exercise against the goods themselves to secure their position, if they are not successful in covering all of the loss in this way, or fail to cover any loss, they are generally entitled to bring an action in the appropriate jurisdiction for damages against the buyers for failure to pay the price, or for delays in making payment (in certain circumstances), or for wrongfully refusing to accept the goods. Damages can be claimed both in contract and in tort, and we shall also give brief consideration to an action for the price and how it is to be distinguished from an action in damages.

Ss. 49(1) and 50(1) of the Sale of Goods Act 1979 provide remedies in three specific circumstances.

Action for the price

This occurs in circumstances where property in goods passes and the buyers accept the goods but do not make payment for them. Then, pursuant to s. 49(1) of the Sale of Goods Act 1979 the sellers can maintain an *action for the price* against the buyers.

For example, the sellers agree to sell FOB to the buyers, payment 30 days from delivery to the vessel. The goods are delivered and the vessel sails. The buyers take the goods and use them but do not pay. The sellers' claim is for the price.

Other provisions

(a) *Property does not pass and the buyer rejects the goods.*
In these circumstances, under s. 50(1) of the Sale of Goods Act 1979 the sellers' action is for *damages*. An example of this would be where goods are sold CIF but the documents are (wrongfully) rejected. The property thereby reverts to the seller, who can seek damages from the buyer

(b) *Property passes, in spite of which the buyer refuses the goods.*
The seller has an *option* to sue for the price or for damages. An example of this would be where, in a simple sale contract, property passes immediately upon a deal being concluded, even though the price is not payable until delivery. The purchaser fails to take delivery of the goods and the seller has the option to seek the price of the goods or damages arising from the breach of contract.

The distinction is important as damages may be substantially more or less than "the price".

There are certain minor exceptions to these general rules.

Damages for wrongful rejection/non-acceptance of goods by the buyer

This is the sellers' sole remedy where property has not passed and they have been left with the goods. It may be that sellers are able to resell the goods at no loss or indeed at a substantial profit. In this case they will have no commercial interest in seeking damages from the original purchaser as they will have to account for any substitute contract that they are able to conclude, and whilst they will be able to establish breach, it will not be possible to prove loss, and they will recover nominal damages only. The sellers are also under a general duty to mitigate the loss, ie to take reasonable and prudent steps to minimise it (although they are not required to go to extreme lengths in the observance of this duty).

The action for damages becomes important where goods are being sold in a volatile market and between the time of conclusion of the contract with the original purchaser and the contract being broken by wrongful rejection of the goods there has been a slump in the market.

The general rule is that sellers may seek damages which flow naturally and directly from the breach of contract. In measuring the damages, recourse may be had to any "available market", and the measure of damages may be judged by the difference between the contract price and the available market price at the time when the goods ought to have been accepted or, if no exact time was fixed, at the time of the refusal to accept (s. 50(3) of the Sale of Goods Act 1979).

An available market is, in some circumstances, quite apparent and in others very difficult to determine. Certainly if goods are being traded on a recognised exchange, then it will be relatively easy to find the appropriate market price for the day of breach. More unusual commodities may not have an available market, or the price may only be ascertainable by reference to expert evidence.

There is a further difficulty where, in spite of there being an available market, the sellers have, in fact, not been able to sell the goods on the day of the breach but have taken several days to conclude an on-sale. If the resale is at market, then the courts will probably be willing to allow them a reasonable time to conclude a substitute contract and award as damages any discrepancy between the substitute sale price and the contract sale price.

If the sellers have made a particularly bad deal and on-sold below market, they will wish to claim the actual loss as opposed to the anticipated loss on the market. By the same token, if they have managed to conclude an especially good deal above the market rate, is the defaulting party able to take advantage of this?

The answer to this question is that if the sellers resell more or less forthwith below market, they will be in difficulty in seeking damages in this increased amount. The sellers will have to establish that they could not have resold at the market price and the duty to mitigate is such that they will be required to establish that reasonable steps were taken in this regard. The sellers are unlikely to be successful in making a full recovery and it will be likely to be assessed at the difference between the market price and contract price only. If the prompt resale is above market, and the sellers can establish that the market price was less advantageous, it is unlikely that the court would allow a further windfall and will simply award damages on the difference between the contract price and the resale price so as to place the sellers in the same position as if the original contract had been performed (ie nominal damages).

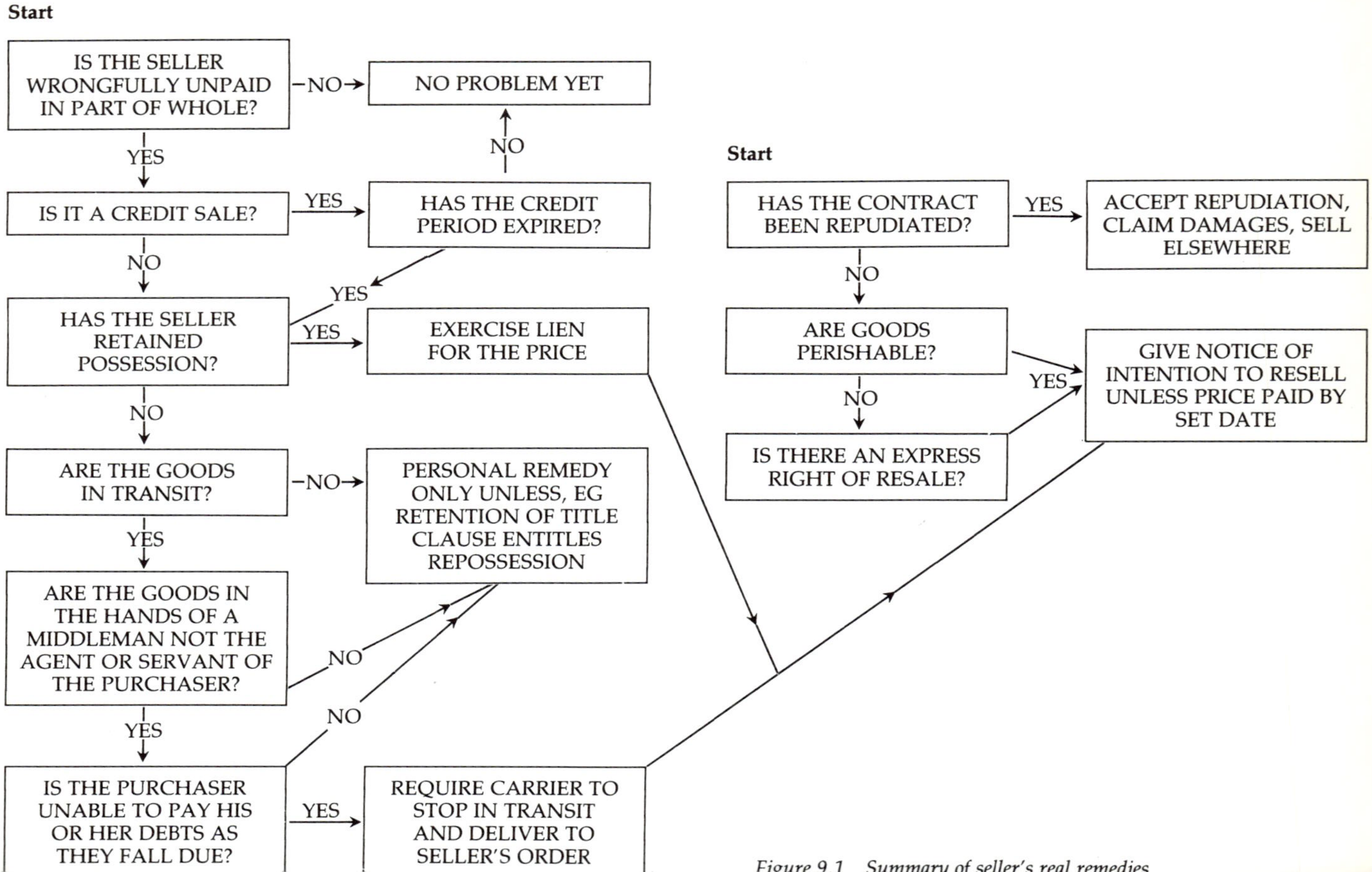

Figure 9.1 Summary of seller's real remedies

If the sellers are not able to resell immediately or prefer to wait for a brief period of time in anticipation of an upturn in the market, this is done at their own risk. That is not to say that the court will not allow the sellers a reasonable opportunity to find an alternative purchaser, but any speculation undertaken by the sellers is entirely at their risk. If the price obtained is ultimately below the market as at the date of breach, the sellers will be unlikely to recover the difference; by the same token, if they manage to sell at a price above market as at the date of the breach, they are unlikely to obtain a windfall. What the sellers are, of course, hoping for is that the market will rise above the original sale price and they will actually make a profit. That is something they are entitled to speculate about, but not to the potential detriment of the buyers if they are wrong.

There are certain circumstances in which the market price rule does not apply. It is only a *prima facie* method of calculating damages, and in certain circumstances it will be inappropriate. It is particularly inappropriate where there is no ready market, or where the goods have some special or unique property. For example, if a seller struck a bargain with a buyer for the purchase of a rare antique clock, and the buyer refused to accept the clock, the amount of damages the seller may seek would be the difference between the contract price and the price which could be obtained on any substitute sale, always provided that reasonable endeavours are used to ensure that the best price is secured.

There may be certain circumstances in which the goods, the subject of the sale, have absolutely no value whatsoever to anybody other than the original purchaser. For example, the goods may consist of specially tailor-made items manufactured to the purchaser's specific requirements. In such circumstances there may be absolutely no market for the goods whatsoever, apart from the original purchaser. In this case the seller's loss will be, effectively, the price.

Delayed payment

The sellers may be in a position where they have sold goods to a purchaser and eventually, after a great deal of difficulty, obtained the price from the purchaser. In the intervening period the sellers may have had to obtain special finance pending payment of the price. There have been a series of cases which establish that, as a matter of English law, sellers are not entitled to claim interest for the late payment of the price from purchasers. There are two exceptions to this rule. The first is where it has been agreed between the parties specifically in the contract that interest will be payable, in which case it can be claimed pursuant to contract. The other exception is where the sellers have been obliged to issue a writ for the price itself. Once a writ has been issued, even if the price itself is subsequently paid, the action for interest can be maintained from the time at which the price fell due until it was actually paid and, moreover, additional statutory interest on that sum may be due.

Example 3
X sues Y for failure to pay the price of goods sold and delivered. Y is served with the writ on Friday 13th June, the same day as the writ was issued, but had made payment of the price in full the previous Thursday. X cannot claim interest for the period of delay. If Y had paid the price on Saturday 14th, as a writ had already been issued, X could press on and sue for interest independently.

Note that if X had included in his contract a term entitling him to specific interest on outstanding accounts (always provided such interest was not at so high a rate as to be "usurious") then X would be entitled to sue for interest due, regardless of when the price was paid.

Buyer's remedies

The buyer is likely to be faced with three types of problem:

(a) non-delivery
(b) delayed delivery
(c) defective quality.

There are three remedies the buyer will have in mind:

(a) an action for the specific performance of the contract or, alternatively, a claim for possession of the goods
(b) rejection of the goods and/or
(c) a claim for damages or return of the price.

Non-delivery

S. 51 of the Sale of Goods Act 1979 provides:

> (1) Where the seller wrongfully neglects or refuses to deliver the goods to the buyer, the buyer may maintain an action against the seller for damages for non-delivery.
> 2) The measure of damages is the estimated loss directly and naturally resulting, in the ordinary course of events, from the seller's breach of contract.
> (3) Where there is an available market for the goods in question the measure of damages is prima facie to be ascertained by the difference between the contract price and the market or current price of the goods at the time or times when they ought to have been delivered, or (if no time was fixed) at the time of the refusal to deliver.

In a case of non-delivery the buyers generally have two options. They can either accept that the sellers are in repudiatory breach of contract, treat the contract as at an end and claim damages or they can seek to enforce the contract, obtaining an order for specific performance.

The measure of damages that buyers may expect depends upon the circumstances of each case. They must be certain that the time for delivery has passed unless (see below anticipatory breach) the sellers have indicated already that they will not be delivering. If the deadline for delivery has passed, buyers may claim damages which result "naturally and directly from the breach". In calculating these, consideration must be given as to whether or not there is an available market. This is a question of fact. If the commodity in question is regularly traded on major international exchanges, then it would be difficult to say that there is not an available market. By the same token if it is a freely available commodity then there will be an "available market". In such circumstances damages are calculated on the basis of the difference between the market price at the latest point delivery could have been made at and the contract price. If no delivery date was agreed, the relevant date in comparison with the contract price is the date of the refusal to deliver.

In the event that there is no available market (the item is unusual or unique) it is material to consider whether buyers are purchasing for their own use or to trade on. If the purchasers are buying for their own use they may claim the additional costs of buying in elsewhere (subject always to their duty to mitigate the loss). Accordingly, if they had contracted to purchase a tailor-made suit from the sellers at a price of £100, they may claim any increased price of procuring an alternative suit of a similar design. If the best offer they can get for a similar suit is at a cost of £120, they are entitled to claim as damages the £20 difference. They would always have had to pay the first £100 in any event, so that would not form part of the claim for damages.

If buyers are purchasing to sell on where there is no available market, the damages they can recover for failure to deliver would be the difference between the "value" of the goods when they should have been delivered and the contract price. "Value" in this context is the price that the buyers could have sold on at, therefore evidence of any existing sub-sale may be very important. In effect buyers are enabled to claim lost profit by way of damages.

In general terms, the existence of a sub-sale is likely to be almost entirely irrelevant and outside the contemplation of the defaulting seller. It rarely has any significance on the extent of damages that may be claimed unless there is no market available for the goods in question and/or where the seller has a specific knowledge of the sub-sale and of the special and specific loss that the buyer may thereby have suffered.

Anticipatory breach

It may sometimes happen that before the date fixed for delivery the sellers make it clear that they will not be performing the contract. In such circumstances the buyers may choose either to accept that position and sue for damages or to treat the sellers as bound by their obligations under the sale contract. The buyers have an absolute choice in this regard. If the anticipatory repudiation of the sellers is accepted, then the above applies. If, however, the buyers choose to hold the sellers to the contract, then the contract continues to bind both parties. There will only be a breach if, on the date fixed for delivery, the sellers fail to deliver. This gives the sellers a chance to take steps to perform the contract and may be a useful option for the buyers to adopt if they think there is a prospect of the sellers complying. Only when the delivery date has come and gone will the buyers be compelled to elect either to treat the contract as at an end and to sue for damages or alternatively to seek an order for specific performance. It is at this stage that a duty to mitigate loss is imposed upon the purchasers.

Specific performance

S. 52 of the Sale of Goods Act 1979 provides:

> (1) In any action for breach of contract to deliver specific or ascertained goods the Court may, if it thinks fit, on the plaintiff's application, by its judgment or decree direct that the contract shall be performed specifically, without giving the defendant the option of retaining the goods on payment of damages.

It should be noted that s. 52 only entitles the disappointed purchaser to an order for specific performance in the event that the goods in question are *specific* or *ascertained*. Accordingly, if the purchaser is interested in a parcel out of a larger parcel of a generic cargo, no such order would be made. Generally speaking the courts are reluctant to make orders for specific performance if a third party's rights are affected (for example if a third party has obtained possession even though it was in breach of the contract between the buyer and seller), or if the purchaser would be adequately compensated by an order of damages. The kind of circumstances where an order for specific performance may be particularly appropriate is in the case of the intended purchase of a very special, perhaps unique, item. In such circumstances the purchaser could argue that damages would not be an adequate compensation.

There is no requirement in seeking specific performance that property in the goods should be vested in the buyers already. Indeed, if property is vested in the buyers they have an alternative application which can be made under s. 3 of the Torts (Interference with Goods) Act 1977. Such an application is likely to be considered on the same terms as an application for specific performance.

Delay

In the event that goods are delayed beyond the time agreed for delivery, disappointed purchasers have a number of options:

(a) in certain circumstances they may elect to treat the contract as having been repudiated by the sellers and brought to an end, and reject the subsequent tender of goods and claim (if appropriate) damages
(b) they can seek an order for specific performance
(c) they can seek damages, although accepting the goods when tendered late.

The measure of damages that buyers may seek for delayed delivery will depend upon whether they are buying for their own use or to trade. If buying for their own use it is possible to claim the cost to them of the period of delay. For example, the hire of a similar replacement chattel for the period of delay. If the buyers are purchasing to trade on they can claim the difference between the market price at the time of actual delivery and the market price at the time of the contractual delivery date. In this instance the *contract price* itself is almost entirely irrelevant because the difference between the two market prices is significant.

Defective quality

Whilst a distinction should be drawn between the defective documents pertaining to the goods (for example a CIF contract) and defects in the goods themselves, in fact there is generally an entitlement to reject for serious defects in either case.

In broad terms purchasers are entitled to reject if the defect in quality is such that it goes to the heart of the contract, in which case they must *in terms* accept the repudiatory breach of the sellers as bringing the contract to an end and reject the goods. If the defect is of a lesser type but nonetheless reduces the value of the goods to the purchasers, they are entitled to seek damages to compensate and to place them in the position they would have been had the contract been performed properly.

The measure of damages to which the buyers may be entitled if goods of a defective quality are delivered to them and accepted can be explained as follows. The buyers may be entitled to set up the loss arising by reason of the breach in diminution or extinction of the price. They can claim the value of the difference between the actual quality delivered and the contractual quality that they bargained for. It may be difficult to establish the different values and expert evidence may well be required. In this context the market itself may be entirely irrelevant.

Difficulties arise when a defect manifests itself at a later stage and it is virtually impossible to reject the goods. A frequent example of this is a late discovery of the back dating of bills of lading so as to ensure that they conform with the documentation specified in the letter of credit. At the time the back dating is discovered the goods may well have been delivered and used and the right to reject the documentation would certainly have been lost. In such circumstances there is authority to

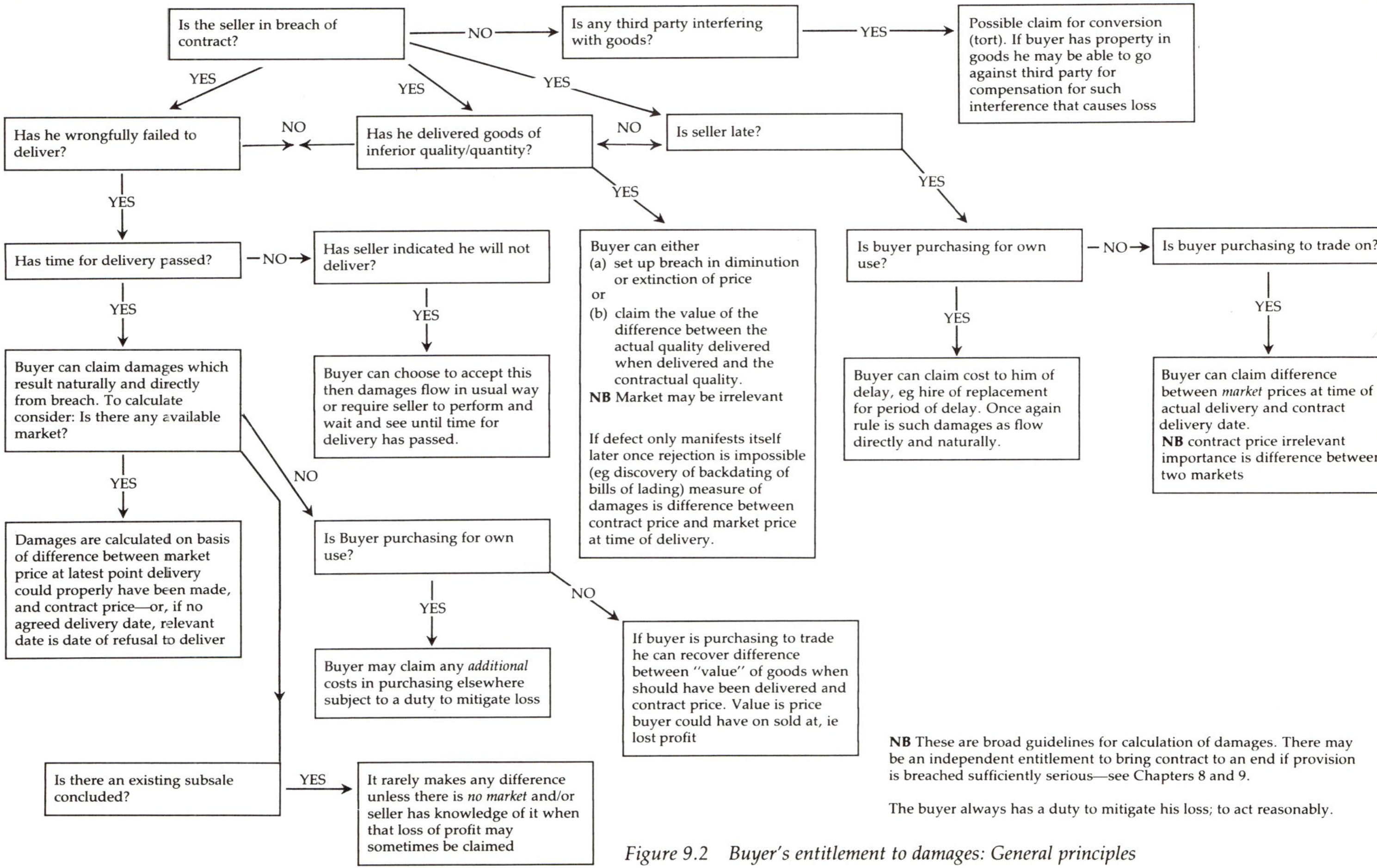

NB These are broad guidelines for calculation of damages. There may be an independent entitlement to bring contract to an end if provision is breached sufficiently serious—see Chapters 8 and 9.

The buyer always has a duty to mitigate his loss; to act reasonably.

Figure 9.2 Buyer's entitlement to damages: General principles

suggest that the measure of damages is the difference between the contract price and the market price at the time of delivery. Whether there is any point in the purchasers seeking damages will, of course, be entirely dependent on any market movement which has occurred, thus making such a claim worthwhile.

Precautionary measures

Many of the difficulties experienced by both buyer and seller in international sale contracts might perhaps be circumvented by judicious wording of sale contracts, or alternatively by clear agreement between the parties in the course of oral negotiations (for example on the telephone) vesting each of them with certain enhanced rights over and above those which pertain in classic CIF or FOB contracts. See Chapter 2 for consideration of the incorporation of terms in contracts.

There is insufficient space in this publication to deal with the type of specific clause that can be agreed and its effect. However, the following are a handful of precautionary measures that warrant consideration by parties when contracting with unfamiliar international partners where they are concerned to preserve their position. There is, of course, no substitute for a detailed contract document drafted on legal advice.

Romalpa clauses (Retention of title clause)

A Romalpa clause represents an attempt by sellers to retain title in goods until such time as the price for those goods has been paid to them in full. The purpose of this is to protect the sellers in the event of the purchasers' bankruptcy when, but for the sellers retaining title in the goods, the goods themselves might form part of the bankrupt estate even though the price had not been paid. Romalpa clauses are becoming increasingly sophisticated, for example:

(a) apparently entitling the sellers to enter property and seize the goods in the event of failure to make payment and to extend the entitlement to reclaim those goods in respect of all unsatisfied accounts;
(b) entitling the sellers moreover to dismantle any other goods which may have become attached to or mixed with the goods in which title is sought to be retained.

The courts have been reluctant to extend the ambit of such clauses significantly. A clause retaining ownership until the full price for those goods is paid is likely to be upheld as long as legal ownership is retained. However, it has proved extremely difficult for sellers to "trace" the goods once their identity is lost in the manufacturing process (when they are transformed into different goods) or they are sold and the sale proceeds themselves spent. Substantial works have been written on the effect and permissible extent of the Romalpa clause, and whilst on balance they are clauses that are beneficial there are certain difficulties that should be borne in mind.

(a) Amendments may be necessary to standard form contracts to provide that *risk* passes to the buyers on delivery even though title does not (unless specified otherwise, risk and title generally pass together), and to enable the sellers to maintain an action for the price even though property has not passed. Otherwise, on a strict construction of s. 49 of the Sale of Goods Act 1979, where a Romalpa clause has been incorporated, and the price is unpaid, the precise cause of action may be difficult to establish.
(b) The potential liability of sellers to sub-purchasers for defects in the goods resold by buyers where title in the goods remains with the sellers because of such clauses.
(c) VAT bad debt relief may be endangered by the use of such a clause to obtain relief if the property is not retrieved; it would be necessary formally to transfer title to any liquidator appointed to claim the VAT bad debt relief.
(d) In certain circumstances, to prevail, the clause may require registration as a charge on the purchasing company. This may not be a realistic option.

A simple Romalpa clause might read as follows:

> All products sold by Mega Co. Ltd shall remain the sole and absolute property of Mega Co. Ltd until such time as all accounts due from the customer to Mega Co. Ltd have been paid in full.

This can be extended so that in the event that products or goods the property of

> Mega Co. Ltd are admixed or comingled with the products or goods the property of the customer, or are processed or attached or incorporated with such goods, the result shall become the property of Mega Co. Ltd and be held by the customer subject to the terms of the clause.

The contractual lien clause

Consideration has already been given to the unpaid seller's right of lien. The right of lien in its common law form extends simply to a right to hold goods until payment of the price in full is made. The right of lien does not extend to other costs associated with the transaction (eg storage charges which have not been met) nor to any previous accounts that remain unsatisfied. By express agreement between the parties the clause can be extended to give the seller a right to lien in those circumstances. Such a clause might provide:

> The seller shall have a lien on the goods the subject-matter of this contract for all outstanding accounts due from or on behalf of the purchaser, and that lien shall extend to storage charges, legal costs, and any other miscellaneous expenditure reasonably incurred in the exercise of the lien for amounts so due. The seller's right to lien under this clause does not restrict their rights of lien under the provisions of s. 41 of the Sale of Goods Act 1979.

In the event of the insolvency of purchasers, a preferential creditor may take the point that both the Romalpa clause and the contractual lien clause do not afford the otherwise unsecured seller any form of priority or preference. To reduce the likelihood of any argument along these lines being successful, sellers would be prudent to ensure that their rights under both these clauses were registered as charges against the purchasing company—in particular if the purchasing company is registered in England or Wales.

Conclusive quality certificate

There is often provision for conclusive quality certificates in CIF contracts or international contracts where the parties are resident substantial distances apart. They have the advantage of streamlining procedure. They may relieve the purchaser of the right to claim damages for defective quality in the goods or to reject for the same reason. The parties will agree that an independent analyst is to provide a certificate of quality (and sometimes quantity) of the commodity usually at the load port and that the certificate is to be binding. This is of some advantage to the sellers as it reduces the likelihood of rejection of the goods. It also effectively renders the sellers immune for any quality claim by the purchasers, whose only remedy is likely to be a negligence claim against the "expert" who gives a certificate which proves to be inaccurate. A typical conclusive quality certification clause might provide:

> The seller shall provide a certificate of quality from an independent analyst of good standing, which certificate shall be conclusive as between the parties of the quality and specification of the material sold. "Independent" means not in the employment of either of the parties.

Letters of credit

The use of the letter of credit has become an almost commonplace financial arrangement for international transactions. The bank effectively acts as the clearing house and will open a letter of credit in favour of the sellers and make payment to them against presentation of documents in conformity with the bank's instructions. This arrangement offers a safeguard to both buyers and sellers. Sellers are assured of the bank having funds available in the event that the documentation is accurate; the purchaser, through the bank, has the opportunity of inspecting the documents before authorising payment. Such arrangements are dealt with in detail in Chapter 4.

Jurisdiction clause

Unless the parties specifically agree an appropriate law and jurisdiction provision for any disputes which arise under the contract, there is a danger that the eventual jurisdiction may be unfamiliar to one or both parties.

Take the example of a purchasing company in Monrovia which concludes a contract through one of its managers, temporarily in Switzerland, who reaches agreement on the telephone with an American seller for goods to be shipped from Australia to Hong Kong, with payment in London. If the vessel were to become stranded *en route* at the Philippines where it was refloated by a German salvage company, there would be very great difficulty in recognising which is the appropriate jurisdiction.

As a matter of English law the jurisdiction which has the closest connection with the contract would probably be the one which should assume responsibility for dealing with the dispute. Which country has the closest connection with the contract is in every case a matter of fact. Important features may be

(a) the place where the contract has to be performed both physically and in so far as the payment of funds are concerned
(b) the place in which most people concerned with the contract are resident or where they were when they concluded the contract and
(c) the place in which the final acceptance of the offer made to the contract is received.

In the example given above, if receipt of the acceptance was received in New York, then *prima facie* the courts in New York might well assume jurisdiction, but the appropriate law might be that which had the closest connection with the contract. In the event that payment was to be made in London and that banking arrangements and shipping arrangements were made through London, the New York courts might be obliged to apply English law, although they might equally consider that Australia had the closest connection with the contract. The uncertainty that can be produced is a matter of concern and the parties for that reason commonly agree either to a sophisticated neutral venue for the determination of disputes or, in any event, for some specific court or arbitration tribunal to have jurisdiction.

In the case of contracts for certain commodities, many of the trade associations have already established sophisticated arbitration procedures which are readily accepted by both buyers and sellers. For example, the Grain and Feed Trade Association (GAFTA), the Federation of Oils, Seeds and Fats Association (FOSFA), the London Metal Exchange (LME), the Refined Sugar Association (RSA) all have such procedures.

Whenever the parties consider determination of disputes they should look separately and specifically at the *place* where any dispute is to be determined, and the appropriate *law* which is to be applied.

A typical London arbitration clause might provide:

> The parties agree that in the event of a dispute arising under this contract the English law will apply, and that there will be arbitration in London according to the "Arbitration Acts".

This provides not only the appropriate *law* but also the appropriate venue.

Interest clause

As explained above, unless specific provision is made for interest, and so long as the principal is paid prior to the issue of a writ, no matter how long the delay in payment of the price sellers are unlikely to be able to claim interest independently of the price. This can be circumvented by a simple interest clause being agreed between the parties. Such a clause might provide:

> The seller is entitled to interest at a rate of 12% per annum on all accounts outstanding 30 days after delivery of the relevant invoice/goods.

(Alternatively the interest rate might be linked to base rate of LIBOR.) The only cautionary note is that interest claimed must not be excessive or the clause will not be upheld. There is no hard and fast rule but the Moneylenders Act 1909 indicates that 48 per cent may well be "grossly exorbitant".

Interim remedies

Apart from the real and personal remedies available to disappointed buyers and sellers already considered above, there are a number of interim procedural remedies available in the English courts to plaintiffs and defendants.

The full scope of these procedural steps available in the context of intended or existing litigation falls outside this publication. They are, moreover, general remedies and not simply confined to transactions concerning the sale of goods. However, because they are so useful and in fairly wide usage, it is appropriate at this stage to touch on them briefly.

The majority of the remedies are contained in Order 29 of the Rules of the Supreme Court, those being the rules governing the procedure and practice within the High Court. Similar remedies may exist in the county court but are not dealt with in this section. Generally speaking the county court deals with small claims, the size of the claim being calculated by its monetary value.

Mareva injunction

Of the remedies referred to above, by far the most commonly invoked injunction is the Mareva injunction (and the very similar provision in s. 25 of the Civil Jurisdiction and Judgments Act 1982). The Mareva injunction is an interlocutory injunction intended to prevent the dissipation of assets. Because litigation can be a time consuming enterprise, often with a substantial passage of time passing between the date of issue of a writ and the final determination of the dispute, a defendant has time within which to try to dissipate or conceal assets so as to make any judgment obtained worthless or difficult to enforce. To illustrate the recognition of this potential difficulty in England it was apparently common practice until the middle of the last century to arrest the defendant at the outset of an action and restrain him or her in prison until security had been found to cover the plaintiff's claim. This draconian procedure remained available to the Crown until 1947.

Until the 1970s Mareva relief was not widely available, in stark contrast to Continental systems where "conservative" injunctions were freely available. The potential difficulty was particularly well illustrated in the case of foreign shipping companies registered under a flag of convenience and owning only one vessel. These companies might incur liabilities from England and maintain a bank account for insurance within London. A claim commenced in London against the shipping company might be vigorously defended unsuccessfully, and at the end of the day the funds that had once been in London might prove illusive.

One answer was to invoke Admiralty jurisdiction and to arrest a vessel to secure the claim, but this was dependent upon it entering a jurisdiction where this was possible. In 1975 the Court of Appeal approved for the first time the making of an injunction restraining defendants from removing assets or disposing of them outside the jurisdiction. The circumstances of the first reported decision concerned foreign based shipowners and the SS "Mareva" lent its name to the injunction.

The procedure subsequently approved by the Court of Appeal was swiftly enshrined in legislation and Mareva relief is now provided for in s. 37(3) of the Supreme Court Act 1981. The section provides:

> 3. The power of the High Court . . . to grant an interlocutory injunction restraining a party to any proceedings from removing from the jurisdiction of the High Court, or otherwise dealing with, assets located within that jurisdiction shall be exercisable in cases where that party is, as well as in cases where he is not, domiciled, resident or present within that jurisdiction.

In broad terms the Mareva jurisdiction extends to cases where there is a danger that assets will be dissipated within the jurisdiction as well as removed out of it.

In general terms there are a number of hurdles that have to be overcome before Mareva relief is available.

(a) The English courts must have jurisdiction to determine the issue (although see Chapter 10 on s. 25 of the Civil Jurisdiction and Judgment Act 1982).
(b) There must be existing or imminently intended proceedings within the jurisdiction.
(c) The plaintiff must give *full* and *frank* disclosure of all material matters, including giving particulars of the claim dealing with any weakness in that claim.
(d) The plaintiff must be able to establish that the defendant has assets to which the Mareva injunction can attach. (It is not sufficient for a blanket order to be made over all assets within the jurisdiction. The order is usually made over a named asset, for example a bank account, and then extended to any other assets.)
(e) The plaintiff must have some ground for believing that there is a risk that the assets will be removed before judgment. Previously it was necessary to show that the removal would be out of the jurisdiction but now any dealing with the asset so as to defeat the ends of justice is sufficient.
(f) The plaintiff must give an undertaking in damages both to third parties affected by the injunction and generally in case the claim fails and/or the injunction turns out to be unjustified. It is increasingly common for the court to make a probing enquiry as to the sufficiency of such undertakings and on occasion to require them to be fortified.

Upon obtaining a Mareva injunction the applicant must without delay notify the defendant and all third parties potentially affected by the order of its terms and serve upon them as soon as possible a copy of the sealed order. Banks may incur administrative costs in ensuring that these orders are complied with. For that reason all possible detail concerning assets, the subject-matter of the order, should be included in its terms and it should contain an undertaking to pay the bank's costs incurred in adhering to the order.

The Mareva injunction is an order granted on an ex-parte application. That is, the plaintiff alone is represented before the court when seeking the injunction. For this reason the court is dependent upon the plaintiff giving a proper and frank account of the events and will seriously criticise anyone who embellishes his or her case or omits relevant details from the affidavit, and indeed may discharge the order in such circumstances. The court has recently indicated that if there is a subsequent change of circumstances, the party obtaining the Mareva injunction has a duty to return to court to explain the change of circumstances. At the very least, the sanction for non-compliance would be an order of costs against the plaintiff.

The effect of the Mareva injunction is to freeze assets up to the amount noted in the order. Unless application is made to the court there can be no dealing with assets whatsoever until the injunction is lifted. The injunction does not afford any form of priority, it simply preserves the assets until determination of the issues between the parties. The courts recognise that the injunction should not take effect so as to preclude the ordinary business of the defendant and should not hamper commerce, and for that reason are sympathetic to applications from defendants for the lifting or modification of Mareva injunctions so as to enable them to carry out their everyday business.

The Civil Jurisdiction and Judgments Act 1986, which came in to force at the beginning of 1987, included a provision (s. 25) similar in effect to the Mareva injunction relief already available.

Broadly it provides that if the parties to a dispute are already engaged in litigation in the courts of another convention country (effectively EC countries), then the English courts may make an order similar in effect to a Mareva injunction to freeze assets of the defendants within the English High Court's jurisdiction as security for the litigation taking place in that convention country.

Anton Piller order and orders for preservation of property

Order 29, rule 2 of the Rules of the Supreme Court provides for retention, preservation, etc of the subject-matter of the cause or matter. Order 29, rule 2 states:

> 2–(1) On the application of any party to the cause or matter the Court may make an Order for the detention, custody or preservation of any property which is the subject matter of the cause or matter, or as to which any question

may arise therein, for the inspection of any such property in the possession of a party to the cause or matter.

(2) For the purposes of enabling any Order under paragraph (1) to be carried out the Court may by the Order authorise any person to enter upon any land or building in the possession of any party to the cause or matter.

Apart from the rules, the court has an inherent power to make an order for the detention or preservation of the subject-matter of the action and of documents and articles relating thereto. The orders made pursuant to this power are potentially draconian in effect. A court may, upon proper request, empower a plaintiff to enter the defendant's premises to search and seize documents or materials which the plaintiff can illustrate are in danger of being destroyed by the defendant. This type of relief is most frequently sought in patent, copyright and passing off actions. It is, however, also material to sale of goods cases where, for example, the quality of the product is disputed and the plaintiff fears that the defendant may dispose of the goods or otherwise try to damage them or documentation concerning them.

Because of the potentially draconian effect of such an order the court requires a high degree of disclosure from the plaintiff and it is necessary for him or her to show an extremely strong *prima facie* case. It is moreover imperative that the plaintiff shows that the damage that would arise if the destruction feared was carried out would be extremely serious. The applicant is invariably required to give an undertaking to pay damages to any third party affected by the order, and to the defendant if the order is misconceived.

The popular conception of an Anton Piller order involves a dawn raid on premises. The court will usually require the inspection to be supervised by the plaintiff's solicitor and for only parties named on the writ or on the order to be in attendance. No damage to property is permitted (eg no battering down of a door which remains locked) although a refusal to comply with the court order will constitute a contempt of court punishable by imprisonment.

In spite of the wording of Order 29, rule 2 the court has further power to grant an Anton Piller order to ensure preservation of a document which does not itself form the subject matter of an action (eg, a survey report on the quality of goods) always provided that the document is important evidence vital to the case.

Anton Piller orders, whilst extremely useful in extreme cases are difficult to obtain; they require early disclosure of a great deal of information by the plaintiff and the level of accuracy required is very high. Accordingly, the amount of preparation required to obtain such an order is high and it is unlikely that the defendant would ever be called upon to pay the costs of the Anton Piller application even if the plaintiff is ultimately successful. The courts are anxious that the Anton Piller order should not be used as some form of sanction to a fishing expedition to inspect the defendant's documents randomly, and for that reason the preferred course is for named documents or items to be specified in the body of the order sought.

Writ of ne regno exeat

The court may, in restricted circumstances, order the arrest of a defendant to be held in prison until security is provided where there is a claim against that defendant in debt and they are about to leave the jurisdiction, thereby potentially prejudicing the prosecution of the claim. It is an extreme measure only truly appropriate against a defendant capable of acting in contempt of other orders that should ensure security is available (eg a Mareva injunction).

Sampling

Order 29, rule 3 permits a party to the action to apply to the court for authority to require a sample to be taken of any property which is the subject matter of the cause or matter. The application can be made after commencement of proceedings and is restricted to the *bona fide* subject-matter of the action. The order will not be available where the subject-matter of the action is not in the possession or control of the defendant, but the court has power to order an article to be sent abroad to be identified on commission. The court may require the sample, or indeed the goods, to be lodged with it.

Order for sale

Order 29, rule 4 provides that the Court may dispose of any property which is the subject-matter of litigation or as to which any question arises therein, which is perishable or is likely to deteriorate if kept or which for any other good reason it is desirable to sell forthwith (eg a wasting asset). It will be appreciated that this procedural remedy is available in the context of existing litigation and is complementary to the

Sale of Goods Act 1979 relief already discussed. The application is made with both parties in attendance.

Delivery up of goods

S. 4 of the Torts (Interference with Goods) Act 1977, where claims are made concerning "interference" with goods under the action (commonly for conversion), empowers the court to make an early order for delivery up of such goods.

Recovery of personal property subject to lien

Order 29, rule 6 provides that where either party claims the recovery of specific property (not land) and the party from whom recovery is sought does not dispute the title to the property, but claims to be entitled to retain it by virtue of a lien, the court can order the party seeking to recover the property to be at liberty to pay in to court money as security (together with appropriate interest and costs) and upon payment that the property claimed be given up to the party claiming it. For example, the repairers of a motor vehicle may be entitled to exercise a lien over it until such time as the account for repairs is met. Order 29, rule 6 may oblige them on application by the customer, to release the vehicle to the customer, who has paid in sufficient funds to court to replace the security afforded by the vehicle.

Usually it would be unnecessary for an application to be made under the provisions of Order 29, rule 6. Most parties would be capable of reaching agreement as to the substitution of adequate cash for a liened commodity. The rule is clearly sensible where the item liened is vastly more valuable than the claim.

Order for inspection

Order 29/7A, ss. 33(i) and 34(3) of the Administration and Justice Act 1970 provide for such an order to be made when proceedings in respect of goods to be inspected are intended or have been commenced. Commonly the applicant will be required to secure the costs of the person who is to permit inspection. The courts may also be concerned to preserve confidentiality.

Order for speedy trial

If claimants can establish that a case is particularly pressing, they may be allowed by the court to "queue jump" and get an early date for trial.

Order for interim payment/summary judgment

If claimants can show a very strong case, but the trial date is far off, they may try and short circuit the process by obtaining an early part-payment if their claim is particularly strong. If the entire claim is very strong they may be in a position to ask for *summary judgment* (ie early judgment without the need for trial) but will have to establish on affidavit evidence that their opponent does not have any arguable defence. If the court is only partly satisfied, an order may be made permitting the defendant to defend but commonly upon payment of funds into court.

10

Taking proceedings

Introduction

Most commercial contracts are performed without any problems. Where disagreement occurs, the problem can usually be settled amicably between the parties, but in some instances they are forced to turn to the law. There are several methods by which a dispute can be resolved:

(a) *Litigation*
Usually High Court proceedings before a single judge.

(b) *Arbitration*
The voluntary submission by prior or *ad hoc* agreement of a dispute to a single person or a tribunal.

(c) *Conciliation*
The intervention of a third party at the invitation of the contestants in order to bring the parties together in an amicable compromise.

Arbitration or litigation

Whether a party chooses arbitration or High Court litigation depends upon the nature of the dispute and the parties concerned.

Arbitration

There are a number of reasons why the parties might prefer to settle their disputes by arbitration. In arbitration proceedings the parties to the arbitration select their own arbitrator/s. Each party can choose someone in whom they have confidence. Usually the arbitrator will be chosen because of familiarity with the commercial practice applicable to the dispute, business acumen or knowledge of the relevant law.

Arbitration proceedings on the whole tend to be more informal, more flexible and less hostile than litigation. The parties themselves will decide on a convenient venue for the arbitration. The arbitration hearing is private and the arbitrator's award is not published. A lack of publicity may be preferred by the parties and could be beneficial to their business relationship.

The cost of arbitration may in some instances (for example an arbitration on documents alone) be cheaper than High Court litigation, but this depends upon the nature of the dispute. Arbitrators are closely involved with the development of the case and as a result have a good knowledge of its factual background. This may result in certain economies as there may be less need for long background explanations and lengthy reading of documents. With arbitration, however, the parties are required to meet the arbitrators' fees charged, usually on an hourly basis, and pay for a convenient venue.

Arbitration may be quicker than litigation, especially when compared to High Court cases where proceedings have to be served abroad. Arbitrators often fix a hearing date at an early stage and, whenever possible, try to keep to it. The final decision, however, may be delivered more quickly in litigation rather than in arbitration; arbitrators can take considerable time before publishing their award.

Arbitration awards are enforceable (with leave of the court) as if they were judgments of the High Court of Justice under s. 26 of the Arbitration Act 1950. Final awards are enforceable abroad if the country where enforcement is anticipated has acceded to the New York Convention or recognises the Enforcement of Foreign Arbitral Awards 1958. High Court judgments, however, depend upon the narrower existence of a statutory provision in the country where enforcement is sought.

Litigation

Although in many instances the parties may prefer arbitration, there are a number of advantages to commencing proceedings in the High Court. An arbitrator's powers in relation to interlocutory proceedings are governed by the Arbitration Act 1979, but are rather less extensive than the equivalent interlocutory powers exercised by a High Court judge. Where a party to High Court litigation has an exceptionally strong case, they may apply under Order 14 of the Rules of the Supreme Court for summary judgment. This allows judgment to be given where a party can prove that there is no defence to their claim. This procedure is not available in arbitration, although early interim awards can be sought in suitable cases.

There are certain advantages in having a commercial arbitrator, but he or she may be without legal qualification. Lack of legal expertise may result in the arbitrator paying insufficient regard to the nature and weight of the evidence and the legal considerations, and render the award liable to appeal. In comparison, High Court proceedings are presided over by a legally qualified professional judge.

High Court litigation is likely to be more advantageous than arbitration where there are more than two parties involved. An arbitration clause is by nature enforceable between the two parties to the contract, but arbitration does not make any provision for third party proceedings unless all the parties agree. Litigation, on the other hand, makes provision for joining any number of defendants and offers an opportunity for commencing third party proceedings.

High Court litigation makes provisions for a judge to refer any question of law to the European Court of Justice. There is no equivalent procedure in arbitration. The arbitrator instead would need to apply under s. 2(1) of the Arbitration Act 1979 or appeal under s. 1(3).

Commercial arbitration

In a commercial arbitration the parties appoint arbitrators of their own choice to settle their disputes. There must be three elements present:

(a) a dispute between two or more parties
(b) an agreement to refer the dispute to arbitration
(c) intention that the decision of the tribunal is legally binding.

The arbitrator's jurisdiction depends upon the arbitration agreement itself. Arbitration has been described by s. 32 of the Arbitration Act 1979 as:

> a written agreement to submit present or future differences to arbitration whether an arbitrator is named or not.

Arbitration clauses

There are a number of standard arbitration clauses. In a shipping context, the charterparty will usually contain a written contractual agreement to arbitrate. In the Baltime Charterparty the arbitration clause states:

> 23. Any dispute arising under the charter to be referred to arbitration in London (or such other place as may be agreed) one Arbitrator to be nominated by the Owners and the other by the Charterers and in case the Arbitrators shall not agree then to the decision of an Umpire to be appointed by them, the award of the Arbitrators or the Umpire to be final and binding upon both parties.

The arbitration clause is, of course, subject to the substantive law. In a number of contracts, provision is made for English law to govern any contractual dispute. Where there is no express clause governing the relevant law in the agreement, generally that system of law with the closest connection to the contract will be chosen. If a dispute is then referred to arbitration in a particular country, the laws of that country will apply. The *lex fori* (the law of the country where the arbitration is held) governs the procedure and conduct of the arbitration. The jurisdiction of the arbitrators can be extended by agreement of the parties. Arbitration therefore allows the parties to reach a commercial settlement to a commercial dispute by commercial agreement.

The Arbitration Acts 1950–1979

Arbitration proceedings in England and Wales are governed by the Arbitration Acts 1950, 1975 and 1979. Although the parties to an arbitration have freedom to appoint and regulate the powers of their chosen arbitrator, the court has an inherent jurisdiction over the arbitration as a whole. The Arbitration Acts apply to any written agreement to subject a dispute to arbitration.

International arbitrations are generally conducted in accordance with the rules of a specified trade association or national, regional or international arbitration association. The London Court of International Arbitrators (LCIA) and the London Maritime Arbitration Association (LMAA) are both examples of bodies which set out a clear framework for conduct of arbitrations.

Appointment of the arbitrator

There are two different ways in which an arbitrator may be appointed. The contract itself may lay down the method of choosing the arbitrator and may even specify a named individual (eg the president of a trade association). Alternatively, the parties may be free to choose their own arbitrator. Where more than one arbitrator is appointed they may, between them, appoint a third arbitrator, perhaps to act as umpire. Once the party has appointed an arbitrator and the appointment has been accepted, all the parties to the arbitration should be notified. Both the notification and the arbitrator's acceptance should be made in writing. The appointment is not complete until the arbitrator has notified the parties of his or her acceptance, although it is not necessary for the arbitrator to accept the appointment before notification is given to the other side (see *Bunge SA v Kruse* [1979]).

S. 8 Arbitration Act 1950 as amended by s. 6 of the Arbitration Act 1979 provides that:

> 1. Unless a contrary intention is expressed therein, every arbitration agreement shall, where the reference is to two arbitrators, be deemed to include a provision that the two arbitrators may appoint an Umpire at any time thereafter, they are themselves appointed and shall do so forthwith if they cannot agree.
>
> 2. Unless a contrary intention is expressed therein, every arbitration agreement shall, where such provision is applicable to the reference, be deemed to include provision that the arbitrators have delivered to any party to the arbitration agreement, or to the Umpire, a notice in writing stating that they cannot agree, the Umpire may forthwith enter on the reference in lieu of the arbitrator.

Where two arbitrators are appointed they may, therefore, mutually appoint a third arbitrator to sit as umpire. The umpire will be present throughout the arbitration but will not be called to decide on the issue unless notified by his or her fellow arbitrators that they are in disagreement. If this situation arises the umpire's decision will be final. In some cases a third arbitrator will have an equal vote, and in this instance a decision by two out of the three arbitrators will be sufficient for a binding award.

The number of arbitrators appointed in each case will depend on the nature of the dispute and the provisions of the arbitration agreement. In a general domestic arbitration the normal practice is for a single arbitrator to be appointed. However, regularly, especially in maritime and international disputes, a tribunal is more likely to consist of three arbitrators in an attempt to ensure that impartiality is retained at all times. It is possible, but more unusual, to have a larger number of arbitrators but this is usually limited to complex technical disputes which require the arbitrators to have a particular expertise and considerable technical experience in the relevant field.

The arbitrators' remuneration is usually agreed by the parties before the hearing commences. For the hearing itself the arbitrators will usually be paid a fixed amount or an amount per day, while for other interlocutory aspects, remuneration will usually be per hour.

Removal of the arbitrator

The arbitrator is usually removed by agreement between all the parties to the dispute and, of course, will be removed automatically when a dispute is settled. A single party may, however, apply to the court to remove an arbitrator. The court will only exercise its discretion if the circumstances demand it, for example, where the arbitrator has an interest in the dispute, is biased or where there has been misconduct. The right of the arbitrator to retire is also limited and in general, unless an arbitrator has the full agreement of all the parties, he or she may only retire if entitled to do so under the arbitration agreement.

Commencement of arbitration

In order to prevent a claim from becoming barred by lapse of time, the claimants must serve notice upon the defendants within any contractual time limit, or if no contractual time limit has been specified, within the six year statutory time limit set out in the Limitation Act 1980 that a claim is made. This notice should be in writing, contain particulars of the dispute and require the defendant to appoint or agree to the appointment of an arbitrator.

Once the arbitrator's consent to the appointment has been obtained, notice should be given to the other party to appoint their arbitrator within the required time—s. 7(b) of the 1950 Act requires seven clear days. If the other party does not appoint an arbitrator within the correct time period, then notice should be given that the person already appointed will act as sole arbitrator.

Once an arbitrator has accepted the appointment, he or she must ensure that he or she is qualified to act and, secondly, secure the agreement of the parties as to what rules the arbitration is to proceed upon (eg London Maritime Arbitration Association (LMAA)).

Example 1
The arbitration clause referred disputes to "commercial men". The appointment of a solicitor would not be within this description and would be invalid unless all the parties agreed the appointment.

Preliminary meeting

In some trade arbitrations preliminary meetings are held at an early stage in proceedings. Both parties and their legal advisers will be encouraged to attend, but the attendance of counsel is not usually necessary except in the most complex disputes. Where the case involves a number of technical issues, both parties will usually agree that their technical experts should attend the preliminary meeting. The purpose of the meeting is to define the nature of the dispute, the areas where the parties are in agreement and clarify the issues. The preliminary meeting is comparable to the High Court summons for directions, although it occurs at a much earlier stage in the proceedings. The meeting is used by the arbitrators as an opportunity to define the areas of disagreement and to issue directions for the future conduct of the case.

Preliminary meetings are uncommon in London maritime arbitration cases. If a meeting is held, it will usually take place at a later stage, for example after discovery has taken place. Until then, any necessary directions will be given in writing on written application. The London Maritime Arbitration Association (LMAA) Rules (1978) provide that where a case is expected to last over five days, the parties' legal representatives should meet and review the progress of the case. Only after this preliminary meeting occurs should a full meeting be arranged with the arbitrators so that the tribunal can issue the directions sought.

Pleadings

Pleadings in arbitration largely correspond with those in the High Court. The pleadings will usually comprise:

(a) *Points of claim or informal submissions of claim*
This is the written statement of the claimants' case. It should set out the background to the dispute, the applicable law and the

relief that the parties require. The "submissions of claim" should be accompanied by the relevant documentation on which the parties wish to rely.

(b) *Points of defence or informal letter of defence*
The points of defence should deal with each and every point raised by the claimants. They should incorporate the defendants' interpretation of the case and if there is a counter-claim this should also be included.

(c) *Reply*
Each party has the chance to comment on the other side's defence submissions. The claimants' reply usually takes the form of reply to defence and counter-claim. There may be further exchanges.

The arbitrators can order whatever pleadings they think are appropriate. Copies of all pleadings should be sent, not only to the arbitrators, but also to the other side. It is good practice to ensure copies of *all* correspondence with the arbitrators are made available to the other side.

Evidence and discovery

Discovery and inspection take place after the close of pleadings. By analogy the Rules of the Supreme Court apply to discovery and inspection, but in arbitration proceedings the process is often more flexible. Discovery may be undertaken by exchange of lists of documents. Each party provides the other with a list of all the documents relevant to the issues in dispute, which are or have been in their possession or control. Privileged documents are excepted. Inspection follows discovery, usually the parties exchange copies of the documents they require, but the parties can request a personal inspection and attend the offices of the solicitor whose documents are being discovered. Most arbitration rules give the arbitrator the right to order discovery. Regularly, in arbitration, formal lists are dispensed with and copies of all relevant documents simply exchanged.

Interlocutory applications

The parties may apply to the tribunal to hear any interlocutory applications. The arbitrators will adjudicate these matters and decide on such applications so as to:

(a) give further directions
(b) amend pleadings
(c) extend time for the production of documents
(d) request further and better particulars of any pleadings
(e) grant interrogatories—a form of written question used to clarify the issues
(f) grant supplementary discovery
(g) order the preparation and exchange of experts' reports
(h) grant security for costs—the arbitrators only have jurisdiction to deal with such an application if all the parties agree—otherwise this matter must be referred to the court.

The parties may call one or more experts, but usually no expert evidence may be given at the hearing unless the party seeking to adduce it has applied to the tribunal to determine whether or not a direction should be given for the substance of the report to be disclosed. Disclosure by mutual exchange of experts' reports usually takes place prior to the hearing so that issues in dispute can be narrowed.

If the parties fail to comply with the arbitrators' directions, they may issue a peremptory notice requiring the parties to comply.

The object of discovery and inspection is to enable the parties to prepare agreed bundles of correspondence and documents for use by the arbitrator and the parties at the hearing. The bundle is usually put before arbitrators prior to the hearing so that they may be fully conversant with the background to the dispute, thereby perhaps negating the need for lengthy submissions on the facts at the hearing.

The hearing

Some cases may be decided without a hearing; the arbitrators may be asked to decide the case simply upon the parties' written submissions and documents. In most cases, however, the arbitrators will, if the dispute cannot be settled amicably, proceed on one or other party's application to an oral hearing. Subject to the rules that bind them, the arbitrators have conduct of the hearing. The date, time and duration of the hearing will be decided upon by the arbitrators after consulting both parties. Normally the claimants' solicitors will make the necessary arrangement and initially bear the cost of the hearing.

The hearing is usually private, with the arbitrators, the parties, their legal advisers and witnesses in attendance. The procedure at the arbitration usually follows that of the High Court. The arbitrators will usually call upon the claimants' advocate to open the case and address the arbitration on the factual background of the case. They will outline the issues and the evidence by which they propose to establish the case, together with the defence to any counter-claim raised. The claimants' witnesses will be called in succession, and will be examined and cross-examined by the other side and perhaps re-examined by the claimants' own counsel. The respondents' advocate will then open the case for the defence and call any witnesses following the same procedure as the claimants. The respondents' counsel will sum up the case to the arbitrators, and the claimants' advocate is then given the chance to reply to the respondents' defence and conclude the hearing. The parties may also be asked to address the arbitrators in respect of both cost and interest.

The tribunal will not usually arrive at its decision immediately. It will consider the evidence and arguments and arrive at a reasoned decision. Both parties will be notified when the arbitrators' decision is ready for collection.

The award

There are no specific requirements in relation to the form of the award, although unless the parties request and receive a "reasoned award" there will be no possibility of appeal. In order to ensure that the award will be enforceable, it should be in permanent form (ie in writing) and signed by the arbitrators, preferably with the attestation of an independent witness. S. 16 of the Arbitration Act 1950 provides that unless a contrary intention is expressed, every arbitration agreement shall be deemed to contain a provision that the award shall be "final and binding on the parties and the persons claiming under them respectively". The arbitrators should therefore ensure that the award covers all aspects of the dispute including interest and costs. Under s. 18 (4) Arbitration Act 1950 the arbitrators can still make provision for interest and costs even after the award has been made. Apart from this exception the award is conclusive between the parties of the facts decided by it.

Generally once the award has been made, the arbitrators cannot go back and alter it. An exception to this is the "slip rule". S. 17 of the Arbitration Act 1950 provides that "unless a contrary intention is expressed in the arbitration agreement, the arbitrators or umpire shall have power to correct in any award any clerical mistake or error arising from any accidental slip or omission". To qualify under the slip rule the error must be one of phraseology; it cannot alter the substance of the award or allow the arbitrators to change their opinion.

Usually, once the award is published it is final to those matters decided in it, but the tribunal has the power under s. 14 of the Arbitration Act 1950 to make an *interim* final award. This award will deal with a number of issues, but the arbitrators are "factus officio" as regards the issues not contained in the award. In other words, they retain the jurisdiction to decide the other issues at a later date. The interim final award is often used where a question of liability must be decided before the question of amount of damages can be considered.

Form of award

As stated above the award should be in writing, dated and signed by the arbitrators in the presence of two witnesses. Generally the award should record:

(a) the parties to the arbitration
(b) the background to the case
(c) the arbitration clause and the appointment of the arbitrators
(d) the various steps taken in the arbitration
(e) the various issues in dispute
(f) the arbitrators' findings of fact and law
(g) the arbitrators' award.

The award only comes into effect on publication. The arbitrators will notify both parties that the award has been published and is ready for collection. Both parties will be invited to collect the award on the payment of the necessary fees and expenses. Once it has been collected, a signed copy of the award will be posted to the remaining parties to the dispute.

Reasons

In most cases the arbitrators will give a reasoned award, however the parties cannot compel them to do so unless they apply to the court under s. 1(5) of the Arbitration Act 1979.

> (5) . . . if an award is made and, on an application made by any of the parties to the reference,—
>
> (*a*) with the consent of all the other parties to the reference, or
> (*b*) subject to section 3 [of the Act], with the leave of the court, it

> appears to the High Court that the award does not or does not sufficiently set out the reasons for the award, the court may order the arbitrator or umpire concerned to state the reasons for his award in sufficient detail to enable the court, should an appeal be brought under this section, to consider any question of law arising out of the award.

One of the aims of the 1979 Arbitration Act was to encourage arbitrators to state the reasons behind their decisions. The Act allows the court to order arbitrators to state their reasons in sufficient detail to enable the court to consider them for the purposes of an appeal on any question of law arising out of the award. In most cases the arbitrators will give a reasoned award, even if they are not requested to do so by the parties. If reasons are not given and the award is unfavourable it will usually be too late for any party to apply to the court for reasons. Despite the provisions of the 1979 Act and the *"Nema"* [1981] guidelines in some London arbitration cases reasons are still supplied separately from the award itself—a consequence of which is that the terms cannot be referred to in any subsequent litigation between the parties.

Costs

S. 18 (1) of the Arbitration Act 1950 provides that the costs of the reference and award are at the arbitrators' discretion. The arbitrators shall decide by whom, to whom and in what manner the costs shall be paid; their discretion is only limited by the principle that they must act judiciously at all times. The same principles apply to arbitration as apply to High Court proceedings, ie costs follow the event. In an arbitration the costs are usually:

(a) costs of the award—arbitrators' fees and expenses including VAT, if applicable
(b) costs of the reference—that is costs which either of the parties will have to pay if the costs are awarded against them.

It is common for the parties to reach an agreement concerning the costs beforehand, which will be fully enforceable provided that it was reached when the parties were already in dispute. If no provision is made by the arbitrators as to costs, it does not mean that the question of costs has not been considered but that both parties will bear their own. In this case the parties may apply within 14 days of publication of the award to the arbitrators under s. 18 (2) of the Arbitration Act 1950 to amend the award. The court has the power to extend the 14 day time limit. If the arbitrators have decided which party should bear the costs of the award, subject to the arbitration agreement, the arbitrators have the power to tax the costs incurred.

Interest

The arbitrators are deemed to have the power to award interest, unless the arbitration agreement provides otherwise. The provision of interest, again, is at the arbitrators' discretion and should be exercised judiciously, but in the absence of any exceptional circumstances they will award simple interest for any period up to, but not after, the award (s. 19A of the Arbitration Act 1950).

Enforcement

S. 26 of the Arbitration Act 1950 as amended by s. 17(2) of the Administration of Justice Act 1977 enables parties to the arbitration to enforce any arbitration award. By this provision an arbitration award can be registered in the United Kingdom and enforced in the same way as a judgment of the High Court. An application should be supported by an affidavit exhibiting the original or true copies of the agreement and the award. Only in exceptional circumstances, eg where there is a question of the validity of the award, will the court refuse to register it.

Appeals

The Arbitration Act 1979 governs applications, made after 1 August 1979, for leave to appeal. S. 1 of that Act gives a qualified right of appeal on questions of law arising out of "an award made on an arbitration agreement". S. 2 gives the court jurisdiction to determine any question of law arising in the course of the reference. The appeal under s. 2 must be made with the consent of either the arbitrator/umpire or the other parties to the arbitration. Notice of an application must be made and served within 14 days of the relevant consent being obtained. However, under ss. 3 and 4 the Court has a discretion whether an appeal should be granted:

> (3) An appeal under this section may be brought by any of the parties to the reference—

(*a*) with the consent of all the other parties to the reference; or
(*b*) subject to section 4 below, with the leave of the court.

(4) The High Court shall not grant leave under subsection (3)(*b*) above unless it considers that, having regard to all the circumstances, the determination of the question of law concerned could substantially affect the rights of one or more of the parties to the arbitration agreement; and the court may make any leave which it gives conditional upon the applicant complying with such conditions as it considers appropriate.

The guidelines for the court to follow in exercising their discretion are set down by the House of Lords in the *"Nema"* [1981] which were subsequently approved in the *"Antaios"* [1985].

In order that an appeal may stand, the arbitrators must give reasons for their award. Applications for leave to appeal under s. 1(2) should be made within 21 days after the award has been published. The court may confirm, vary, set aside the award or remit the question back to the arbitrators for consideration, together with the court's opinion on the relevant law. Under s. 1(8), where the award is varied by the court, it will still take effect as if it had been made by the arbitrators.

The 1979 Act also makes provision for *exclusion agreements*. An exclusion agreement is a written agreement between the parties excluding a right of appeal under s. 1 of the Act. In domestic arbitrations the right of appeal cannot be excluded by the parties before the arbitration has commenced. In international cases, however, the parties can exclude the right of appeal at any time before or after the commencement of the arbitration.

International arbitrations

International arbitrations are those in which one or both parties are resident out of the jurisdiction. It is not uncommon for foreign parties to choose to have their dispute resolved under English law as a sophisticated neutral forum. As with any domestic arbitration the starting point is always the agreement between the parties which will indicate the proper law governing the contract. An arbitration clause may provide the rules under which an arbitration should be governed, such as the rules of the London Court International Arbitration (LCIA) or the International Chamber of Commerce (ICC) or Unicitral. In international arbitration it is common for more than one arbitrator to be appointed, in order to ensure that there is complete impartiality.

A foreign award is one defined by Part 2 of the Arbitration Act 1950 or an award governed by the 1958 New York Convention on Recognition of Foreign and Arbitral Awards. Enforcement of an unpaid award is governed by s. 26 of the Arbitration Act 1950, while foreign awards are also enforceable under the Administration of Justice Act 1920 or the Foreign Judgment (Reciprocal Enforcement) Act 1933.

High Court litigation

Where there is no agreement to arbitrate, commercial litigation will usually be conducted in the High Court of Justice. In most cases actions involving breach of contract will be conducted in the Queen's Bench Division, either in the Queen's Bench itself or one of its specialised courts (ie the Commercial Court or the Admiralty Court).

Proceedings in the High Court are of an adversarial nature, counsel for both parties addressing the various issues and presenting the relevant evidence.

Any interlocutory disputes will be dealt with by the master (or judge in the commercial court) or, if the case is conducted outside London, the High Court registrar.

The Commercial Court

The Commercial Court derives its jurisdiction from Order 72 of the Rules of the Supreme Court. It has jurisdiction over "commercial actions" which include

> . . . any cause arising out of the ordinary transactions of merchants and traders and, without prejudice to the generality of the foregoing words, any case relating to construction of a mercantile document, the export or import of merchandise, affreightment, insurance, banking, mercantile agencies and mercantile notice.

The aim of the Commercial Court is to deal with commercial disputes quickly and simply. The cases that are dealt with by the court are predominantly ones where there is a great deal of money in issue and where one or both of the parties is resident out of the jurisdiction. The court is manned by Queen's Bench judges, but there are notable differences from the Queen's Bench procedures (eg interlocutory applications are dealt with by the judge rather than a master, applications are more likely to be heard outside court hours and the judges are specialists in commercial matters). The aim of the Commercial Court is to offer an efficient and streamlined specialist service to the international commercial community.

Commencement of proceedings

There are a number of stages in a typical High Court case.

Letter before action

Prior to the commencement of proceedings it is usual and sensible for a letter before action to be sent, setting out the nature of the claim and indicating that if it is not met within a specified time limit, proceedings will be instituted. Except in respect of a claim for specific delivery of goods or where an express contractual clause requires a formal demand to be made in advance of legal proceedings being commenced, there is no legal obligation to send such a letter. However, such a letter may have the desired effect in resolving the dispute, thereby saving considerable costs.

Issue and service of the writ

Actions commenced in the High Court of Justice are usually begun by the issue of a writ of summons. In a small number of cases, generally where the issues concern a point of law rather than a question of fact, the proceedings may be commenced by an originating summons. If the action is commenced by writ, the statement of claim, setting out the facts on which the parties' claim is based, may be endorsed on the writ as a full statement of claim (a specially endorsed writ). Alternatively, the statement of claim may be served separately and in this case the writ should be endorsed with a brief summary of the claim. The writ is then issued and a copy of it, together with the acknowledgement of service form, should be served on the defendant either personally or by first class post at the last known address if he or she is an individual, or for a company at its registered office.

If the defendant wishes to contest the proceedings he or she must return a completed acknowledgement of service form to the Court Office within 14 days (or specified extended period if resident abroad) stating the intention to defend the action. If the defendant fails to do this, then the plaintiff is entitled to enter judgment in default of service provided that he or she can prove service of the writ on the defendant, usually by affidavit.

The pleadings

The aim of the pleadings is to set out the facts upon which each party intends to rely and to define the legal issues. The pleadings should narrow and clarify issues in dispute so that the parties need only call evidence in relation to the contested issues.

(a) *Statement of claim*
If a party serves a separate statement of claim it should be served within 14 days after the defendants have given notice to defend. The statement of claim should describe concisely the factual background of the case and each and every issue on which the plaintiffs rely. The plaintiffs should try wherever possible to particularise a claim. In some cases the claim will be simply for damages (an unliquidated claim), but in others the plaintiffs will be able to particularise the amount of loss (a liquidated claim). Apart from the plaintiffs' claim for relief in the form of damages, the pleadings should also claim interest pursuant to s. 35A of the Supreme Court Act 1981, or if based upon a contract at the contractual rate stated therein. The plaintiffs must set out all the grounds upon which they rely in the statement of claim, as only the grounds pleaded (unless pleadings are amended at a later stage) can be relied upon at the trial.

(b) *Defence*
The defendants should serve a defence within 14 days of the final date for acknowledging service of the writ, where the claim is endorsed on the writ. Where the statement of claim is served separately, the defence should be served within 14 days of this date. If the defendants fail to serve the defence within this time, the plaintiffs can enter judgment in default of service of the defence; commonly, however, the parties agree to extend the deadline. The defence should answer each and every point raised by the plaintiffs by means of an admission, denial or a non-admission. If any point raised is not answered in the defence then the defendants are taken to admit that issue. As well as defending the plaintiffs' claim, the defence usually includes any

counter-claim that the defendants may wish to make. This is a separate claim against the plaintiffs and any other party the defendants may wish (with the court's permission) to join and the points raised in the counter-claim need not necessarily relate to those in the defence.

(c) *Reply and defence to counter-claims*
The plaintiffs may reply to any points raised in the defence and counter-claim. As with the defence itself, if the plaintiffs fail to deny the points made in the counter-claim then they are taken to admit those areas. In the reply the plaintiffs may raise any points in response to the issues raised in the defence. A reply is not an essential pleading and unless there is a specific issue that the parties wish to deal with then a reply will not generally be necessary as the plaintiffs are deemed to deny any points raised in the defence.

(d) *Further and better particulars*
A party may request further details of the pleadings if their opponents have not given sufficient information to enable them to deal with the issues raised. If a request for further and better particulars is made and the party does not voluntarily furnish the particulars then an application can be made to a High Court master for an order requiring their production. Particulars are not "pleadings" as such.

Evidence and discovery

As with arbitration, discovery is undertaken by the exchange of lists of documents and inspection of the documents thereafter. Discovery should take place within 14 days after the close of pleadings (Order 18, Rule 12(3) of the Rules of the Supreme Court) with inspection taking place at the offices of the party producing the documents within seven days thereafter. It is usual, however, in many cases for the parties to dispense with personal inspection, their opponents merely supplying copies of the documents requested by the other side.

The aim of discovery is to enable each party to assess the strengths and weaknesses of their opponents' case and thereby narrow and clarify the issues involved. It is hoped that once the parties have seen their opponents' case, it will encourage them to settle the dispute amicably and save further time and costs.

Under Order 24 of the Rules of the Supreme Court the parties must disclose all documents which are or have been in their possession, custody or power and are relevant to the issues in the case, unless such documents are privileged. Privileged documentation is covered by Order 24 Rules of the Supreme Court which includes legal communications between the parties, their legal representatives (probably excluding in-house legal staff) and a third party provided that they are prepared for the purpose of pending litigation. "Without prejudice" documents qualify for privilege if such documents are guaranteed to encourage settlement between the parties and, lastly, documents whose production is considered to be contrary to the public interest.

Once discovery and inspection have taken place, if either party suspects that the opponents have not disclosed all relevant documentation, they can ask for an order for further discovery or specific discovery, asking for identifiable documents that they believe are in their opponents' possession, or serve interrogatories (written questions requiring an answer by affidavit).

Summons for directions

Under Order 25 of the Rules of the Supreme Court, within one month after close of pleadings the plaintiff should take out a summons for directions. Directions are a stock-taking exercise by which both parties go before the master in order to obtain the necessary instructions in order to take the case to trial. In most cases the parties are able to agree directions and the master can make the order by consent. The most common directions often cover the following points:

(a) allowing either party to amend their pleadings
(b) discovery and inspection (if not completed)—time limits will usually be set within which this is to be done
(c) any outstanding further and better particulars of pleadings
(d) directions for expert evidence, including the number of experts, and the time within which their reports must be exchanged
(e) place, length and mode of trial.

The Commercial Court commonly requires proofs of factual witnesses to be exchanged and to stand on evidence in chief.

Preparation for trial

A number of steps must be taken to ensure that the case is set down for trial. The parties must ensure that all proofs of evidence, ie witness statements, are taken and any Civil Evidence Act notices required are served. These are used if a party is obliged to submit of witnesses' written statements rather than calling the witnesses themselves (eg if they are abroad). In respect of any witnesses the parties wish to call, if they will not attend voluntarily then a subpoena must be served to ensure attendance at the hearing. Finally the court bundles, which should contain all documents relevant to the issues being heard, must be prepared and copies must be lodged at court. Counsel for both parties must be briefed for the hearing.

The trial

Litigation in the High Court is conducted in front of a single High Court judge, with (at present) only counsel or the litigant in person having the right of audience. The procedure in the High Court has largely been followed by the arbitration process. The claimants/plaintiffs open their case and call their witnesses who will be examined, cross-examined and perhaps re-examined. Counsel for the defendants then opens the defence case and calls witnesses for the defence. Both counsel will make closing speeches and unlike arbitration, the High Court judge may give a judgment immediately. In the Commercial Court this timetable may be abridged, with witnesses' statements replacing examinations in chief, and with the prospect of final speeches being reduced to writing in the future.

Costs

The general principle upon which costs are awarded is that costs follow the event. Costs are, however, awarded at the discretion of the High Court judge. The unsuccessful party will usually pay not only their own costs, but the costs of the successful party. However, the judge has a discretion to apportion the costs between the two. Costs are awarded to the successful party on a "standard" basis, which under Order 62, Rule 12(2) entitles costs in respect of all expenses reasonably incurred. Generally this will not cover the whole of the successful party's costs but, say, 80 per cent. In exceptional cases costs may be awarded on an "indemnity" (ie full) basis.

The costs between the party and their own solicitor are based upon the "solicitor and their own client" basis, which allows all costs unless they are of "an unreasonable amount or have been unreasonably incurred". Costs will usually be reasonably incurred if this happens with the knowledge and approval of the client. The solicitor's costs will not be taxed automatically, but only at the request and on the initiative of the client.

Judgment without a trial

In certain circumstances a party may obtain judgment at an early stage in the action, without taking the case to trial.

Judgment in default

A party may obtain judgment in default of acknowledgement of service or alternatively judgment in default of service of defence, if the defendants fail to comply with the relevant time limits in each case. Such judgments in default are final judgments but it is possible for the defaulting party to have them set aside if they can show good cause or an arguable defence, in which case judgment will be set aside and they will proceed to serve their defence.

Order 14—summary judgment

Order 14 of the Rules of the Supreme Court allows a party to obtain summary judgment where it can be proved that there is no defence to the cause of action. Applications for summary judgment are made by summons to the master supported by an affidavit identifying the cause of action and stating the deponents' belief that there is no defence. Such a summons can be served at any time after the defendants have acknowledged service and they may respond with their own affidavit in reply. The master will decide the issue after considering both the affidavit evidence and the oral submissions of the parties. If it can be shown that the defendants have no reasonable defence to the claim then the master will give judgment which the plaintiffs can enter immediately. If there is evidence of a defence, the master may give leave unconditionally to defend, or, if there is some doubt, upon fulfilment of a condition (regularly the payment of the disputed sum into court).

Settlement

The parties may settle the action at any stage in the litigation process. Settlement may be made by means of a "without prejudice" offer either orally or in writing. This offer is privileged (until accepted) and will not be brought to the attention of the court, unless the parties have made such an offer "without prejudice except as to costs", when they may be drawn to the court's attention after judgment for argument on costs.

The defendants may make a payment into court in order to protect their position as to costs. This payment may be in respect of the claim as a whole. If the payment is accepted, the claimants will also be entitled to all costs to the date that payment in was made. If the claimants do not accept the sum then they will run a risk as to subsequent costs if they fail "to better" the payment in on judgment.

Security

Security for costs

Under Order 23, of the Rule 1 of the Supreme Court the plaintiffs may apply in certain circumstances for security for costs. The main circumstances where security will be given are where the plaintiffs are ordinarily resident outside the EC, or are nominal plaintiffs, or where there is reason to believe that they will be unable to pay the costs of the application if ordered to do so, or have incorrectly stated their address in the writ, or have changed their address during the course of the litigation in order to evade any costs consequences. Security may be ordered to ensure the defendants are adequately covered for their costs if they succeed in the action. Security is provided by means of a payment into court of the sum awarded or agreed or, commonly, by means of a bank guarantee. Security may also be ordered against the defendants where they claim relief by means of an independent counter-claim.

Security for the claim

Security for costs must be distinguished from any applications by the plaintiffs for security for the claim as a whole. In maritime cases security can be obtained by arresting a ship—in some cases, under the Supreme

Court Act 1981, ss. 20–21 there is a statutory right to arrest a ship. For example, where there is a claim as to ownership of a vessel, or costs of goods supplied to the ship, then the Admiralty Court has jurisdiction to arrest the ship or a sister vessel under the same ownership until the dispute is resolved, or until provision of a bail bond or other acceptable security.

Security may be provided by a Mareva injunction (see Chapter 9).

Appeal

Final decisions from the High Court can be appealed, generally without leave, to the Court of Appeal. The Court of Appeal is usually presided over by three judges and the case will be heard by re-hearing. The final decision of the Court of Appeal can be appealed to the House of Lords in certain circumstances. Provision is also made for reference to the European Court of Justice.

Application of the Civil Jurisdiction and Judgments Act 1982

Scope of the Act

The Civil Jurisdiction and Judgments Act came into force on 1 January 1987. The Act is based on the EC Convention on Jurisdiction and Enforcement of Judgment in Civil and Commercial Matters 1968. The Convention aims to provide a uniform set of rules to determine jurisdiction and enforcement of judgments in contracting Member States.

The Act is limited in its application, being confined to "civil and commercial matters", an all embracing term covering contractual, tortious and other disputes, but it expressly excludes four categories of dispute:

(a) the status or capacity of natural persons, rights in property arising out of matrimonial relationships, wills and succession
(b) bankruptcy proceedings relating to the winding up of insolvent companies or other legal, judicial arrangements, compositions and analogous proceedings
(c) social security
(d) arbitration—merely by commencing proceedings in arbitration,

rather than High Court litigation, takes the dispute outside the scope of this Act.

The 1982 Act makes a number of substantial changes to English law:

S. 2(1) of the 1982 Act, gives the 1968 Convention (as amended by the Accession Convention) force of law in the United Kingdom. The text of the Convention is set out in Schedule 1 of the Act.

To summarise, the Convention sets out the principles relating to the jurisdiction of the courts in contracting states:

(a) S. 1 of the Convention provides domicile as the basis of the provisions relating to jurisdiction.
(b) S. 2 provides rules relating to jurisdiction in special circumstances. These rules relate to questions concerning contract, maintenance, tort, civil claims and criminal proceedings, branches and agencies, trust and disputes relating to salvage of cargoes or freights together with provisions relating to domicile of co-defendants and third parties.
(c) Ss. 3 and 4 make provisions for jurisdiction in matters relating to insurance and consumer contracts.
(d) S. 5 includes the exclusive jurisdiction provisions.
(e) S. 6 relates to jurisdiction agreements.
(f) S. 7 sets out provisions for the examination by the particular Court of its jurisdiction.
(g) S. 8 deals with circumstances where actions are pending in more than one contracting state.
(h) S. 9 gives the court jurisdiction to order protective and provisional measures.

Ss. 41 and 42 of the 1982 Act, introduce a new definition of "domicile". This definition is substantially different from that previously provided under English law and is more akin to the English definition of "habitual residence". The provisions as to domicile are discussed in more detail later.

Ss. 4 and 5 of the 1982 Act make provisions for the recognition and enforcement of judgments of contracting states. Under Article 26 of the Convention a judgment of a contracting state would be automatically recognised and enforced in another contracting state. The grounds for non-recognition are set out in Article 27 and are limited to:

(a) public policy
(b) failure to comply with requirements relating to notice
(c) judgments irreconcilable with the judgment of a contracting state where enforcement is sought
(d) cases involving preliminary questions such as to status or legal capacity
(e) judgments irreconcilable with earlier judgments of non-contracting states.

S. 16 and Schedule 4 of the 1982 Act provide for rules as to the jurisdiction of the courts of the United Kingdom in cases where the defendant is "domiciled" in another part of the United Kingdom.

Ss. 18 and 19 and Schedules 6 and 7 of the Act relate to enforcement of United Kingdom judgments in other parts of the United Kingdom.

S. 20 and Schedule 8 of the Act make provision for jurisdiction involving foreign defendants in Scottish cases.

S. 25 of the 1982 Act provides for interim relief in the United Kingdom in the absence of substantive proceedings. It is, therefore, no longer a bar to the court's powers to provide interim relief that the main proceedings have been commenced in another contracting state. This removes the restriction placed by the House of Lords in the *"Siskina"* [1979] that interim relief is not available in England unless the English Courts have jurisdiction in the substantial dispute.

S. 34 of the 1982 Act provides that a judgment given by an English or foreign court is a bar to further proceedings in the United Kingdom on the cause of action in respect of which the judgment was given.

Jurisdiction

The aim of the Act is to provide a uniform code relating to jurisdiction applicable in all contracting states. The rules are broadly based on the concept of domicile, but the definition of domicile differs from the traditional criteria applied in the United Kingdom and can be more closely associated with the concept of "habitual residence".

The general rule under Article 2 of the 1968 Convention, is that a defendant can be sued in the court of the state in which the defendant is domiciled.

Article 2

Subject to the provisions of this Convention, persons domiciled in a Contracting State shall, whatever their nationality, be sued in the courts of that State.

Persons who are not nationals of the State in which they are domiciled shall be governed by the rules of jurisdiction applicable to nationals of that State.

The concept of domicile under the 1982 Act, depends upon a "substantial connection with the Contracting State". S. 41 of the Act provides:

Domicile

Domicile of individuals

41.—(1) Subject to Article 52 (which contains provisions for determining whether a party is domiciled in a Contracting State), the following provisions of this section determine, for the purposes of the 1968 Convention and this Act, whether an individual is domiciled in the United Kingdom or in a particular part of, or place in, the United Kingdom or in a state other than a Contracting State.

(2) An individual is domiciled in the United Kingdom if and only if—
- (*a*) he is resident in the United Kingdom; and
- (*b*) the nature and circumstances of his residence indicate that he has a substantial connection with the United Kingdom.

(3) Subject to subsection (5), an individual is domiciled in a particular part of the United Kingdom if and only if—
- (*a*) he is resident in that part; and
- (*b*) the nature and circumstances of his residence indicate that he has a substantial connection with that part.

(4) An individual is domiciled in a particular place in the United Kingdom if and only if he—
- (*a*) is domiciled in the part of the United Kingdom in which that place is situated; and
- (*b*) is resident in that place.

(5) An individual who is domiciled in the United Kingdom but in whose case the requirements of subsection (3)(*b*) are not satisfied in relation to any particular part of the United Kingdom shall be treated as domiciled in the part of the United Kingdom in which he is resident.

(6) In the case of an individual who—
- (*a*) is resident in the United Kingdom, or in a particular part of the United Kingdom; and
- (*b*) has been so resident for the last three months or more,

the requirements of subsection (2)(*b*) or, as the case may be, subsection (3)(*b*) shall be presumed to be fulfilled unless the contrary is proved.

(7) An individual is domiciled in a state other than a Contracting State if and only if—

(*a*) he is resident in that state; and
(*b*) the nature and circumstances of his residence indicate that he has a substantial connection with that state.

Article 42 sets out the provisions relating to the domicile of a Company or Association:

DOMICILE AND SEAT OF CORPORATION OR ASSOCIATION

42.—(1) For the purposes of this Act the seat of a corporation or association (as determined by this section) shall be treated as its domicile.

(2) The following provisions of this section determine where a corporation or association has its seat—

(*a*) for the purpose of Article 53 (which for the purposes of the 1968 Convention equates the domicile of such a body with its seat); and
(*b*) for the purposes of this Act other than the provisions mentioned in section 43(1)(*b*) and (*c*).

(3) A corporation or association has its seat in the United Kingdom if and only if—

(*a*) it was incorporated or formed under the law of a part of the United Kingdom and has its registered office or some other official address in the United Kingdom; or
(*b*) its central management and control is exercised in the United Kingdom.

(4) A corporation or association has its seat in a particular part of the United Kingdom if and only if it has its seat in the United Kingdom and—

(*a*) it has its registered office or some other official address in that part; or
(*b*) its central management and control is exercised in that part; or
(*c*) it has a place of business in that part.

(5) A corporation or association has its seat in a particular place in the United Kingdom if and only if it has its seat in the part of the United Kingdom in which that place is situated and—

(*a*) it has its registered office or some other official address in that place; or
(*b*) its central management and control is exercised in that place; or
(*c*) it has a place of business in that place.

Part V

(6) Subject to subsection (7), a corporation or association has its seat in a state other than the United Kingdom if and only if—

(*a*) it was incorporated or formed under the law of that state and has its registered office or some other official address there; or

(b) its central management and control is exercised in that state.

(7) A corporation or association shall not be regarded as having its seat in a Contracting State other than the United Kingdom if it is shown that the courts of that state would not regard it as having its seat there.

(8) In this section—

"business" includes any activity carried on by a corporation or association, and "place of business" shall be construed accordingly;

"official address", in relation to a corporation or association, means an address which it is required by law to register, notify or maintain for the purpose of receiving notices or other communications.

Under Article 2(1) of the 1968 Convention, persons domiciled in a contracting state must be sued in that state, although Article 3 sets out the requirements by which a person domiciled in one state can be sued in another contracting state.

Generally, however, the rules relating to jurisdiction depend upon domicile in a contracting state. Article 5 of the 1968 Convention provides special rules in relation to a number of specific areas including contractual questions, maintenance, tort, agency and others:

Article 5

A person domiciled in a Contracting State may, in another Contracting State, be sued:

(1) in matters relating to a contract, in the courts for the place of performance of the obligation in question;

(2) in matters relating to maintenance, in the courts for the place where the maintenance creditor is domiciled or habitually resident or, if the matter is ancillary to proceedings concerning the status of a person, in the court which, according to its own law, has jurisdiction to entertain those proceedings, unless that jurisdiction is based solely on the nationality of one of the parties;

(3) in matters relating to tort, delict or quasi-delict, in the courts for the place where the harmful event occurred;

(4) as regards a civil claim for damages or restitution which is based on an act giving rise to criminal proceedings, in the court seised of those proceedings, to the extent that that court has jurisdiction under its own law to entertain civil proceedings;

(5) as regards a dispute arising out of the operations of a branch, agency or other establishment, in the courts for the place in which the branch, agency or other establishment is situated;

(6) in his capacity as settlor, trustee or beneficiary of a trust created by the operation of a statute, or by a written instrument, or created orally and evidenced in writing, in the courts of the Contracting State in which the trust is domiciled;

(7) as regards a dispute concerning the payment of remuneration claimed in respect of the salvage of a cargo or freight, in the court under the authority of which the cargo or freight in question:

   (*a*) has been arrested to secure such payment, or

   (*b*) could have been so arrested, but bail or other security has been given;

provided that this provision shall apply only if it is claimed that the defendant has an interest in the cargo or freight or had such an interest at the time of salvage.

Appendix A
Glossary

arrival. This is very similar to the DES contract and is generally followed by the named vessel and port of arrival. The seller is to pay freight and procure the delivery of the goods to the vessel and thence to the appropriate destination port. The purchaser pays the price of the goods upon arrival of the goods, and if the goods are lost is not obliged to make payment.

CFR (formerly C&F). Cost and freight—see detailed description in section on "Classic International Sale Contracts" (Chapter 2).

CIF. Cost, insurance, freight. The duties and responsibilities have been listed in the section on "Classic International Sale Contracts" (Chapter 2).

CIF & E. Cost, insurance, freight and exchange. The "e" element is used variously to denote that the risk of an exchange rate fluctuation is built in to the price and/or that the bank's commission is inclusive.

CIF & C. Cost, insurance, freight and commission. The commission in question is usually the export merchant's commission charged when acting as a buying agent for an overseas buyer.

CIF & C & I. Cost, insurance, freight and commission and interest. The commission and interest referred to are charges made by a bank to the seller on negotiation of the bill of lading where there is an hiatus before payment is received whilst monies are awaited from a foreign bank. The "i" indicates to the buyer that the contractual price extends to such interest and commission. It is particularly appropriate for trade with a distant partner.

CIP. Carriage and insurance paid to (named destination); as CPT but seller must also insure goods during carriage and clear goods for export.

CPT. Carriage paid to (named place). Seller pays freight and risk passes to buyer on delivery of goods to carrier.

DAF. Delivered at frontier. This is usually followed by the named place of delivery at the chosen frontier. It is a regularly used contract in continental export trade where no carriage by sea is envisaged. An alternative description is "franco frontier" or "rendu frontier". The frontier in question is the seller's frontier and there is no obligation on the seller to deliver the goods across the frontier. There is no obligation on the seller to insure although he or she will retain responsibility for the goods until delivery has been effected and, therefore, would be wise to place his or her own insurance until that time.

DDP. Delivered duty paid. The name of the place of destination in the importing country is usually inserted between "delivered" and "duty paid". The contract is alternatively described as "free delivery" or "franco, domicile" or "rendu . . . droits acquitte". It is one of the least onerous contracts from a buyer's point of view. The seller is required to procure the delivery of the goods to the chosen place by the purchaser and to pay all associated costs up until delivery, and to bear the risk and expense of the goods until the buyer's disposal at his or her chosen place. The buyer is only obliged to make payment against actual delivery of the goods. The quality and quantity of the goods are to be judged in accordance with their state upon arrival.

DDU. Delivered duty unpaid. As above, save that the seller's obligations are fulfilled when goods are made available at a named place in the country of import; it is for the buyer to obtain all import licences and comply with necessary customs formalities.

delivered at container collection depot. This description is usually followed by the named place of depot. The seller is to pay all costs up until acceptance of the goods by the combined transport operator at the container depot agreed by the parties. Risk of loss and damage of the goods remains with the seller until then and he or she will usually insure this risk. The seller's responsibility is ended when the goods reach the depot and are taken up by the combined transport operator. The responsibility is likely to end before the goods are placed into a container. The buyer is liable for procuring transportation of the goods after they have been placed in the possession of the combined transport operator at the depot and this will extend to procuring transportation to the overseas destination. The buyer will liaise with the combined transport operator in this regard. He will pay freight insurance and other charges and bear the risk from the time of the delivery of the goods to the depot until arrival.

DES (formerly ex-ship). Delivered ex ship. The seller has to procure shipment and pay freight. The buyer is only bound to pay the purchase price if actual delivery is made to him or her at the agreed delivery port. The phrase "ex ship" is usually followed by the named ship and chosen port of arrival. This is not a sale of documents in any respect; delivery of the goods themselves has to be made, against which the purchase price is tendered. Delivery of an endorsed bill of lading to the buyer is generally not given with the intention of passing property, and property passes only when the goods are handed over on their arrival from the ship. Goods are, therefore, not at the buyer's risk in the course of transit and the seller is not obliged to the buyer to insure the goods although he or she would be well advised to insure them for his or her own purposes.

DEQ (formerly ex quay). Delivered ex quay. This is usually followed by the named port of destination. The seller is obliged to ensure the delivery of the goods to the named quay which will include procuring carriage of the goods and payment of freight for such carriage. The seller's duties are the same as for an arrival or DES contract with the additional responsibility of paying import duties and discharging costs. The format is infrequently used unless the seller is familiar with the delivery port's idiosyncrasies.

ex store. Similar considerations apply as for EXW. "Store" may refer sometimes to a certain type of storage, for example refrigerated storage.

ex warehouse. Very similar considerations apply for an ex warehouse contract as for an EXW contract.

EXW (formerly ex works). This is the least onerous format of contract for the seller. The buyer must collect the goods from the seller's works. The purchase price is due on delivery of goods and all the seller is obliged to do is to pack the goods in their customary packaging and await collection by the purchaser against payment of the price. Strictly an EXW contract may not constitute an international sale contract at all and may be simply a domestic arrangement. The expression "EXW" is usually followed by the works address.

FAS. Free alongside ship. This phrase is usually followed by the named vessel in the port of shipment. The goods are at the seller's responsibility and risk until they are carried alongside the named ship so that they may be loaded by the ship's tackle, by shore crane or by some other means. Loading of the goods is the buyer's responsibility. It is for the buyer to nominate an effective ship.

In a container context FAS represents "free arrival station". Such a contract is effectively an arrival contract (see description above), the carrier agreeing to deliver containers to the arrival station specified, ready for customs clearance and unpacking by the purchaser.

FCA. Free carrier—and then named place. The seller must deliver export cleared goods to the buyers' nominated carrier at a named place.

FOB. Free on board. (See full description in Chapter 2.) Title and risk pass at the ship's rail on loading.

free on lighter. This provision is often included in an FAS contract where the seller's responsibility to place goods alongside the ship extends to placing goods "free on lighter", extending the seller's responsibility until such time as the goods are delivered over the lighter's side.

FOR. Free on rail. This is a relatively simple form of contract from the seller's point of view. In this country the seller's obligations are discharged when they have placed goods on British Rail's collecting vehicles. Whilst the seller cannot sit back and await collection of the goods by the purchaser, all he or she has to do is deliver the goods to the custody of the railway authority at the agreed locality. The abbreviation "FOR" is usually followed by the named point of departure agreed. It would be for the seller to use best endeavours to procure the wagons by negotiation with the railway authority. The seller must give immediate notice of the placing of the goods with the railway authorities. The seller must load the goods and correctly address them. The purchaser must pay the purchase price once the goods have been placed in the railway authority's custody. The "free on" element of an FOR contract is frequently known by its french equivalent "franco".

FOT. Free on truck. This is a very similar form of contract to FOR. The seller is responsible for charges up to and including the loading of the goods on the railway wagon. It is a slightly more extensive obligation than under FOR where delivery to the railway authority would probably be sufficient. Apart from that the obligations and duties are virtually identical.

franco (quay). This is a commonly used word. Franco simply denotes "free". Accordingly franco quay relieves the seller, in making the goods available at the specified quay, from bearing the cost of charges imposed by the quay authority.

free to docks. Dock dues become payable when goods enter the docks, and similar charges such as wharfage, porterage and lighterage may become payable. In a typical FAS contract these would have to be borne by the seller in bringing the goods to the side of the ship. The parties can agree to the contrary, and to require the charges to be paid by the buyer agreeing that delivery is to be "free to docks" or "delivery to docks".

NB Many of the abbreviations above are contained in Incoterms, the latest version of which became effective on 1.7.90.

Appendix B

CMR International Consignment Note

An example of this form is provided overleaf.

LETTRE DE VOITURE INTERNATIONALE (CMR) INTERNATIONAL CONSIGNMENT NOTE

Sender (Name, Address, Country) Expediteur (Nom, Addresse, Pays) 1

Customs Reference/Status Reference/designation pour mise en douane 2

Senders/Agents Reference Reference de l'expediteur/de l'agent 3

Consignee (Name, Address, Country) Destinataire (Nom, Addresse, Pays) 4

Carrier (Name, Address, Country) Transporteur (Nom, Addresse, Pays) 5

Place & date of taking over the goods (place, country, date)
Lieu et date de la prise en charge des marchandises (Lieu, pays, date) 6

Successive Carriers Transporteurs successifs 7

Place designated for delivery of goods (place, country)
Lieu prevu pour la livraison des marchandises (lieu, pays) 8

This carriage is subject, notwithstanding any clause to the contrary, to the Convention on the Contract for the International Carriage of Goods by Road (CMR)
Ce transport est soumis nonobstant toute clause contraire à la Convention Relative au Contrat de Transport International de Marchandises par Route (CMR)

Marks & Nos; No & Kind of Packages; Description of Goods* Marques et Nos; No et nature des colis; Designation des marchandises* 9

Gross weight (kg) Poids Brut (kg) 10

Volume (m³) Cubage (m³) 11

Carriage Charges Prix de transport 12

Senders Instructions for Customs, etc Instructions de l'Expediteur (optional) 13

Reservations Reserves 14

Documents attached Documents Annexes (optional) 15

Special agreements Conventions particulieres (optional) 16

Goods Received/Marchandises Reçues 17

Signature of Carrier/Signature du transporteur 18

Company completing this note Societe emettrice 19

Place and Date Signature Lieu et date Signature 20

COPY 1 SENDER
COPY 2 CONSIGNEE
COPY 3 CARRIER

Approved by FTA/RHA SITPRO UK 1981

*NB FOR DANGEROUS GOODS

INDICATE
1 CORRECT TECHNICAL NAME (PROPER SHIPPING NAME)
2 HAZARD CLASS
3 UN NUMBER
4 FLASHPOINT (IF ANY) IN ºC

730

Index